J. Dianne Garner
Editor

Fundamentals
of Feminist Gerontology

Fundamentals of Feminist Gerontology has been co-published simultaneously as *Journal of Women & Aging,* Volume 11, Numbers 2/3 1999.

Pre-publication
REVIEWS,
COMMENTARIES,
EVALUATIONS . . .

"**T**his volume provides a much needed feminist perspective in the field of gerontology. The authors consistently offer a strong feminist analysis of issues and populations that have been kept invisible or marginalized in pre-feminist approaches. This book is a must for the informed practitioner."

Ellyn Kaschak, PhD
Professor of Psychology
San Jose State University

"**F**undamentals of Feminist Gerontology is highly readable and important. It provides valuable insight into the paradigm of feminist gerontology. It introduces the reader to the theory of feminist gerontology, and illustrates how this framework can be applied to better understand important topics for older women. The volume emphasizes practical strategies that can be used to improve the health of older women, as well as their economic and psychic well-being. It increases the reader's awareness of how we can help older women take charge of their lives.

Particularly informative topics include feminist strategies that can help older women to more effectively navigate the health care system and achieve better outcomes, how feminist theory can be used to effectively intervene in the treatment of abused older women, and ways in which feminist theory can be used to help us achieve greater equity for women in the caregiving process."

Sarah B. Laditka, PhD
Assistant Professor
Health Services
Management Director
Center for Health and Aging
State University of New York
at Utica/Rome

"**T**his is a thoughtful discussion of how to assist older women with their health and well being. The major strength of this book is the documentation and acknowledgement of the unique needs of older women, including cultural, ethnic, and lifestyle differences. A chapter on health and alternative therapies documents the need for further efforts among gerontological and health professionals, as well as families. The chapter on caregiving enhances the discussions of the contributions of elder caregivers to society. Overall, the information provides lay persons and professionals different ways of knowing, caring, and serving older women."

Debra C. Wallace, PhD, RN
University of Tennessee
College of Nursing
UT Knoxville

The Haworth Press, Inc.

Fundamentals
of Feminist Gerontology

Fundamentals of Feminist Gerontology has been co-published simultaneously as *Journal of Women & Aging,* Volume 11, Numbers 2/3, 1999.

The *Journal of Women & Aging* Monographic "Separates"

Below is a list of "separates," which in serials librarianship means a special issue simultaneously published as a special journal issue or double-issue *and* as a "separate" hardbound monograph. (This is a format which we also call a "DocuSerial.")

"Separates" are published because specialized libraries or professionals may wish to purchase a specific thematic issue by itself in a format which can be separately cataloged and shelved, as opposed to purchasing the journal on an on-going basis. Faculty members may also more easily consider a "separate" for classroom adoption.

"Separates" are carefully classified separately with the major book jobbers so that the journal tie-in can be noted on new book order slips to avoid duplicate purchasing.

You may wish to visit Haworth's website at . . .

http://www.haworthpressinc.com

. . . to search our online catalog for complete tables of contents of these separates and related publications.

You may also call 1-800-HAWORTH (outside US/Canada: 607-722-5857), or Fax 1-800-895-0582 (outside US/Canada: 607-771-0012), or e-mail at:

getinfo@haworthpressinc.com

Fundamentals of Feminist Gerontology, edited by J. Dianne Garner, DSW (Vol. 11, No. 2/3, 1999). *Strives to increase women's self-esteem and their overall quality of life by encouraging education and putting a stop to age, sex, and race discrimination.*

Old, Female, and Rural, edited by B. Jan McCulloch (Vol. 10, No. 4, 1998). *"An excellent job of bringing together experts from four different disciplines to illuminate the basic interdisciplinary nature of gerontology." (Dr. Jean Turner, Associate Professor, Human Development and Family Services, University of Arkansas, Fayetteville, Arkansas)*

Relationships Between Women in Later Life, edited by Karen A. Roberto (Vol. 8, No. 3/4, 1996). *"Provides an impressive array of issues about women's social networks. . . . Important, up-to-date empirical studies that will fill a significant gap in our understanding about the great diversity in the lives of older women today." (European Federation of the Elderly)*

Older Women with Chronic Pain, edited by Karen A. Roberto (Vol. 6, No. 4, 1994). *"Readers interested in the health concerns of older women, and older women themselves, will appreciate the insight and information in this book." (Feminist Bookstore News)*

Women and Healthy Aging: Living Productively in Spite of It All, edited by J. Dianne Garner and Alice A. Young (Vol. 5, No. 3/4, 1994). *"For those who are not aged themselves, it helps to bring about insights that are not possible when one holds the commonly taught view that disability of any degree is strictly debilitating." (Linda Vinton, PhD, Associate Professor, School of Social Work, Florida State University; Research Affiliate, Pepper Institute on Aging and Public Policy)*

Women in Mid-Life: Planning for Tomorrow, edited by Christopher L. Hayes (Vol. 4, No. 4, 1993). *"Contains illuminating insights into aspects of women's mid-life experiences." (Age and Ageing)*

Women, Aging and Ageism, edited by Evelyn Rosenthal (Vol. 2, No. 2, 1990) *"Readers should find this book helpful in gaining new insights to issues women face in old age. . . Enlightening." (Educational Gerontology)*

Women as They Age: Challenge, Opportunity, and Triumph, edited by J. Dianne Garner and Susan O. Mercer (Vol. 1, No. 1/2/3, 1989). *"Offers Provocative insights into the strengths, dilemmas, and challenges confronting the current and future cohorts of older women." (Affilia: Journal of Women and Social Work)*

Fundamentals of Feminist Gerontology

J. Dianne Garner, DSW
Editor

Fundamentals of Feminist Gerontology has been co-published simultaneously as *Journal of Women & Aging*, Volume 11, Numbers 2/3, 1999.

The Haworth Press, Inc.
New York • London • Oxford

Fundamentals of Feminist Gerontology has been co-published simultaneously as *Journal of Women & Aging*, Volume 11, Numbers 2/3 1999.

The development, preparation, and publication of this work has been undertaken with great care. However, the publisher, employees, editors, and agents of The Haworth Press and all imprints of The Haworth Press, Inc., including The Haworth Medical Press® and Pharmaceutical Products Press®, are not responsible for any errors contained herein or for consequences that may ensue from use of materials or information contained in this work. Opinions expressed by the author(s) are not necessarily those of The Haworth Press, Inc.

The Haworth Press, Inc., 10 Alice Street, Binghamton, NY 13904-1580 USA

Cover design by Jennifer M. Gaska

Library of Congress Cataloging-in-Publication Data

Fundamentals of feminist gerontology/J. Dianne Garner, editor.
       p. cm.
    " . . . co-published simultaneously as Journal of women & aging, volume 11, numbers 2/3, 1999."
    Includes bibliographical references and index.
    ISBN 0-7890-0761-4 (alk. paper).–ISBN 0-7890-0762-2 (alk. paper)
    1. Gerontology. 2. Aged women. 3. Aging. 4. Feminist theory. I. Garner, Dianne J.
HQ1061.F83 1999
305.26–dc21
                                                99-27703
                                                    CIP

INDEXING & ABSTRACTING

Contributions to this publication are selectively indexed or abstracted in print, electronic, online, or
CD-ROM version(s) of the reference tools and information services listed below. This list is current
as of the copyright date of this publication. See the
end of this section for additional notes.

- *Abstracts in Anthropology*
- *Abstracts in Social Gerontology: Current Literature on Aging*
- *Abstracts of Research in Pastoral Care & Counseling*
- *Academic Index (on-line)*
- *AgeInfo CD-ROM*
- *AgeLine Database*
- *Behavioral Medicine Abstracts*
- *BUBL Information Service: An Internet-Based Information Service for the UK Higher Education Community*
- *Cambridge Scientific Abstracts*
- *CINAHL (Cumulative Index to Nursing & Allied Health Literature), in print, also on CD-ROM from CD PLUS, EBSCO, and SilverPlatter, and online from CDP Online (formerly BRS), Data-Star, and PaperChase. (Support materials include Subject Heading List, Database Search Guide, and instructional video)*
- *CNPIEC Reference Guide: Chinese National Directory of Foreign Periodicals*
- *Combined Health Information Database (CHID)*
- *Contemporary Women's Issues*
- *Current Contents*
- *Family Studies Database (online and CD-ROM)*
- *Family Violence & Sexual Assault Bulletin*
- *Feminist Periodicals: A Current Listing of Contents*
- *Gender Watch*

(continued)

- *Guide to Social Science & Religion*
- *Human Resources Abstracts (HRA)*
- *IBZ International Bibliography of Periodical Literature*
- *Index Medicus*
- *Index to Periodical Articles Related to Law*
- *Institute for Scientific Information*
- *MasterFILE: updated database from EBSCO Publishing*
- *Mental Health Abstracts (online through DIALOG)*
- *National Center for Chronic Disease Prevention & Health Promotion (NCCDPHP)*
- *National Clearinghouse for Primary Care Information (NCPCI)*
- *New Literature on Old Age*
- *Periodical Abstracts, Research II (broad coverage indexing & abstracting data-base from University Microfilms International (UMI) 300 North Zeeb Road, P.O. Box 1346, Ann Arbor, MI 48106-1346)*
- *Periodical Abstracts Select (abstracting & indexing service covering most frequently requested journals in general reference, plus journals requested in libraries serving undergraduate programs, available from University Microfilms International (UMI), 300 North Zeeb Road, P.O. Box 1346, Ann Arbor, MI 48106-1346)*
- *Social Planning/Policy & Development Abstracts (SOPODA)*
- *Social Science Citation Index*
- *Social Work Abstracts*
- *Sociological Abstracts (SA)*
- *Studies on Women Abstracts*
- *Women Studies Abstracts*
- *Women's Healthbeat*
- *Women's Studies Index (indexed comprehensively)*

(continued)

*Special Bibliographic Notes related to special journal issues
(separates) and indexing/abstracting:*

- indexing/abstracting services in this list will also cover material in any "separate" that is co-published simultaneously with Haworth's special thematic journal issue or DocuSerial. Indexing/abstracting usually covers material at the article/chapter level.
- monographic co-editions are intended for either non-subscribers or libraries which intend to purchase a second copy for their circulating collections.
- monographic co-editions are reported to all jobbers/wholesalers/approval plans. The source journal is listed as the "series" to assist the prevention of duplicate purchasing in the same manner utilized for books-in-series.
- to facilitate user/access services all indexing/abstracting services are encouraged to utilize the co-indexing entry note indicated at the bottom of the first page of each article/chapter/contribution.
- this is intended to assist a library user of any reference tool (whether print, electronic, online, or CD-ROM) to locate the monographic version if the library has purchased this version but not a subscription to the source journal.
- individual articles/chapters in any Haworth publication are also available through the Haworth Document Delivery Service (HDDS).

DEDICATION

In memory of the joy, caring, and compassion of 21 year old Chris Hooyman, spirited adventurer and son of Nancy Hooyman who died assisting a fellow mountain climber on Denali.

In a recent letter to a friend paralyzed in a swimming accident, Chris wrote the following:

> The things you do are not half as important as the way you feel–and it seems that if you feel loved and know you love others, you will always feel moments of happiness.

Fundamentals of Feminist Gerontology

CONTENTS

ABOUT THE EDITOR

J. Dianne Garner, DSW, is Co-Owner of Key West Information Systems, Inc., in Key West, Florida. In addition, she is Editor of the *Journal of Women & Aging* (The Haworth Press, Inc.) and Senior Editor of the Haworth feminist book program. Her previous positions include Professor and Chair of the Department of Social Work at Washburn University in Topeka, Kansas, and Director of the Department of Medical Social Work at Cedars-Sinai Medical Center in Los Angeles, California. Dr. Garner is the co-editor of *Women & Healthy Aging: Living Productively in Spite of It All* (1995, The Haworth Press, Inc.), *Geriatric Case Practice in Nursing Homes* (1991), and *Women as They Age: Challenge, Opportunity, and Triumph* (Haworth Press, Inc., 1989). She has also published multiple book chapters, articles, editorial columns, and booklets. A prolific speaker, Dr. Garner has given many international, national, regional, state, and local professional presentations, including keynoting the national meeting of the Alzheimer's Association in 1993, and the Women's Health Congress in 1990 and giving one of the keynote addresses at the annual meeting of Canadian social workers. Dr. Garner has also served as issues expert at the White House Conference on Aging and has earned many honors and awards including Arkansas Social Worker of the Year.

Oldest Camper

Ruth Harriet Jacobs, PhD

Lithe and beautiful at eighty
she must swim in every lake
stream, river, or ocean.
Before the others awake
she thinks about her day
picks roses and daisies
starts her discoveries.

They fantasize futures
she reviews reminiscences
wasting no present moment
knowing all flowers fade
even the most vibrant.

[Haworth co-indexing entry note]: "Oldest Camper." Jacobs, Ruth Harriet. Co-published simultaneously in *Journal of Women & Aging* (The Haworth Press, Inc.) Vol. 11, No. 2/3, 1999, p. 1; and: *Fundamentals of Feminist Gerontology* (ed: J. Dianne Garner) The Haworth Press, Inc., 1999, p. 1. Single or multiple copies of this article are available for a fee from The Haworth Document Delivery Service [1-800-342-9678, 9:00 a.m. - 5:00 p.m. (EST). E-mail address: getinfo@haworthpressinc.com].

Feminism and Feminist Gerontology

J. Dianne Garner, DSW

We have systematically denigrated old women, kept them out of the mainstream of productive life, judged them primarily in terms of failing capacities and functions, and found them pitiful. We have put old women in nursing homes with absolutely no intellectual stimulation, isolated from human warmth and nurturing contact, then condemned them for their senility. We have impoverished, disrespected, and disregarded old women, and then dismissed them as inconsequential and uninteresting. We have made old women invisible so that we do not have to confront our patriarchal myths about what makes life valuable or dying painful.

Having done that, we then attribute to the process of aging per se all the evils we see and fear about growing old. It is not aging that is awful, nor whatever physical problems may accompany aging. What is awful is how society treats old women and their problems. To the degree that we accept and allow such treatment we buy the ageist and sexist assumptions that permit this treatment.

What then does it really mean for a woman to grow old? For me, first of all, to be old is to be myself. No matter how patriarchy may classify and categorize me as invisible and powerless, I exist. I am an ongoing person, a sexual being, a person who struggles, for whom there are important issues to explore, new things to learn, challenges to meet, beginnings to make, risks to take, endings to ponder. Though some options are diminished, there are new paths ahead. (Healey, 1994, p. 83)

[Haworth co-indexing entry note]: "Feminism and Feminist Gerontology." Garner, J. Dianne. Co-published simultaneously in *Journal of Women & Aging* (The Haworth Press, Inc.) Vol. 11, No. 2/3, 1999, pp. 3-12; and: *Fundamentals of Feminist Gerontology* (ed: J. Dianne Garner) The Haworth Press, Inc., 1999, pp. 3-12. Single or multiple copies of this article are available for a fee from The Haworth Document Delivery Service [1-800-342-9678, 9:00 a.m. - 5:00 p.m. (EST). E-mail address: getinfo@haworthpressinc.com].

3

To become old in Western societies is to be devalued. While devaluation with age is true for women and men, there is clearly a difference. Much of western society's view of women's worth is associated with a socially defined physical attractiveness which clearly equates youth with beauty and values youthful beauty and the ability to attract men. Therefore, women lose their social value simply by growing old. Men are more likely to be evaluated and rewarded for what they do. As long as they are able to achieve, age alone has little bearing on social value (Nielsen, 1990). Men with graying hair may be viewed as attractive and sophisticated, while women with graying hair are unattractive and old. There has been much written on the almost desperate attempt by millions of women to continue to look young through use of "age defying" products and surgical procedures. Yet men spend very little on products designed to hide the signs of aging. Women's earnings do not increase with age in the same way that men's earnings increase. In fact the disparity in earnings becomes more pronounced with age. Women, therefore, enter old age with significantly fewer resources than do men. In fact, women constitute more than 75% of the elderly poor. While women outlive men, women encounter more health problems that interfere with activities of daily living than do men. It is not surprising, then, that many women approach old age with a sense of foreboding.

FEMINISM

There are a variety of theories and frameworks which, although not always consonant with one another, contribute to the feminist literature. There is not one feminism, but many feminisms. Feminists across the disciplines work from within a multitude of intellectual paradigms and political positions (Ray, 1996, p. 674). Saulnier (1996) provides a summary sentence attempting to articulate the gist of several separate feminist theories.

> Radical feminism argues that society is psychologically structured on male needs, and that to maintain that order women's needs are subjugated, and that the fabric of society must be fundamentally altered. Lesbian feminism challenges the organization of society around both heterosexual and male dominance and the ongoing enforcement of that arrangement. Cultural

feminism holds that women are more peaceful, cooperative, and nurturing than men, probably because women reproduce and nurture the species. Ecofeminism is the application of women's culture to efforts toward peace and ecology. Socialist feminism blames the economics of capitalism in combination with patriarchy for women's subordinate position in society. Womanism defines sexism as one of multiple, interlocking systems of oppression functioning simultaneously and interdependently, inextricable from each other theoretically or experientially. Postmodern feminism argues that, since *woman* is a socially defined and inherently distorted term, which cannot be defended on empirical or theoretical grounds, we have no reason to think females have an inherent nature or role. Thus, social organization rooted in gender is based on an invented concept. Global feminism seeks to explain the interconnectedness of disparate feminist struggles by examining how worldwide economic factors combine with national histories of colonialism, religion, and culture to oppress women. (pp. 173-174)

Liberal feminism holds that women are equal to men and should be treated as such in public spheres and that societies violate the liberal concept of equal rights with respect to women. The liberal women's movement attacked women's lack of political equality, lack of economic equality and the interference in women's reproductive freedom by governments (Saulnier, 1996, p. 10).

Whether liberal feminism or radical feminism or further refined in theories or frameworks such as cultural feminism, Marxist feminism, womanism, post-modern feminism, global feminism, or ecofeminism, feminism seeks to increase the awareness of all individuals regarding the realities of the oppression of women. Consciousness raising is an integral part of feminist theories. Further, most feminist frameworks attempt to provide the basis for increasing the self-esteem of women, increasing their active participation in decision making and social action, empowerment, and facilitating the recognition by societies of the intrinsic value and worth of women.

FEMINIST GERONTOLOGY

Gerontology and feminism share common goals: development of social consciousness about inequities, utilization of theories and methods that accurately depict life experiences, and promotion of change in conditions that negatively impact older people or women (Reinharz, 1986). Feminism recognizes the intrinsic value of women, their right to equal treatment, and their right to be viewed as individuals. Gerontology recognizes the intrinsic value of older people, their right to equal treatment, and their right to be viewed as individuals. However, much of the feminist literature has focused on issues of younger and middle aged women such as reproductive rights and child care. Until recent years, the gerontological literature has tended to focus on older people without making distinctions by gender. In fact, much of the early research in the field of gerontology, particularly in the medical arena, was conducted using only older men as subjects. It is not surprising that the interest in feminist gerontology is now gaining momentum. The increasing interest in feminist gerontology may be partially related to the aging of feminists themselves as they confront the combination of the myths, stereotypes, and discrimination based on age coupled with the still present myths, stereotypes, and discrimination based on gender.

It is interesting to note that Betty Friedan (1993) postulates that what initiated the women's movement of the 1960s and 1970s was the additional years of women's lives. She points out that women's life expectancy at the turn of the century was 46 and now it is nearly 80. "Our growing sense that we couldn't live all those years in terms of 'motherhood' alone was the problem that had no name" (p. 96). Although the activism of the 1960s and 1970s declined in the 1980s and 1990s as the country's political mood shifted toward conservatism and a return to individual culpability (Saulnier, 1996), feminism continues to seek social change and individual empowerment as mechanisms for enhancing the lives of women while gerontologists also recognize the dual importance of social action and individual empowerment as mechanisms to enhance the lives of older people.

There are approximately 19.5 million women over the age of 65 in the United States (American Association of Retired Persons, 1994). Many of these older women were socialized from an early age to defer decision making to men, especially in the area of finances, to keep their opinions silent, and to place the needs of husbands and children above their own. As many women outlive the men with whom they have had relationships and children grow up and move away, they are left with the sometimes overwhelming tasks of managing finances and making decisions alone which were previously made by others or made collaboratively. Women whose children were raised viewing their mothers as unable to make decisions may step in and take over, contributing to a sense of lack of control and helplessness. Women whose life experiences within families or among friends have included active decision making, freedom to voice opinions, and the ability to meet their own needs as well as the needs of others, are nonetheless plagued by societies which view them as less valuable and less capable than men. Hence, the concept of empowerment, rooted in feminist theory and practice, is critical to feminist gerontology.

"Empowerment oriented practice developed based on the principles of egalitarian client-worker relationships, strengths-based assessment, the promotion of empowerment through education and skills development, consciousness raising, self-help, and the use of collective and social action" (Cox and Parsons, 1996, p. 142). As feminists have struggled to empower women, it is also important to strive to empower older women through assisting them in developing new roles, in identifying their abilities and strengths, and in utilizing their knowledge. Feminist practice defines the linkages between personal and social change and provides strategies and methods for empowering women to make meaningful changes in their lives (Kravetz, 1986). Feminist gerontologists facilitate the processes of older women learning to care about themselves as valuable human beings and to become empowered.

According to Marilyn Mason (1991) empowering women to work together is the first step toward the healing process. Older women, with the assistance of feminist practitioners, join together with one another to explore new options for productivity and fulfillment. Increasing awareness of societal biases and the resulting barriers to women's success facilitates movement away from inappropriate self blame. Working with older women, singularly or collectively, it is important to convey respect and recognition of their value and worth as human beings. Egalitarian, collaborative relationships cannot totally obliterate the reality of a power differential between practitioner and client; however, the power differential is minimized and active client participation is elicited. A thorough assessment and recognition of strengths facilitates collaboration, assists clients in identifying their own problem-solving skills, and frequently results in an improved sense of worth thereby diminishing the overwhelming nature of identified problems to be addressed and beginning the empowerment process.

A variety of group interventions have emerged as a result of feminism. Assertiveness training, self-help groups, support groups, consciousness raising groups, survivors groups, and consensus building are all rooted in feminist theories. Women are frequently sustained by women, especially as they age (Thone, 1992). It is, therefore, in keeping with the natural experiences of women to use feminist group interventions in working to empower older women. In applying a feminist approach to life review, older women not only connect with one another through telling stories of their lives, but they validate their current worth through collective problem-solving using skills and strengths identified in sharing life stories. Older women are thereby valued, not only for who they have been, but for who they are today. Cox and Parsons (1996), in their study on the influence of empowerment oriented group interventions on the relationships of older women, found empowerment oriented interventions enhanced the quality of life of older women, including the development and support of meaningful interpersonal relationships. They also concluded that the use of small groups is a viable strategy for work with older women, including those who are frail, and that ongoing participatory strengths-based problem assessment and participation in self-help and mutual-help activities promotes competence in coping with late life challenges. "Empowerment interventions promote egalitarian, strengths-based relationships through education, self-help, mutual support, consciousness raising, and social action activities" (Cox and Parsons, 1996, p. 129).

Feminist gerontologists also recognize the need to work with other practitioners in the use of empowering techniques and skills. While talking with an old women in a retirement center recently, she nodded in the direction of a staff person and whispered, "I'm tired of being patted like a dog." As I watched the staff person move through the room, I became acutely aware how she patted residents and spoke to them as if they were children. Rather than sit beside them, she always stood over them. She most likely viewed herself as a caring professional and had little or no awareness of the messages she conveyed through tone of voice, patting, and stance. While a mutual hug, holding of hands, and other therapeutic forms of touch can enhance a sense of collaboration and mutual problem solving, patting generally does not. Most helping professionals do not address colleagues or clients of their own age cohort in the manner just described. Unfortunately, old women are all too often approached by practitioners in a manner which is unintentionally demeaning. If the majority of professionals approach old people as if they were children, a single feminist practitioner may be unsuccessful in facilitating empowerment. Working effectively with colleagues to increase the collective staff's success in the use of feminist skills may be as important as working with older women.

Alyn and Becker (1984) state that feminist practice is not a political view or a therapeutic technique but a perspective that they bring to their work which recognizes and validates women's experiences. In essence, a feminist perspective, seeks to enhance self-esteem, raise consciousness, empower, and validate recipients of treatment or services. Feminist practice focuses on respect and the value of women for their intelligence, support, skills, talents, and abilities. Feminist practitioners explain techniques and share insights as part of a mutual problem-solving partnership with their clients (Sancier, 1981). A feminist approach includes honestly and openly giving opinions, options, and feedback as well as asking questions. It means collaborative as opposed to hierarchical interaction, and being challenging rather than confrontational (Pasick and White, 1991). A feminist approach to treatment includes appropriately responsible support. Feminist practitioners encourage independence and self sufficiency while supporting their clients' basic rights to services and resources. It is not atypical for feminist practice to draw simultaneously from several areas of feminist theory while assisting women in understanding the realities of oppression and providing support for individual and social change. Feminist gerontology adheres to those principles of feminism and applies them to the aging cohort.

Advocacy for women is an inherent component of feminist practice (Abbott, 1994). Although most geriatric practitioners are primarily concerned with individual, family, and small group interventions, advocacy is also an important part of feminist gerontology. Not only is there a responsibility for feminist gerontologists to advocate for old women, but there is a responsibility to facilitate advocacy efforts by older women themselves. One need only consider the advocacy and social change efforts of the Gray Panthers to recognize that old women need not be excluded from advocating for themselves and others. The

Gray Panthers was organized by Maggie Kuhn and six other women over the age of 65. Their original purpose was to oppose the Vietnam War. It has now become a global network advocating for the rights of people of all ages. Since 1970 the Gray Panthers have effectively advocated for multiple societal changes. They exposed and documented nursing home abuse, with Ralph Nader they exposed a hearing aid scam, they were largely responsible for the Age Discrimination Employment Act for an intergenerational amendment to the Older Americans Act that increased opportunities for old people to nurture and assist children through volunteer programs (Friedan, 1993), and they continue advocacy efforts today although most of the original founders, including Maggie Kuhn, have died or are advocating elsewhere. Advocacy may include such efforts as linking self help groups to create an avenue for broad based social criticism or assisting groups in becoming agents of social change (Whithorn, 1994). Advocacy from a feminist gerontological perspective includes pressuring organizations or governments to respond to the needs of older women and working to eliminate stereotypes, change societal attitudes, and broaden the range of roles available to aging women.

OVERVIEW:
FUNDAMENTALS OF FEMINIST GERONTOLOGY

There is no attempt in this work to select a particular branch of feminism or to specifically define feminism. Rather, much like practitioners, authors draw on a variety of feminist frameworks and adapt them to feminist practice with aging women. We have chosen to address, from a feminist perspective, a number of issues that effect aging women and are frequent problem-solving areas for practitioners and their clients. N. Jane McCandless and Francis P. Conner discuss how basic feminist principles such as education, egalitarianism, empowerment, and inclusion can be used to improve older women's experiences in the health care system. Susan Gaylord addresses empowering older women through alternative health care strategies and includes an assessment of how conventional medicine serves to disempower aging women. Virginia E. Richardson develops a feminist approach to assisting older women in dealing with retirement. Retirement is conceptualized as a process which includes three stages: preretirement, the retirement decision, and retirement adjustment. Dr. Richardson focuses on feminist conceptions of retirement, economic issues, psychological issues and social issues. Using case examples, feminist practice approaches are incorporated, including interventions ranging from individual empowerment and awareness to advocacy. Karen A. Roberto, Katherine R. Allen, and Rosemary Blieszner incorporate a feminist perspective to describe and interpret strategies for enhancing older women's relationships with their children and grandchildren. They address the strengths women develop throughout their life course as active players in their families and how older women utilize these strengths to adapt to contemporary family challenges. Linda Vinton assists all of us in using feminist theory and individual and group practice techniques with abused, neglected, or battered older women. N. Jane McCandless and Francis P. Conner addresses feminist practice as a sensitive, empowering modality for work with terminally ill older women and their families.

Working from a feminist perspective with three specific populations are also included in this volume. These particular populations were selected, not because they are inclusive, but because there are considerations that must be attended to based on culture, lifestyle, or the nature of the tasks at hand. Kate Conway-Turner focuses on the application of feminism in assisting African American and other minority older women. Elise M. Fullmer, Dena Shenk, and Lynette J. Eastland present the social construction of lesbianism for older women and the use of feminist practice with lesbian older women. Nancy R. Hooyman and Judith G. Gonyea examine women's experiences in caring for older family members and apply feminist theories and practice skills to working with caregivers.

Finally Ruth E. Ray addresses feminist research, defining empowering research and argues the need for critical gerontology informed by feminist theories. While that may at first glance seem a strange inclusion for a work of this nature, one must recognize that much of practice theory and techniques are based on research findings. When research is male biased, as in the case of the vast majority of earlier medical research, the resulting theories and techniques are not terribly likely to apply to women. It is, therefore, critical for practitioners to be able to assess research findings for biases and, when involved in research themselves, to be able to eliminate biases, hopefully, through the use of feminist research techniques.

This volume presents new feminist knowledge and strategies and a reshaping of old feminist knowledge and strategies to assist aging women in more fully developing, enhancing, and enjoying their later years. The focus on empowerment throughout is not by accident. "We must seek the empowerment of age, new roles for people over sixty, seventy, eighty, in work and business, public and private sectors, churches, synagogues, and in the volunteer cutting edge of the community" (Friedan, 1993). Empowerment is a fundamental mechanism which allows human beings to grow. To borrow from the tone of Harriet Tubman's 1851 presentation "Ain't I a Woman": Ain't old women human?

REFERENCES

American Association of Retired Persons. (1994). *A Profile of Older Americans: 1994*. Washington, DC (PF3049. D996).

Abbott, A. (1994). A feminist approach to substance abuse treatment and service delivery. *Social Work in Health Care*, 19 (3/4), 67-83.

Alyn, J. & Becker, L. (1984). Feminist therapy with chronically and profoundly disturbed women. *Journal of Counseling Psychology*, 31(2), 202-208.

Cox, E. O. & Parsone, R. R. (1996). Empowerment-oriented social work practice: Impact on late life relationships of women. In K. A. Roberto (Ed.), *Relationships between women in later life* (pp. 129-143). NY, NY: Harrington Park Press.

Ray, R.E. (1996) A postmodern perspective on feminist gerontology. *The Gerontologist*, 36 (5), 674-680.

Friedan, B. (1993). *The fountain of age*. New York, NY: Simon & Schuster.

Healey, S. (1994). Growing to be an old woman: Aging and ageism. In E. P. Stoller and R. C. Gibson (Eds.), *Worlds of difference: Inequality in the aging experience* (pp. 81-83). Thousand Oaks, CA: Pine Forge Press.

Kravetz, D. (1986) Women and mental health. In N. Van Den Berg & I. Cooper (Eds.), *Feminist visions for social work* (pp. 101-127). Washington, DC: NASW.

Mason, M. (1991) Women and shame: kin and culture. In C. Bepko (Ed.), *Feminism and addiction* (pp. 175-194). Binghamton, NY: The Haworth Press, Inc.

Nielsen, J.M. (1990). *Sex and gender in society*, 2nd ed. Prospect Heights, IL: Waveland Press, Inc.

Pasick, P. & White, C. (1991). A feminist stance in substance abuse treatment and training. In C. Bepko (Ed.), *Feminism and addiction* (pp. 87-102). Binghamton, NY: The Haworth Press, Inc.

Reinharz, S. (1986). Friends or foes: Gerontological and feminist theory. *Women's Studies International Forum*, 9, 503-514.

Sancier, B. (1981). Beyond advocacy. In Weick A. & Vandiver S. (Eds.) *Women, power and change* (pp. 186-196). Washington, DC: NASW.

Saulnier, C. F. (1996). *Feminist theories and social work: Approaches and applications*. Binghamton: The Haworth Press, Inc.

Thone, R. R. (1992). *Women and aging celebrating ourselves*. New York, NY: Harrington Park Press.

Older Women
and the Health Care System:
A Time for Change

N. Jane McCandless, PhD
Francis P. Conner, ACSW

SUMMARY. In spite of women's active involvement in a woman's health care movement, the mainline health care system continues to hold tight to its androcentric focus. If women are to be subjected to a health care system that employs sexist and ageist practices, the quality of life in their later years will continue to be jeopardized. The purpose of this paper is to first, recognize the existing health care practices which limit the health care opportunities and choices of older women; and secondly, to discuss how such basic feminist principles as education, egalitarianism, empowerment, and inclusion can be used to improve an older woman's experience. *[Article copies available for a fee from The Haworth Document Delivery Service: 1-800-342-9678. E-mail address: getinfo@haworthpressinc.com]*

KEYWORDS. Aging women, elderly women, older women, feminist health care, health care, medical care, women's health care

"One of the most striking aspects of the history of women's organizations and feminist movements is the degree to which these groups were active very early in trying to improve the quality and quantity of health care in America" (Sapiro, 1994, p. 177). An early pioneer

[Haworth co-indexing entry note]: "Older Women and the Health Care System: A Time for Change." McCandless, N. Jane, and Francis P. Conner. Co-published simultaneously in *Journal of Women & Aging* (The Haworth Press, Inc.) Vol. 11, No. 2/3, 1999, pp. 13-27; and: *Fundamentals of Feminist Gerontology* (ed: J. Dianne Garner) The Haworth Press, Inc., 1999, pp. 13-27. Single or multiple copies of this article are available for a fee from The Haworth Document Delivery Service [1-800-342-9678, 9:00 a.m. - 5:00 p.m. (EST). E-mail address: getinfo@haworthpressinc.com].

13

among health care advocates was Margaret Sanger, who fought for a woman's right to control her reproductive capabilities. "In a series of articles called 'What Every Girl Should Know,' then in her own newspaper *The Woman Rebel*, and finally through neighborhood clinics that dispensed women-controlled forms of birth control, Sanger put information and power into the hands of women" (Steinem, 1998, p. 93). Women less well known than Margaret Sanger include Dr. Juliet Nathanson who was teaching women about their bodies 25 years before the second wave of the women's movement inspired the feminist health centers (Anonymous, 1998). In fact, "Nathanson began a 50-year career of holistic and feminist health care that helped thousands of women and their families" (Anonymous, 1998, p. 37). As noted by Fugh-Berman (1994, p. 36) "women have a substantial history to draw upon–mainly the women's health movement of the sixties and seventies, when women opened feminist health centers, established the National Women's Health Network, demystified gynecological exams, and redefined their relationships with their bodies and their health care practitioners."

In spite of women's active involvement in the women's health movement, our health care system continues to hold tight to its androcentric focus, and sexist and ageist practices. The need to improve a woman's experience in the health care system, especially an older woman's experience, has never been more pressing. Women, more frequently than men, seek health care services and account for two out of every three health care dollars spent (Kadar, 1994, p. 68). Furthermore, this pattern of seeking health care continues to increase across the life span as the need for such care follows logically from women's longevity. However, if women are to be continually subjected to an androcentric health care system that employs sexist and ageist practices, the quality of life in their later years will continue to be jeopardized. Health is a major determinant of the quality of life, and for the elderly, a significant predictor of life satisfaction. And "a male-dominated medical profession, left-brained and mechanistic, enamored of gadgetry and novelty, always seeking to repair things, sometimes misses the point about the inner workings of someone with a medical condition" (Edelberg, 1997, p. 39).

"Fortunately, interest in improving women's health care has never been higher" (Fugh-Berman, 1994, p. 35), and "there is an emerging call for a feminist approach to health promotion for aging women"

(Ward-Griffin and Ploeg, 1997, p. 280). Unfortunately, feminists do not agree on the universal principles of a feminist health care perspective, and thus it would be presumptuous of us to suggest there are exact principles to guide such an approach. Instead we will argue that what is important to this discussion is first, to recognize the existing health care practices which limit the health care opportunities and choices for older women; and second, to discuss how such basic feminist principles as education, egalitarianism, empowerment, and inclusion can be used to improve an older woman's experience in the health care system.

THE PRINCIPLE OF EDUCATION

Education can help older women come to understand the sexist assumptions made about their health and their health care needs. As stated by Salk, Sanford, Swenson, and Luce (1992, p. 387):

> It is not enough to provide or improve medical care, to have more women physicians, to stop the abuses or to increase access to existing health and medical care for the poor and elderly–even though we support absolutely equal access to care for all classes and groups. We want to reclaim the knowledge and skills that the medical establishment has inappropriately taken over.

A striking example of sexism within the health care system is the way in which women's normal life processes have been medicalized. Consider for a moment, menstruation. Menstruation has been subjected to a variety of medical interventions and has even been used to "make a charge of mental instability," most notably, "premenstrual phase dysphoric disorder in the *Psychiatric Diagnostic and Statistical Manual*" (Hunter College Women's Studies Collective, 1995, p. 103-104). Consider, too, the process of childbirth which has been transformed into a major medical event, with pregnant women losing control over the birthing process as they are turned into patients. "Studies have shown that 95 to 98 percent of women could give birth to healthy babies without medical intervention if they had proper prenatal care, nutrition, and so forth" (Keville, 1993, p. 130). Today, however, childbirth is plagued by an increasing use of caesarians, though "the Centers for Disease Control maintain that about 36 percent of caesarian deliveries are medically unnecessary" (Renzetti and Curran, 1995, p. 450). But the medicalization of women's lives extends far beyond the processes of menstruation and childbirth. As stated by Fugh-Berman (1994, p. 34) "the American Society of Plastic and Reconstructive Surgeons reached a new low when it suggested that small breasts be considered a disease–they named it 'micromastia.'"

This pattern of medicalizing the normal life processes of women continues across the life span. "Although menopause is typically acknowledged to be a normal part of the aging process, it is at the same time treated as an abnormality, a disease" (Belgrave, 1993, p. 191). "The biological shifts that come with menopause, seen through this medical perspective, are regarded as pathological and in need of medical management–dosing with hormones, even surgical removal of the uterus, among other measures" (Hunter College Women's Studies Collective, 1995, p. 412). Today, hysterectomies remain the second most frequently performed major surgical procedure in this country, though only 10.5 percent of all hysterectomies performed in the U.S. between 1970 and 1984 were necessary and medically indicated (Schumacher, 1990, p. 54).

When we argue for education, we are arguing that an essential goal of a feminist health care approach must be to educate older women to the ways in which the patriarchal health care system has medicalized their normal life processes. Such an understanding is particularly important for women during the aging process, especially when we begin to consider how many aspects of a woman's life might be medicalized. Aging women experience so many changes in their skin, hair, body tissues, senses, muscles, bones, joints, hearts, lungs, and nervous system, that medical intervention could become a daily task. In fact, there is evidence that the natural aging process has already boosted the medical field of surgical beautification. As stated by Chrisler and Ghiz (1993, p. 68):

> Because of society's creation of beauty culture and insistence that women pursue an illusive beauty ideal, and because of the tendency to see youth and beauty as synonymous and to define "woman as body," one can expect to find many mid-life and older women experiencing body image disturbance as they encounter the effects of aging.

It is also important to point out that the medicalization of women's lives extends far beyond the health care system. Today a variety of industries and businesses misrepresent health benefits of cancer cures and medical devices. No doubt, older women fear cancer and would do whatever necessary to find relief from the aches and pains associated with arthritis. Still, such medical quackery robs older women of their time, their energy, and their limited financial resources.

Just as important in the educational process is understanding that even when medical intervention is deemed to be necessary, older women cannot automatically assume that such intervention is going to be beneficial. Until recently, medical researchers have systematically excluded women from most clinical studies.

> In some instances, the degree of bias borders on the absurd. A research project ostensibly aimed at determining the impact of obesity on breast and uterine cancer was conducted with male subjects. According to an NIH official, the narrow focus of the study was the effects of certain nutrients on estrogen metabolism, which researchers believed to be similar in men and women–a tenuous rationale, to say the least. (Keville, 1993, p. 126-127),

"Females also get short shrift because such problems as contraception, breast cancer, and postpartum depression don't receive the attention of male ailments" (Abramson, 1992, p. 87).

> From 1986 to 1987, the proportion of the NIH budget devoted to research on "women's health issues," very broadly defined, grew by 8 percent. It sounds like a lot. However, it grew to only 13.6 percent of the NIH budget, though women are more than 50 percent of the population. (Berney, 1990, p. 24)

Simply put, although traditional medical care may, at times, be imperative, "the lack of research exploring whether men and women, blacks and whites, respond differently to the same treatment means that doctors in communities all over America don't have the information they need to treat their patients correctly" (Berney, 1990, p. 26).

A feminist approach to health care does not assume that older women cannot understand, nor do not want to have access to information as it affects their health. A feminist approach to health care places great emphasis on giving older women as much medical knowledge and information as is available, whether through literature, self-help groups, or focused seminars. While the distribution of such materials is, necessary, it is, at the same time, not always sufficient. First, we must question whether such information is presented in ways that older women can easily understand the information itself. Secondly, we must begin to fill the gaps in the literature and come to recognize the paucity of information regarding many age-specific illnesses and diseases and how such illnesses and diseases affect women. It is also perplexing that the information on some common injuries during the life span do not take the variable of age into account. Breaking an arm at 50 years of age is certainly different from breaking an arm at 15 years of age. "The key purpose of information. . . . is not to educate women in a didactic way but to enable them to make more informed choices for themselves" (Foster, 1989, p. 342).

THE PRINCIPLE OF EGALITARIANISM

The relationship between a woman and her physician has been described as a relationship of profound inequality; "a paternalistic encounter that incorporates both benevolence and social control" (Sharpe, 1995, p. 10). Because of such inequitable interactions, it is not surprising to find that women's complaints of medical problems are not always taken seriously and, sometimes, are trivialized or discounted.

> A study released by the Physician Insurers Association of America in July, 1990, revealed a disturbing tendency for doctors to minimize patients' discoveries of breast lumps. It noted that, in 69% of malpractice cases which resulted in payment to the patient, the physician delayed action after the patient discovered a breast lump. In more than half the cases, the doctors said their own physical findings were at odds with the patients. (Abramson, 1992, p. 89)

This common lack of disregard for the opinions of women further complicates matters when the illness is life threatening.

> Boston-area medical research institutions produced some dismaying results when they gathered 13 male doctors to review

videotapes of a man and a woman complaining about chest pains. Both patients were 40 years old, smoked, and said they had high-stress jobs. Two thirds of the internists urged additional tests and evaluation for the male patient, but only one-third thought the female should have further tests. All the doctors said the man should stop smoking, but not one thought the woman should quit. Two of the 13 felt she was a candidate for psychiatry. (Abramson, 1992, p. 88)

Based upon such evidence it is not surprising to find that "women (are) less likely to be referred for cardiac catheterization and coronary bypass surgery . . . (and) are only about half as likely as men to receive the most current medical treatments–such as 'clotbuster' drugs and balloon angioplasty–for heart attacks" (Keville, 1993, p. 128-129). Because women's symptoms are treated less seriously it is also not uncommon for physicians to attribute physical symptoms to psychosomatic causes. In a few cases this may be an accurate diagnosis, but in far too many cases such conclusions result in the dispensing of prescription drugs. In fact, women "consume about 60% of all prescriptions drugs used in the U.S. every year" (Abramson, 1992, p. 87).

The problems associated with prescription drugs for older women are many. First, older women often take several medications, from several different physicians, for various chronic conditions, which can, and sometimes do, lead to drug-induced disorders. Secondly, "until a few years ago drug trials were performed exclusively on men" (Fugh-Berman, 1994, p. 35). Take, for example, "the news of a 1988 study of 22,071 volunteers (which) produced banner headlines announcing that small amounts of aspirin on a regular basis can reduce the chances of a heart attack" (Abramson, 1992, p. 87). This recommendation, unfortunately, is only applicable to men, as not one woman participated in the study. Even today the "use of calcium after menopause, directed at prevention of osteoporosis, has been growing despite the lack of a firm evidentiary basis for the practice" (Muller, 1986, p. 40).

Another very common pattern is for physicians to attribute a woman's chronic conditions to the "natural aging process," thereby creating a situation where physicians are less willing to treat such symptoms. "Although most urinary incontinence can be prevented, improved, or cured through medical or behavioral techniques, there is a persistent belief among professionals and lay people that it is an expected part of the aging process" (Sharpe, 1995, p. 15).

The first step toward changing this all too common interactional pattern between patient and physician requires that attention be paid to the rights of the patient.

> Everyone should maintain that sense of a patient's basic right–a right to express one's own opinion, to be treated with respect, and to be taken seriously . . . A patient should be able to make a request without having to apologize . . . One pays for the providers services and certainly is entitled to receive information that affects one's health and well being. (Rogers, 1987, p. 141)

A second step toward changing the patient-physician interaction is for health care professionals to reevaluate their own sexist and ageist stereotypes and come to understand how such stereotypes negatively affect the lives of older women seeking health care services. It would be just as rewarding if physicians could learn to listen to women, learn to help women express their feelings, and take notice of their pain. It has been argued that "health professionals must have a clear understanding that the client is, in fact, the elderly person (and) to communicate clearly and directly with that individual is the appropriate ethical action" (Bata and Power, 1995, p. 150). Unfortunately, geriatric medicine is not a requirement in most medical schools (Henderson, 1997), and "the current medical system remains deficient indeed when it comes to the care of women" (Fugh-Berman, 1994, p. 34). The question of how physicians should be trained to care for their female patients has led to much unresolved discussion. As stated by Fugh-Berman (1994, p. 35):

> Fellowships, residencies, master's programs, and continuing education courses in women's health have all been proposed, and in some cases implemented. No proposal, however, has drawn more fire than the recommendation that a new specialty in women's health be established–some of the most outspoken women in medicine are on opposite sides of the question.

Changes in the relationship between patient and physician also requires that older women challenge what society has defined as appropriate female behavior. Here, deference, dependency, and passivity have negative consequences regarding an older woman's health.

Many older women are, in fact, intimidated by physicians. As stated by Sharpe (1995, p. 11) "although older health care consumers express desire for more information from physicians than they receive and endorse medical consumerism in theory, they appear less likely than younger people to actually challenge physician authority." It is imperative that older women come to understand that their health is dependent upon their active involvement in the patient-physician interactional process. Older women must learn to ask questions and expect answers. Should they be denied access to the information requested, then women must exercise their option of choosing a physician who will meet their needs. We must help older women feel comfortable enough to voice their concerns and explore their choice; to "incorporate fully into their thoughts and actions a sense of their rights as patients" (Rogers, 1987, p. 141).

EMPOWERMENT AND INCLUSION OF ALL WOMEN

"The Public Health Service Task Force on Women's Health Issues reported that fundamental changes in the health care system and significant improvement in the individual's health status no longer come from technological breakthroughs, but from interpersonal changes, such as the way people participate in their own health care" (Rogers, 1987, p. 141). Indeed, empowerment–the ability to meet our needs, solve our problems, and organize the resources necessary to take control of our lives–is a central idea within the feminist perspective, and a central principle for reforming older women's experience in the health care system. As stated by Sharpe (1995, p. 14) "level of perceived control in old age is positively associated with health-related behaviors, psychological coping, functioning of the immune and neuroendocrine systems, and decreased mortality."

Older women must take responsibility for their health, as they, and they alone, are the "major stake-holders in health care" (Anderson, 1996, p. 697). Aging women must come to understand that fitness, healthy eating, smoking cessation, moderate alcohol consumption, and stress reduction are all constructive steps to take as they continue to age. It is the woman herself who can identify her own needs, for it is she who is an expert on her own body.

But older women cannot take control of their health without the guidance and assistance of those who are experts on matters of health.

Thus mutual aid is extremely important when we speak of empowerment.

It is imperative that health professionals seek to enhance the knowledge of their clients and help them take control over factors that affect their health. Unfortunately, "the health promotion movement . . . has been targeted primarily at young rather than older persons, at men rather than women" (Ward-Griffin and Ploeg, 1997, p. 280), and thus "has been slow to pay attention to older women in the planning of health promotion and disease prevention programs" (Sharpe, 1995, p. 16). Furthermore, among the health promotion programs that do exist, "many of the individual-level health promotion programs do not create a sense of control or empowerment, but tend to 'blame' the older person for their situation" (Ward-Griffin and Ploeg, 1997, p. 284).

Programs that do not create a sense of control, programs that are overprotective in nature, and programs that blame the victim for her situation do not flow from the principle of empowerment. Rather, a health promotion program based on the premise of empowerment does just the opposite.

Interestingly, Anderson (1996, p. 699) asks "whether empowerment, with its focus on enabling the individual, deflects our attention from the structures that perpetuate social inequities." As such, we must recognize that we have an ever expanding diversity in our aging population. Language differences, ethnic differences, racial differences, cohort differences, economic differences, educational differences, occupational differences, and sexual preference differences have all captured the attention of scholars, and now lay the foundation for, and recognition of, a diverse population of people. Yet, we have been slow to recognize issues of diversity among those who are aging, preferring instead to treat the aging as a homogeneous group of people.

"The ideal health care system for elderly women is one that is sensitive to individual needs in light of this cohort's heterogeneity" (Henderson, 1997, p. 113). We must therefore be sensitive to the issues that will impact a woman's experience in the health care setting. As Ward-Griffin and Ploeg (1997, p. 287) "there is a need to first identify the social dimensions and structures that are constraining older women's life choices, and second, to decrease or eliminate the barriers to social inequality."

A case in point is the position that older women occupy within the economic institution. For decades women have been subjected to occupational segregation, resulting in economic discrimination and limited resources, such as health care benefits. Elderly women are particularly disadvantaged as a lifetime pattern of economic discrimination results in fewer resources during the later years of life, making the management of an illness more difficult. "Women who are 65 years old today are still paying for the wage and social discrimination they suffered when 30 or 40 years old" (Barrow, 1992, p. 167). In fact, elderly women have the highest poverty rate for any age group in the U.S., comprising more than 70 percent of the elderly poor.

A disturbing pattern, yet common within the health care system, is that older women's health care coverage is often inadequate. "Contrary to popular belief, Medicare and Medicaid do not cover all medical expenses for those over age 65" (Barrow, 1992, p. 161). "One study demonstrated that Medicare offers superior coverage for the acute conditions that more frequently appear in older men–such as lung cancer, prostate disorders, and heart attacks–than for the chronic medical problems that commonly afflict elderly women–for example, breast cancer, depression, and arthritis" (Keville, 1993, p. 139). Even for women who have the luxury of private health insurance, it is not unusual for women to be charged more for individual coverage (Baylis and Nelson, 1997), or to be shortchanged when it comes to reimbursements:

> . . . medicare reimburses patients for male specific surgeries about 44 percent more in sheer dollar amount than for comparable female-specific procedures, according to a recent study published in the Journal Gynecologic Oncology . . . These findings should be of concern to women on all types of insurance plans, says David M. Gershenson, M.D., former president of the Society of Gynecologic Oncologists, because many private insurance carriers use the Medicare system to determine reimbursement. (Richardson, 1997, p. 24)

Race is another position within the system of stratification that has ramifications for elderly women seeking health care. Suffice it to say, elderly black women are among the most severely disadvantaged as the interaction of sex, age, and race further limits their health and their treatment in the health care system.

> Women of African descent carry a greater burden of morbidity and mortality than white women, with higher rates for virtually every major illness . . . the mortality rate from coronary heart disease is 22% higher for black women . . . black women die of heart attacks at a younger age . . . hypertension in black women is 21.2% compared with 4.8% in white women . . . black women's death rate from stroke is 78% higher than white women's . . . More than half of all women with AIDS in this country are black . . . the incidence of breast cancer has been increasing more rapidly in black than in white women. (Kielich and Miller, 1996, p. 61)

Elderly black women do have more health-related problems than do elderly white women. The most important question to ask is: why?

No doubt black elderly women are worse off financially than elderly white women. Black elderly women have lower incomes than their white counterparts, as well as lower levels of education and occupational status (Coke and Twaite, 1995). Furthermore, "the health problems experienced by elderly blacks are made more serious by their tendency to underutilize health care delivery systems" (Coke and Twaite, 1995, p. 12), explained, in part, by the fact that such facilities are staffed by white professionals who may appear intimidating and may lack the ability to communicate effectively with older blacks (Downing and Copeland, 1980).

A feminist approach to health care rests on the premise of inclusion for all women, despite class or race, or language-ethnic-cohort-sexual preference differences. It is an approach that is sensitive to those women who have been excluded from the conversations and practices that directly impact their lives; it is an approach that cannot continue to perpetuate discriminatory practices.

CONCLUSION

"In the 1990s, women's health is an issue with political cache. It is an issue that resonates with voters across economic, racial and partisan lines, and no member of Congress wants to pass up the opportunity to be seen as its champion" (Howes and Allina, 1994, p. 7). Thus, the time is now to eliminate the impact that both sex and age has upon older women who seek health care services. And a feminist framework is one alternative that can successfully challenge the ways older women have been defined by the health care system, confront the paternalistic nature of physician-patient relationships, and focus attention on the health care concerns of all older women. It is this framework that will create for women a sense of empowerment.

We must note, however, that not everyone who claims to use a feminist approach to health care, is in fact, doing so. Many of us have become aware of the newfound "women's health center" in our communities. Even in small towns, women's health clinics have begun to appear around the corner from the local hospital. Yet, Lundy and Mason's (1994) exploratory study of women's health care centers identified two primary concerns: (a) the problem in defining women's health care, and (b) access to adequate health care for all women.

Regarding the definition of women's health care centers, Lundy and Mason (1994) pointed out:

> From our inquiry it appears that women's health care centers more often serve younger women with a focus on reproductive functions. This is not to deny the need; indeed, many young women lack adequate reproductive care. Rather, it raises the question of whether the need for and resultant definition of comprehensive medical care for all women is falling prey to the more acceptable focus of prenatal care and childbirth, excluding other medical needs. (p. 116)

Regarding access to such health care centers, the authors further noted "with one exception, only centers with a reproductive focus provide sliding scale fees and accept Medicaid" (p. 118). As Lundy and Mason (1994, p. 118) conclude "perhaps women are led to believe that their medical care is changing when it is just being packaged differently."

Interesting, but not a new phenomenon. In an effort to boost sales and profits, businesses do follow the latest trends. And, health care, "constrained by the demands of the capitalist system in general and the profit orientation of drugs companies" is no exception to the rule. If "women's health care centers" are what will attract business, by all means, a change in a clinic's name is a very small investment. The lesson that we learn is as old as that of supply and demand: "buyer beware." There are no guarantees that what is labeled as "women's health care" is in fact based upon basic feminist principles, and worse, no guarantee that a woman's health needs will be met in a nonsexist, egalitarian fashion.

"Women's health advocates now have an uncommon opportunity to use the political power they have built to advance women's health goals . . . The timing is fortuitous, since women's health advocacy is now at a point of unprecedented strength" (Howes and Allina, 1994, p. 6-7). It is then our challenge and our responsibility to work towards change in the health care system which will ensure that all women receive the health care that they need during their aging process.

REFERENCES

Abramson, L. (1992). Women and health care: unneeded risks. *USA Today: The Magazine of the American Scene, 121*, 87-89.

Anderson, J. (1996). Empowering patients: issues and strategies. *Social Science Medicine, 43*, 697-705.

Anonymous. (1998). Juliet Nathanson: Pioneer in feminist health care. *Ms., 8*, 37.

Bata, E. and Power, P. (1995) Facilitating health care decisions within aging families. Pgs. 143-157, in G. Smith, S. Tobin, E. Robertson-Tchabo, and P. Power (Eds.) *Strengthening Aging Families*. CA: Sage.

Barrow, G. (1992). *Aging, the Individual, and Society*. NY: West.

Baylis, F. and Nelson, H. (1997). Access to health care for women. *The New England Journal of Medicine, 336*, 1841.

Belgrave, L. (1993). Discrimination against older women in health care. *Journal of Women & Aging, 5*, 181-99.

Berney, B. (1990). In research, women don't matter. *Progressive, 54*, 24-27.

Chrisler, J. and Ghiz, L. (1993). Body image issues of older women. Pgs. 67-76, in N. Davis, E. Cole, E. Rothblum (Eds.) *Faces of Women and Aging*. NY: Harrington Park Press.

Coke, M and Twaite, J. (1995). *The Black Elderly: Satisfaction and Quality of Later Life*. NY: The Haworth Press, Inc.

Downing, R. and Copeland, E. (1980). Services for the black elderly: national or local problems? *Journal of Gerontology, 28*, 497-502.

Edelberg, D. (1997). Women's health. *Total Health, 19*, p. 39.

Foster, P. (1989). Improving the doctor/patient relationship: a feminist perspective. *Journal of Social Policy, 18*, 337-361.

Fugh-Berman, A. (1994). Training doctors to care for women. *Technology Review, 97*, 34-30.

Henderson, J. (1997). Issues in the medical treatment of elderly women. *Journal of Women & Aging, 9*, 107-115.

Howes, J. and Allina, A. (1994). Women's health movements. *Social Policy, 24,* 6-14.

Hunter College Women's Studies Collective. (1995). *Women's Realities, Women's Choices.* NY: Oxford.

Kadar, A. (1994). The sex-bias myth in medicine. *The Atlantic Monthly, August,* 66-70.

Keville, T. (1993). The invisible woman: gender bias in medical research. *Women's Rights Law Reporter, 15,* 123-142.

Kielich, A. and Miller, L. (1996). Cultural aspects of women's health care. *Patient Care, 30,* 60-64+.

Lundy, M. and Mason, S. (1994). "Women's health care centers: multiple definitions." *Social Work in Health Care, 19,* 109-122.

Muller, C. (1996). Women and men: quality and equality in health care. *Social Policy, 17,* 39-45.

Pearson, B. and Beck, C. (1989). Physical health of elderly women. Pgs. 149-175, in D. Garner and S. Mercer (Eds.) *Women as They Age.* NY: The Haworth Press, Inc.

Richardson, V. (1997). Women pay more for medicine. *Shape, 17,* 24.

Renzetti, C. and Curran, D. (1995). *Women, Men, and Society.* MA: Allyn and Bacon.

Rogers, P. (1987). Improving communication between women and health care providers. *Public Health Reports, 102,* 141-142.

Salk, H., Sanford, W., Swenson, N., and Luce, J. (1992). The politics of women and medical care. Pgs. 387-405, in S. Ruth (Ed.) 1998. *Issues in Feminism.* CA: Mayfield.

Sapiro, V. (1994). *Women in American Society.* CA: Mayfield.

Schumacher, D. (1990). Hidden death: the sexual effects of hysterectomy. Pgs. 49-67, in E. Rosenthal (Ed.) *Women, Aging, and Ageism.* NY: Harrington Park Press.

Sharpe, P. (1995). Older women and health services: moving from ageism toward empowerment. *Women and Health, 22,* 9-23.

Steinem, G. (1998). Margaret Sanger." *Time, 1512,* 93-94.

Ward-Griffin, C. and Ploeg, J. (1997). A feminist approach to health promotion for older women. *Canadian Journal on Aging, 16,* 279-296.

Alternative Therapies and Empowerment
of Older Women

Susan Gaylord, PhD

SUMMARY. There has been a striking increase in Americans' awareness and use of alternative therapies over the last decade. Women, in
particular, have been drawn to explore these unconventional health
practices, which include herbal medicine, acupuncture, homeopathy,
manual therapies, energy healing, and mind-body therapies. From a
feminist perspective, the rise in alternative therapies' use in the United
States represents a shift in cultural concepts of health from an outmoded patriarchical model which disempowers older women, to a more
feminine, holistic model which can reempower older women. Throughout history, older women have developed, applied, and taught the principles and practices of what are now considered alternative healing modalities, in their roles as mothers, expert herbalists, midwives, wise
women, and shaman. By becoming familiar with these therapies, older
women can increase their control over their health, enhance prevention
and self-care, and enjoy a health-care pathway that leads to wholeness
in body, mind, and spirit. *[Article copies available for a fee from The
Haworth Document Delivery Service: 1-800-342-9678. E-mail address:
getinfo@haworthpressinc.com]*

KEYWORDS. Alternative medicine, women, aging, elderly, control,
health beliefs

INTRODUCTION

Alternative therapies, known also as complementary or unconventional therapies, are often defined in terms of what they are not:

[Haworth co-indexing entry note]: "Alternative Therapies and Empowerment of Older Women." Gay-
lord, Susan. Co-published simultaneously in *Journal of Women & Aging* (The Haworth Press, Inc.) Vol. 11,
No. 2/3, 1999, pp. 29-47; and: *Fundamentals of Feminist Gerontology* (ed: J. Dianne Garner) The Haworth
Press, Inc., 1999, pp. 29-47. Single or multiple copies of this article are available for a fee from The Haworth
Document Delivery Service [1-800-342-9678, 9:00 a.m. - 5:00 p.m. (EST). E-mail address: getinfo@
haworthpressinc.com].

"Those medical interventions not taught widely at U.S. medical schools or generally available at U.S. hospitals" (Eisenberg, Kessler, Foster, Norlock, Calkins & Delbanco, 1993). They include such practices as herbal medicine, acupuncture, homeopathy, manual therapies, energy healing, and mind-body therapies. Although these therapies are "alternatives" to conventional Western medicine, they have been used throughout the world for hundreds or thousands of years, and are still the primary form of health care practiced in many countries today. Throughout history, older women, in the roles of family healer, expert herbalist, midwife, wise woman and shaman, have developed, applied, and taught the principles and practices of these therapies, in their many cultural variations (Stein, 1990). Older women today have the opportunity to reclaim this knowledge and to be empowered to use these practices for the benefit of themselves and others.

The striking growth in Americans' awareness and use of alternative therapies has caught the medical establishment by surprise. A landmark national survey, published in *The New England Journal of Medicine*, found that in 1990 one-third of U.S. adults, and about a quarter of older people, used alternative therapies (Eisenberg et al., 1993). That year, Americans made an estimated 425 million visits to providers of unconventional therapies, compared with 388 million visits to all primary care physicians, and spent about $13.7 billion dollars, of which $10.3 billion was paid out of pocket. Women are the main users of alternative medicine, with two studies finding the majority of users to be women aged 30-49 years, and another study, women aged 45-64 years (Drivdahl & Miser, 1998; Lloyd, Lupton, Wiesner, & Hasleton, 1993; Thomas, Carr, Westlake, & Williams, 1991). The public's use of alternative and complementary therapies continues to soar, with some therapies–for instance, St. John's Wort to alleviate depression and Ginkgo biloba to enhance memory–competing in use with standard treatment.

What are the reasons for the phenomenal increase in popularity of these alternative healing modalities? And how can use of these therapies enhance well-being in older women? The answers to these questions are explored here from the feminist perspective of empowerment and its positive effects on well-being. It is argued that the rise in alternative therapies' use in the United States represents a shift in our cultural concepts of health (Kleinman, 1978), from an obsolete patriarchical model to a more holistic model. It is also argued that integrating alternative and conventional health practices within this holistic paradigm will better meet the health needs of older women.

DISENCHANTMENT
WITH THE FORMAL HEALTH CARE SYSTEM

There is growing disenchantment with many aspects of the formal health-care system in the United States. Gratitude for life-saving technologies is offset by dissatisfaction with high costs and lack of success in treatment of chronic disease. These issues particularly affect older women because (1) older women are the predominant users of the health-care system; (2) their incomes are lower, on average, compared with other groups; and (3) elderly women, who live longer than elderly men, may contend for more years with chronic health problems. Increasingly, there are complaints about dehumanization and ineffectiveness of the physician-patient relationship: the doctor doesn't spend enough time with patients, listen well or resolve problems. From a feminist perspective, this dissatisfaction is largely due to the conventional health-care system's continuing to operate within an outmoded patriarchical framework, dominated by the biomedical model. This model, and its manifestations, are described below.

THE BIOMEDICAL MODEL AS A DOMINANT,
PATRIARCHICAL MODEL OF HEALTH CARE

Elements of a cultural model of a health-care system include our definitions of health, what we experience as illness, our beliefs about the cause and prevention of illness, how we manage our illness, including selection of treatment and health-care providers, and how we deal with treatment failure, recurrence, chronic illness, and dying. Culturally based explanatory models of health care not only provide meaning for our illnesses, but determine our pathways towards healing (Kleinman, 1978).

The biomedical model has been the officially sanctioned, dominant explanatory model of health and illness in twentieth century Western technologically developed societies (Engel, 1977). Although Engel called for health professions to embrace a new biopsychosocial model, in which psychological and sociological factors would be included as explanations of cause and treatment of illness, the biomedical model continues to dominate education and practice in the medical community.

The biomedical model is a patriarchical model in that it is hierarchical, reductionist, mechanical and aggressive. It is hierarchical in that the doctor is in charge, and his (or her) view of health and illness has predominated. The patient's perspective has been viewed as subjective, and perhaps naive. Communication is often too brief and one-sided; the patient's story is not fully heard.

Disease, rather than the individual with the disease, is the focus of the biomedical model. It reduces explanations of cause of disease, including mental illness, to biochemical or neurophysiological processes, or to attack by external agents. It often explains disease-processes in mechanistic terms; the body is analogized as a machine, with parts that can be removed and replaced. Diagnosis involves identification of the pathogen or process responsible; treatment involves removing (e.g., surgery), destroying (e.g., antibiotics), or modifying (e.g., hormone therapy) the disease-causing agent. Sanctioned healers are highly trained experts (stereotypically white males or other white-lab coated ones) who diagnosis and treat in sterile settings with scientifically-tested agents and procedures. Words such as "attack," "aggressive," "target," "fighting," and "battle" describe treatment approaches, with the "magic bullet" as the illusive holy grail.

Any belief system influences one's perception of the world. Engel (1977) described the biomedical model as being raised to the level of powerful cultural dogma, such that any new phenomena must fit into the model or be rejected. Thus, diseases that do not fit the biomedical model may be viewed as imaginary or nonexistent. For example, chronic fatigue syndrome and Gulf War Illness are conditions for which the search continues for pathogens which, until found, will deny the reality of the illness. Another example is the syndrome "hypochondriasis," which *Stedman's Medical Dictionary* defines pejoratively as "a morbid concern about one's own health and exaggerated attention to any unusual bodily or mental sensations; a delusion that one is suffering from some disease for which no physical basis is evident" (Spraycar, 1995, p. 834). Even the term "psychosomatic," while strictly defined as mind-body interaction, is more commonly used to belie the objective reality of someone's experience of pain or illness. Entire healing systems may be rejected or reinterpreted within the dominant framework of biomedicine. For example, both faith healing and homeopathy, to be discussed later, have been described as merely the placebo effect.

HOW CONVENTIONAL MEDICINE DISEMPOWERS OLDER WOMEN

In a patriarchical system, the dominant belief system automatically suppresses, disregards, and denigrates other systems of belief in attempts to disempower those who hold those beliefs. The American Medical Association, for instance, has since its inception waged war against alternative medicine, with slanderous attacks on the integrity of its practitioners and ridiculing of its practices (Zwicky, Hafner, Barrett, & Jarvis, 1993). In true paternalistic fashion, the medical profession has attempted to deter the public from use of non-conventional practices by painting the frightening picture of uneducated, desperate, vulnerable people–often older women–being duped by unscrupulous charlatans eager to take their money without offering any hope of cure. In fact, there is greater use of alternative medicines among more highly educated than lesser educated Americans (Eisenberg et al., 1993).

Elements of the biomedical model are themselves disempowering. Focus on disease, rather than on the individual with the disease, robs people of meaning in their illness and thus in their lives. Viewing the body as a machine subtlety dehumanizes and deemphasizes the body-mind's ability to heal itself. And aggressive language and treatment strategies represent an overemphasis on the masculine approach and deemphasize the gentler, often more effective strategies of prevention and self-care.

The hierarchical relationship between doctor and patient can make the patient feel like a second-class citizen in her own body. Particularly when doctors are male, and their patients older women, power differentials and divergent perspectives may occur. If her perceptions and perspectives are not honored, self-confidence and self-esteem may suffer. If her own self-care strategies are belittled or ignored (as is often the case when patients tell their physicians about their use of alternative therapies) her sense of control over her own health care may decrease. Perhaps this is why, according to the Eisenberg study, two-thirds of those who visited alternative care providers did not tell their primary-care physicians about these visits (Eisenberg et al., 1993).

Conventional medicine also disempowers by making older people dependent on the formal health-care system. For example, how many older women have been told that they will be on hypertensive medication "for the rest of their life" or that there is nothing that can be done other than suppressive or palliative pharmaceutical therapies to treat a particular disease?

Finally, conventional medicine disempowers by divesting the family and tribal culture of many of their own healing traditions, which have often been the province of mothers, sisters, and grandmothers. These include the domains of children's health, midwifery, and care of the old. For example, in one study, older women living in an impoverished rural area were queried about family traditions of health care. They shared childhood memories of their mothers' and grandmothers' gathering herbs from surrounding areas, for use in teas, poultices, and tonics, and of only rarely seeing the doctor. When asked whether they had made a conscious effort to pass on these healing practices to their own children or grandchildren, they often replied that there was no need of it now that there were so many doctors and such good modern medicine. There was sadness and resignation in this loss of knowledge of their own tradition, and evidence of disempowerment. As more than one older black woman said about these traditional self-care practices, "They just don't work like they used to." One older Native American woman supplied a striking metaphor for loss of cultural knowledge as she mused wistfully, "You know, back in the old days, there used to be a lot of herbs and such out in the fields, but now they're just weeds" (Gaylord, unpublished study).

ALTERNATIVE THERAPEUTIC SYSTEMS: PAST AND PRESENT USERS

Alternative systems of healing have existed throughout history in all societies. Older women, as well as older men, have often been the holders of knowledge of these traditions, and have enjoyed the accompanying power and privilege as well as the responsibility of preserving and transmitting this cultural wisdom (Boulding, 1975; Stein, 1990). When these alternative health traditions co-exist with the "official" health care system, they are called "folk medicine." While these folk health systems have lower status than officially recognized health-care systems, they nevertheless empower the knowledgeable user. Their continued popularity (Hufford, 1992), even in the United States, may be due to the fact that they provide coherent, culturally relevant, systems of meaning for their users, healing the whole person: body, mind, and spirit.

To varying degrees in all cultures, older women have attended to the ills of themselves, their families and others, performed as midwives, and cared for the old and frail. Their ministries may have been the only source of health care in some communities. The combination of folk-knowledge and power in a patriarchical milieu has sometimes earned them the titles of medicine women or witches. Women have been denounced, tortured, burned at the stake, and otherwise put to death, particularly in the middle ages in Europe, for their presumed witchcraft (Boulding, 1975).

Poor people and those in rural areas, including the United States, who have had less access to the modern health-care system, still utilize various folk systems of healing in addition to available biomedical personnel and technology. For example, a study in West Virginia found folk remedies in use by 76% of patients attending rural primary care clinics, and 70% attending urban clinics (Cook & Baisden, 1986). As typical of the biomedical perspective, the authors of the study, rather than expressing any positive regard for patients' self-care initiatives, warned only of the remedies' "potential for causing serious morbidity or mortality" (Cook and Baisden, 1986, p. 1098).

Members of cultural minorities whose beliefs about illness and healing differ from that of mainstream medicine are often users of alternative therapies. For example, root work, a medical tradition still prevalent among subcultures of African-Americans in the American South, involves the belief that supernatural forces can be controlled and manipulated by humans to heal or harm (Mathews, 1992). Older women as well as older men may be practitioners of rootwork, with the power of the practitioner said to increase with advancing age.

Religious beliefs and alternative health practices are often linked, as in the example of faith healing, still widely practiced among certain fundamentalist Christian denominations in the United States. In one study of patients attending a family practice clinic in rural North Carolina (King, Sobal, & Deforge, 1988), 56% reported watching faith healers on television, 29% believed that faith healers can help some people whom physicians cannot help, 21% reported attending a faith healing service, and 6% reported being healed by faith healers. Women, as well as men, may be inspired to become faith healers, many practicing well into old age.

Other population groups using alternative medicine in high numbers include those suffering from chronic or incurable diseases such as cancer, arthritis, and Alzheimer's disease. Interviews with caregivers of Alzheimer's patients found that 55% had tried one or more alternative treatments in efforts to improve patients' memories, with 40% perceiving some benefit from the remedy (Coleman, Fowler, & Williams, 1995). Again, the authors, two of them physicians, expressed concern that use of the unproven remedies "exposes vulnerable people to possible side effects, increased costs, and possible exploitation" (Coleman et al., 1995, p. 747).

Those who seek out alternative therapies may subscribe to an alternative explanatory model of health and illness. For a client who uses rootwork, the cause of a illness which is unresponsive to treatment by conventional means includes the possibility that an enemy has placed a root on or near the individual; the cure involves removal of the root by expert root doctors with counteracting potions. Faith healing involves the belief that while some illnesses are due to natural causes, others may be a punishment from God and that cure may be effected by belief in, and surrender to, God's power to overcome all afflictions. Others who take alternative pathways to healing may believe that true healing must involve fundamental, far reaching changes in their lives, including spiritual and emotional growth as well as lifestyle changes, as emphasized by many alternative healing systems.

PRINCIPLES AND PRACTICES
OF ALTERNATIVE THERAPIES

Many alternative therapies emphasize the following principles to a greater extent than allopathic medicine (Gaylord, 1998). These principles are aligned with a holistic, feminine healing perspective.

1. Emphasizing self-care and preventive strategies;
2. Stimulating the body's self-healing abilities, with recognition that healing can be a gentle and gradual, developmental process;

3. Preventing illness by strengthening homeostatic balance and remaining in harmony with the psychosocial and physical environment;
4. Individualizing treatment to the particular patient, rather than focusing on the disease condition;
5. Addressing the underlying causes of illness, including emotional, environmental, and spiritual factors, rather than simply eliminating (suppressing) its surface manifestations;
6. Using natural non-pharmaceutical substances or techniques, while avoiding use of prescription medications (particularly those which might suppress symptoms or compromise the body's self-healing abilities);
7. Enhancing wellness with optimal diet, exercise, and stress-reducing regimens;
8. Viewing the mind, body, and spirit as interactive and inseparable;
9. Acknowledging the electromagnetic energy field that permeates the human organism and the role of the vital force in healing.
10. Appreciating the importance of intuitive understanding in both the patient and healer.

Some of the therapies that incorporate these principles, and their relevance to the health of older women, are briefly discussed below (Gaylord, 1998; Burton Goldberg Group, 1994).

Mind-Body Therapies

These interventions involve an understanding of the inseparability and interaction of cognitive and emotional processes with the body organ-systems, and the underlying psychobiological mechanisms by which communication occurs, including immune and neurotransmitter substances. Included are hypnosis, biofeedback, guided imagery, relaxation therapies, mindfulness meditation and mindful exercise, all of which have been used successfully by older women to enhance self-care. Through *biofeedback training*, a woman can learn to modify her own vital functions, such as breathing, skin temperature, heart-rate or even EEG brain-waves, to prevent, control, and treat a range of dysfunctions often seen in old age, including sleep disorders, incontinence, back-pain, heart dysfunction, gastrointestinal disorders, difficulty swallowing, ringing of the ears, migraine and tension headaches, asthma, and hypertension (Danskin & Crow, 1981).

Hypnosis uses the power of suggestion to induce trance-like states so as to access deep, often unconscious levels of the mind to effect positive behavioral change. Hypnosis has been used effectively to treat such conditions as ulcers, migraine and tension headaches, sleep disorders, anxiety, phobias, depression and substance abuse. Important uses of hypnosis and guided imagery in older populations include their substitution for anesthesia during surgery and in pain control (Lang, Joyce, Spiegel, Hamilton, & Lee, 1996).

Meditation practices have been used and taught by older women throughout the ages, in spite of their often being enmeshed in patriarchal religious frameworks. In meditation, the practitioner continually brings the attention back to the present moment, so that the mind is not preoccupied with thoughts and feelings of the past and future. Concentrative meditation techniques include focus on an image or sound, or simply the breath. Mindfulness meditation involves expanding the attention to include awareness of thoughts and emotions without being distracted by them. Both techniques have been shown to reduce such stress markers as heart-rate, pulse-rate, and plasma cortisol, and to enhance EEG alpha state. Meditation can enhance immune function and decrease anxiety, hypertension, and chronic pain (Kabat-Zinn, Lipworth, & Burney, 1985).

Mindful exercise includes such practices as yoga, tai chi, Alexander Technique, and Feldenkrais, some thousands of years old, others quite new. *Mindful* exercise is more beneficial than simple physical exercise, in terms of certain physiological responses. Most of these exercises can be adapted for use by older women with a wide range of abilities, and have been found to improve function. For example, tai chi was found to reduce frailty and falls in older people (Wolf, Huiman, Kutner, McNeely, Coogler, Xu, & Atlanta FICSIT Group, 1996).

Chiropractic

Chiropractic is based on the understanding that structural distortions can cause functional abnormalities. Vertebral subluxation of the spine is an important structural distortion which disturbs body function primarily through neurologic pathways. Chiropractic adjustment is a specific and definitive system for correcting vertebral subluxation, harmonizing the neuronal function and stimulating the body's innate healing potential, focusing primarily on manual adjustment or manipulation of the spine. Chiropractic, the third largest independent health profession in the western world, following allopathic medicine and dentistry, includes a growing number of women. Older women patients visit chiropractic physicians particularly for the prevention and treatment of neuromusculoskeletal conditions of low back pain, neck pain, and headaches, conditions for which spinal manual therapy has been shown to be safe and effective. Chiropractic treatment reduces the need for potentially harmful drug-therapies for chronic pain, while improving function.

Bodywork

Bodywork techniques range from traditional massage to a variety of contemporary and energy-based systems. Bodywork practitioners include women as well as men, and many of their clients are older women.

Therapeutic massage can relieve muscle pain, headaches, and tension-related respiratory syndromes such as bronchial asthma and emphysema. Massage can promote relaxation, alleviate swelling, correct poor posture, and improve circulation. It can increase lymphatic circulation, thus alleviating chronic inflammatory conditions and facilitate the removal of toxins from the body, thus promoting rapid recovery from illness. It can be used as adjunctive therapy in treatment of cardiovascular, neurological and gynecological and gastrointestinal disorders, reducing the need for pharmacological treatment (Van Why, 1997).

The Alexander Technique, pioneered by Frederick Matthias Alexander, uses awareness, movement and touch to change habitual movement patterns that interfere with proper body functioning. The *Feldenkrais Method*, founded by Moshe Feldenkrais, involves altering the self-image along with corresponding negative habitual patterns of movement. Group exercise programs, called "Awareness Through Movement," guide participants through slow, gentle sequences of movement designed to replace old patterns with new ones. *Functional Integration* involves individualized hands-on touch and movement, in which the practitioner directs the client's body through movements tailored to the client's needs. *Structural Integration*, commonly called *Rolfing*, was founded by Ida Rolf in 1970, and is based on the philosophy that proper alignment of body segments (head, torso, pelvis, legs, feet) via manual manipulation and stretching of the body's fascial tissues, improves body movement and function. Research has show that Rolfing does indeed reduce chronic stress, promote change in body function and enhance neurological function (Burton Goldberg Group, 1994).

Touch therapies are energy-based healing systems which include laying on of hands, Reiki, and therapeutic touch. *Laying on of hands* is an ancient art found in various spiritual traditions, in which the practitioner directs healing energy, often proported to come from a universal force, to the patient or to the site of illness. *Reiki*, which traces its origins from Tibet, is one form of this therapy; *Therapeutic Touch*, another variation, was developed by Dolores Krieger, Ph.D., R.N. and Dora Kunz, a healer, and is now being used in U.S. hospitals, particularly by the nursing profession. Therapeutic Touch can decrease anxiety, reduce pain and promote wound healing. Physiological changes include altered enzyme activity and increased hemoglobin levels (Micozzi, 1996; Burton-Goldberg Group, 1994; Wirth, 1992).

Acupuncture

Acupuncture and acupressure are part of a complete system of healing developed in China over 5,000 years ago. In this system, health is dependent on the balanced flow of chi or qi, the vital life energy, throughout the body, and illness is due to a disturbance of chi. Acupuncture treatment balances the chi by inserting needles at points on the body where the chi flows, through one of twelve channels or meridians. Diagnosis involves inspection (visual assessment of the patient, particularly their spirit, form and bearing), feeling the pulse, observing the tongue and eyes, and questioning the patient about her physical and social environment. Acupuncturists or practitioners of Chinese medicine include many women, and older women themselves have found acupuncture treatment to be useful for maintaining health and dealing with illnesses ranging from common colds and flus, to pain management, to addictions, to chronic fatigue. Acupuncture has been found to be useful in treating such conditions as migraines, back pain, knee pain, nausea and vomiting, withdrawal from substance abuse, bronchial asthma, and chronic bronchitis (Burton Goldberg Group; Micozzi, 1996).

Alternative Dietary Therapies

Older women have been leaders in the natural foods movement, with its emphasis on the importance of whole, organic foods and the elimination from food products of pesticides, antibiotics, hormones, and food additives such as preservatives, dyes, and artificial flavors, substances that may play a role in decreased immune function, increased food allergies, increased chemical sensitivities and other disorders. There are a variety of natural nutritional prescriptions for healing and preventing illness. The simplest is an organic, plant-based, whole-foods diet, which decreases the body's burden of chemical additives, maximizes natural vitamin and mineral intake, decreases fat and sugar, and increases fiber. *Macrobiotics* is a dietary prescription formulated by Michio Kushi based on the ancient Chinese philosophy and practice of balancing yin and yang, and emphasizing whole foods. A *vegetarian* diet calls for the elimination of all meat; a *vegan* diet goes further, eliminating all animal products, including milk and eggs. *Juice therapies* provide supplementary nutrients, particularly vitamins and minerals, both to prevent illness (i.e., during times of stress) and to restore the body to health. *Fasting* has been used for centuries in all societies to purge the body of toxic substances, enhance immune function and increase spiritual awareness. Extreme fasts (not recommended for vulnerable older women) may involve drinking only pure water; modified juice fasts include fresh organic vegetable and sometimes fruit juices (Burton Goldberg Group, 1994).

Herbal Medicine

In feminist health tracts, women's knowledge of herbal and plant therapies is traced back to pre-patriarchical times, to the era of the matriarchies (Stein, 1990). Herbs and plants are portrayed as a sacred expression of Gaia, the earth-mother, and women's instinctive connection with the Goddess is said to have given her dominion over this earliest of healing systems. Traditionally, women shared with each other their knowledge of herbs and other medicinal plants for use as tonics for preventing illness, and as remedies for most functional disorders known to humankind, (i.e. dyspepsia, respiratory disorders, menstrual disorders, anxiety, and depression) as well as treatments for more serious organic disorders such as cancer. Even as patriarchical systems gained ascendancy and the formal practice of medicine was dominated by men, women continued to practice herbal medicine in the vast informal health-care system. Herbal preparations disappeared from physicians' armamentarium with the growth of manufactured drugs, and the medical profession's knowledge and use of herbs has practically ceased in the United States. Meanwhile, many women have begun to reawaken their connection with this ancient practice, often purchasing raw herbs and learning to make their own remedies. Although the usefulness of many herbal preparations has been established by tradition, there is growing research confirming the efficacy of herbal preparations in specific conditions (e.g., Mowrey, 1986; Murray, 1996). For example, research has recently established the efficacy of St. John's Wort for depression (Linde, Ramirez, Mulrow, Pauls, Weidenhammer, & Melchart, 1996).

Aromatherapy

Plant essences, including essential oils, have been used therapeutically for thousands of years particularly by Egyptians, Greeks, and Romans. Aromatherapy is a term coined in 1937 for this ancient practice by the French chemist Rene Maurice Gattefosse. Women have been drawn to aromatherapy for the treatment of such conditions as immune deficiency, bacterial and viral infections, and skin disorders, and as a tool for stress management. The oils transmit their healing properties not only by inhalation but by absorption through the skin, exerting much of their effect through their pharmacological properties and small molecular size. Aromatic molecules interacting with the cells of the nasal mucosa transmit signals to the limbic system through which they connect with parts of the brain controlling heart-rate, blood pressure, breathing, memory, and hormone balance (Burton Goldberg Group, 1994; Micozzi, 1996).

Homeopathy

Since ancient times, in India and Greece, it has been known that a remedy can cure a disease if it produces in a healthy person symptoms similar to those of the disease. Samuel Hahnemann, a German physician who in the early 1800's became disheartened with the medical practice of his day, formally tested this principle–*similia similibus curentur*, "like is cured by like"–and subsequently established it as the basis of a system of medicine. Central to homeopathic therapeutics is the infinitesimal dose, the smallest dose necessary to produce a healing response. Through experimenting with lower and lower doses of drugs in efforts to minimize side effects, Hahnemann developed a technique called potentization, in which the original substance is repeatedly diluted and succussed (shaken vigorously after each dilution) to produce a medicinal substance diluted in many cases to the point where there is unlikely to be a single original molecule left.

Homeopathic treatment involves selection of a homeopathic preparation that produces in a healthy person symptoms similar to that of the patient's complete symptom picture. Even for acute conditions, prescribing takes into account the individualized response to illness. Particularly in chronic conditions, constitutional prescribing may incorporate the person's entire symptomatology not only with regard to the present complaint, but over the course of a lifetime. Illness is viewed as a disturbance of the vital force, as manifested in its physical, mental, and emotional responses that is unique to each patient. Symptoms are viewed as the organism's expression of its life energy and are not suppressed, but used in the cure of the whole person. Although the mechanism by which the similar remedy acts is unknown, homeopathic theory maintains that in some way it stimulates the organism's own innate healing capacities. Homeopathy is useful for a wide range of acute conditions (e.g., cold, influenza, poison ivy rash) as well as chronic illnesses (e.g., a lingering cough, allergies, asthma, chronic fatigue, depression, anxiety, phobias) (Lockie & Geddes, 1994).

Although homeopathy was rejected by many in the orthodox medical community of the day, it was very popular among lay-people, particularly the women healers in the households across Europe, as a safe, inexpensive, and effective therapy. In fact, it is said that women kept homeopathy alive, just as homeopathy accepted women as healers prior to their acceptance by the orthodox medical community. Today, homeopathy is growing steadily in use in the United States. Women are flooding study groups, as they learn to appreciate homeopathy for its safe, gentle, and inexpensive approach to healing.

Shamanism

A shaman is a person who journeys outside time and space via an altered state of consciousness, often to perform healing rituals. The term "shaman" applies equally to men and women, and cross-culturally, both genders have been found fulfilling the role. Traditionally, shaman have been called upon to diagnosis and treat illnesses, perform divinations, and communicate with the spirit world. Recently, in the United States, there has been a revival of shamanism due particularly to the work of Michael Harner and his students (Ingerman, 1991). A number of women, including middle-aged and older women, are beginning to study shamanic rituals and journeying, and to become healers who perform "soul retrivals" for clients suffering from illnesses of the spirit.

HOW ALTERNATIVE AND COMPLEMENTARY THERAPIES CAN EMPOWER OLDER WOMEN

The philosophy and mechanisms of action of many alternative therapies reflect a feminine, rather than a masculine perspective on healing. The biological capacity for motherhood would seem well aligned with an appreciation for gentle nurturance and gradual development over time, rather than the harsh, forced, and arbitrary treatments, such as surgery and powerful drugs, that are often used in conventional medicine.

Use of alternative therapies enhances sense of control, which is known to enhance health. Self-determination is a hallmark of empowerment (Stein, 1997). Many alternative therapies require for their use an attitude of self-determination, self-motivation, and independence. For example, mind-body and body-work therapies require discipline of both mind and body over a long period of time, working to change habitual patterns of behavior or learn a new skill. The philosophy of many alternative therapies encourages self-education through reading books, listening to tapes, or searching the Internet.

Use of alternative therapies often requires courage to go it alone against the conventional medical establishment. For example, the primary-care provider may believe that one's desired health-care pathway is worthless. Frequently, he or she may know little or nothing about a particular therapy. Patients who use alternative and complementary systems of health care in addition to biomedicine are often the managers of their own "team" of health professionals, which may include one or more alternative care providers. For example, in addition to a family physician, a patient may be visiting an herbal specialist or making regular visits to a chiropractic physician. Some members of the patient's "team" may not even know of the existence of other members.

Many of these therapies represent "alternatives" to merely palliative pharmaceutical products or to the threat of iatrogenic illnesses. True healing mechanisms stimulate the body-mind's self-healing capacity, strengthening and balancing the system, and making it more resistant to stress. Thus prevention is emphasized and encouraged over treatment. Costs of many alternative therapies may be lower than conventional care, particularly when prevention and reversal of chronic illness is factored into the equation.

Finally, in-depth knowledge about alternative-care strategies such as herbal or homeopathic medicine empowers the user to effectively care for oneself and family members rather than offer merely suppressive over-the-counter therapies. Such skill reinstates the older women in her role as family healer. In addition, widespread use of alternative therapies should further empower the practitioners of these therapies, many of whom are, or will be, older women.

HOPE FOR THE FUTURE: EMPOWERMENT FOR ALL THROUGH INTEGRATIVE MEDICINE

The patriarchical model of health care is narrow and passe. The feminine, holistic model represented by many alternative therapies, should be the primary method of health care practiced and taught, since it is the first line of defense in maintaining health and preventing disease. But there is still the need, sometimes, for the masculine element of health-care, as represented by much of conventional health practice. Antibiotics and surgery, for example, are life-saving tools when used judiciously and as a last rather than a first resort.

A truly integrative healing system would involve an appropriate balance of the masculine and feminine healing arts and sciences, and a mutual appreciation of their strengths and uses. There is no place for a hierarchical, suppressive relationship between healer and patient. A patient-centered approach should involve acknowledgement of the powerful role of beliefs in healing and health-care pathways, respect for other members of the patient's team of care providers, and encouragement of self-determination and the health-giving benefits of empowerment. With such a health-care system in place, we can hope to provide the best possible health care for people of all ages.

REFERENCES

Boulding, E. (1975). *The underside of history. A view of women through time.* Boulder, CO: Westview Press.

Burton Goldberg Group, (Eds). (1994). *Alternative medicine. The definitive guide.* Fife, WA: Future Medicine Publishing.

Coleman, L.M., Fowler, L.B., & Williams, M.E. (1995). Use of unproven therapies by people with Alzheimer's disease. *Journal of the American Geriatrics Society, 43,* 747-750.

Cook, C. & Baisen, D. (1986). Ancillary use of folk medicine by patients in primary care clinics in Southwestern West Virginia. *Southern Medical Journal, 79,* 1098-1101.

Danskin, D.G. & Crow, M. (1981). *Biofeedback. An introduction and guide.* Palo Alto, CA: Mayfield Publishing Company.

Drivdahl C.E. & Miser W.F. (1998). The use of alternative health care by a family practice population. *Journal of the American Board of Family Practice, 11,* 193-199.

Eisenberg, D.M., Kessler, R.C., Foster, C., Norlock, F.E., Calkins, D.R., Delbanco, T.L. (1993). Unconventional medicine in the United States. Prevalence, costs, and patterns of use. *New England Journal of Medicine, 328,* 246-252.

Engel, G.L. (1977). The need for a new medical model. A challenge for biomedicine. *Science, 196,* 129-135.

Gaylord S. (1998). Complementary therapies in family practice. In P.D. Sloane, L.M. Slatt, P. Curtis, & M.H. Ebell, (Eds.), *Essentials of Family Medicine,* 3rd Edition (pp. 191-200). Baltimore, MD: Williams and Wilkins.

Gaylord, S. Unpublished interviews with older women in Northampton and Halifax Counties, North Carolina about health beliefs, health practices, and care pathways, 1992-1995.

Hufford, D.J. (1992). Folk medicine in contemporary America. In J. Kirkland, H. Mathews, C.W. Sullivan, III, & K. Baldwin (Eds.), *Herbal and magical medicine. Traditional healing today* (pp. 14-31). Durham: Duke University Press.

Ingerman, S. (1991). *Soul retrieval.* San Francisco, CA: HarperCollins Publishers.

Kabat-Zinn, J., Lipworth, L., & Burney, R. (1985). The clinical use of mindfulness meditation for the self-regulation of chronic pain. *Journal of Behavioral Medicine, 8,* 163-190.

King, D.E., Sobal, J., & DeForge, B.R. (1988). Family practice patients' experience and beliefs in faith healing. *Journal of Family Practice, 27,* 505-508.

Kleinman A. (1978). Concepts and a model for the comparison of medical systems as cultural systems. *Social Science and Medicine, 12,* 85-93.

Lang, E.V., Joyce, J.S., Spiegel, D., Hamilton, D., & Lee, K.K. (1996). Self-hypnotic relaxation during interventional radiological procedures: Effects on pain perception and intravenous drug use. *International Journal of Clinical and Experimental Hypnosis, 44,* 106-119.

Linde, K., Ramirez, G., Mulrow, C.D., Pauls, A., Weidenhammer, W., & Melchart, D. (1996) St. John's Wort for depression–an overview and met-analysis of randomised clinical trials. *British Medical Journal, 313,* 253-258.

Lloyd P., Lupton D., Wiesner D., & Hasleton S. (1993). Choosing alternative therapy: an exploratory study of sociodemographic characteristics and motives of patients resident in Sydney. *Australian Journal of Public Health*, *17*, 135-144.

Lockie, A. & Geddes, N. (1994). *The women's guide to homeopathy*. New York: St. Martin's Press.

Mathews, H. (1992). Doctors and root doctors: Patients who use both. In J. Kirkland, H.F. Mathews, C.W. Sullivan, III, and K. Baldwin, (Eds.), *Herbal and magical medicine. Traditional healing today*. Durham, NC: Duke University Press.

Micozzi, M.S. (Ed.). (1996). *Fundamentals of complementary and alternative medicine*. New York: Churchill Livingstone.

Mowrey, D.B. (1986). *The scientific validation of herbal medicine*. New Canaan, CN: Keats Publishing, Inc.

Murray, M.T. (1996). *Natural alternatives to Prozac*. New York: William Morrow and Company.

Spraycar, M. (1995). *Stedman's medical dictionary*, 26th ed. Baltimore, MD: Williams and Wilkins.

Stein, D. (1990). *All women are healers*. Freedom, CA: The Crossing Press.

Stein, J. (1997). *Empowerment and women's health*. London: Zed Books.

Thomas, K.J., Carr, J., Westlake, L., Williams, B.T. (1991). Use of non-orthodox and conventional health care in Great Britain. *British Journal of Medicine*, *302*, 207-210.

Van Why, R. (1997). *The body work database*. Evanston, IL: American Massage Therapy Foundation.

Wirth D.P. (1990). The effect of non-contact therapeutic touch on the healing rate of full thickness dermal wounds. *Subtle Energies*, *1*, 1-19.

Wolf, S.L., Huiman, X.B., Kutner, N.G., McNeely, E., Coogler, C., Xu, T., & Atlanta FICSIT Group. (1996). Reducing frailty and falls in older persons: An investigation of tai chi and computerized balance training. *Journal of the American Geriatrics Society*, *44*, 489-497.

Zwicky, J.F., Hafner, A. W., Barrett S., & Jarvis, W.T. (1993). *Reader's guide to alternative health methods*. Milwaukee, WI: American Medical Association.

Women and Retirement

Virginia E. Richardson, PhD

SUMMARY. A feminist analysis of retirement is presented by questioning the applicability of traditional definitions and theories of retirement to retired women. The effects of marriage, caregiving and other family obligations on women's retirement are examined within the context of salient social, psychological and economic factors. An empowerment-oriented perspective that considers interactions and connections between family and work roles, public and private and personal and political levels are recommended to alleviate the high poverty rates among older women, to promote parity among men and women during retirement and to emancipate women from substantial involvement in unpaid work, specifically, caregiving and home labor. *[Article copies available for a fee from The Haworth Document Delivery Service: 1-800-342-9678. E-mail address: getinfo@haworthpressinc.com]*

KEYWORDS. Women and retirement, feminist gerontology, gender differences in retirement, retirement and caregiving, marriage and retirement, older women, poverty among older women

INTRODUCTION

The labor force participation rates for working-age females have nearly doubled since 1950 (Leavitt, 1996). In 1993, they were 47.3% for women between the age of 55-64 and 8.2% for those over the age of 65. Women's labor force participation rates have increased dramatically among the 55-64 female age group. Although the rates for males

[Haworth co-indexing entry note]: "Women and Retirement." Richardson, Virginia E. Co-published simultaneously in *Journal of Women & Aging* (The Haworth Press, Inc.) Vol. 11, No. 2/3, 1999, pp. 49-66; and: *Fundamentals of Feminist Gerontology* (ed: J. Dianne Garner) The Haworth Press, Inc., 1999, pp. 49-66. Single or multiple copies of this article are available for a fee from The Haworth Document Delivery Service [1-800-342-9678, 9:00 a.m. - 5:00 p.m. (EST). E-mail address: getinfo@haworthpressinc.com].

are higher in both of these age categories, the gap narrows with age; more men than women are leaving the work force early. In contrast to men, early retirement has minimally affected women's employment patterns.

Despite these advances in labor force participation rates among women, substantially more older women live in poverty than older men (Caputo, 1997). Although they constituted 58% of the older population in 1990, women comprised 74% of the elderly poor (Hess & Markson, 1995). With age, women become at even greater risk for poverty. Fifty-one percent of all women over 85 live in or near poverty (Devlin & Ayre, 1997).

The situation is especially grave among older women from diverse backgrounds. For example, older African American women are twice as likely as older white women to be poor and five times more likely than older white men. The percentage of African American women who are between the age of 65-74 who live in poverty is 33.6%; the rate is 43.9% for African American women over the age of 75. These rates of poverty for older African American women exceed not only older white women but also older women from Spanish speaking backgrounds. These circumstances are even worse when one considers those close to the poverty level, i.e., those between 100 and 150 percent of the poverty line (Devlin & Ayre, 1997). Despite the increases in the number of women who have worked long enough to receive retirement benefits, discriminatory work and retirement policies keep many older women impoverished.

The purpose of this chapter is to expose "patriarchal" influences that contribute to women's poverty in late life. I first question the applicability of traditional definitions and theories of retirement to women's experiences. Next, I identify and discuss salient concerns of women and retirement. They include economic, caregiving, marriage, and psychological issues that greatly influence retired women. I conclude with recommendations for changes in policy and practice.

TRADITIONAL DEFINITION OF RETIREMENT

Retirement has traditionally been defined economically, that is, when a persons ceases working and begins collecting retirement benefits. Atchley (1988), who offers the most comprehensive definition of retirement defines a "retired person" as (1) any person who performs no gainful employment during a given year; (2) any person who is receiving a retirement pension benefit, or (3) any person who is not employed year round.

The appropriateness of this definition to women and for many people from diverse ethnic backgrounds is questionable. It fails to consider the multidimensional nature of retirement culturally and personally. It presumes a linear work path, and it fails to consider other roles. The definition excludes the many women who work intermittently, i.e., take time off work for caregiving responsibilities, or who work part-time, and it depreciates "home" work. We need fluid definitions of retirement that recognize the multiple roles that women occupy and consider how these roles interact and intersect.

A feminist analysis that recognizes interchanges between family and work roles, between public and private, and between personal and political will illuminate how and why women experience retirement in ways that are often very different from men's experiences. Hooyman and Gonyea (1995) endorse a holistic perspective that considers the interconnections between different spheres, such as the interactions between the larger economic and social context and family caregiving.

Similarly, Cox and Parsons (1994) propose an empowerment-oriented practice model that recommends increased attention to the interconnections between person and environment, private and public, and between institutions and individuals. They state, "Perhaps the most intriguing aspect of empowerment-oriented practice is that the focus is not exclusively on the personal or the environmental aspect of problem solving, but rather on the connection and interaction between the two"(Cox and Parsons, 1994, p. 39).

Below is an example of one woman's retirement experience. Her words reveal why we must consider multiple roles and life events when defining or conceptualizing women's retirement.

I hadn't worked for over thirty years when I went to work, and I only had a high school education. My husband died after 27 years of marriage after a long, 4 1/2 year illness which drained our savings. The mortgage was still unpaid. I realized I needed to go to work to try to pay for my bills. Everyone at work was excited about this early retirement incentive program. I also decided to retire early but I didn't realize until after I retired and I applied for my Social Security benefits that there was some kind of law, I still don't understand it, which took $200 off the top of my Social Security. It had something to do with being retired on my husband's Social Security. Now, if I had been retired on my own Social Security I would have gotten the full amount. It's been very difficult to make ends meet. My retirement income is less than half of what I was making.

Ms. Anderson is an example of a woman who returned to work later in life. When she retired, she was poorly informed and ill-advised about her Social Security and other retirement benefits. Ms. Anderson's experience illustrates how inadequate narrow traditional definitions of retirement are for most older women. Retirement is, ultimately, a subjective concept that includes both personal as well as objective indicators. Practitioners working with older women must determine how each woman defines her retirement, what it symbolizes and means to her, and how it affects her feelings about herself, her family, and others.

THEORIES OF RETIREMENT

Traditional theories of retirement insufficiently explain how many older women experience retirement. For example, continuity theory, which was the primary theory used to understand retirement for many years, suggests that individuals develop habits, commitments, preferences, and other dispositions that become a part of their personalities and persist over time (Atchley, 1977). Proponents of this theory assume that given the opportunity, people will tend to maintain earlier life-style patterns, previous levels of self-esteem, and long-standing values. Although Atchley (1988) and others have proposed more dynamic theories of continuity, they still fail to adequately consider the experiences of many older women who encounter substantial reductions in their resources, especially economic, after they retire.

An alternative theory of retirement that better explains why some people experience more discontinuity in retirement resources than others is critical gerontology, which is based on critical theory. According to Best and Kellner (1991) critical theory is concerned with identifying fundamental relations of domination and exploitation, and the ways that hierarchy, inequality, and oppression underlie social patterns and relations. They state that, "a critical social theory also

305.26 S897

305. 26 A267

detects and illuminates crucial social problems, conflicts, and contradictions, and points toward possible resolutions of these problems and progressive social transformation" (Best & Kellner, 1991, p. 264). All critical theorists, including Habermas (1976) as well as those from the Frankfurt School, e.g., Horkheimer and Adorno (1972), would concur that helping retired women achieve an emancipatory ideal, that is to identify and overcome oppressive forces dominating them and or preventing them from achieving "autonomy, wisdom, and transcendence," is a preeminent goal (Held, 1980; Moody, 1988).

Atchley (1993) proposed a critical gerontological perspective on retirement in which he argued that such a perspective would provide us with a more integrated view of the retirement experience by considering social structural and economic factors along with individual and human development viewpoints.

Overbo and Minkler (1993) were one of the first to appreciate critical gerontology's understanding of older women's life transitions, and, specifically, connections between gender and aging. They asserted that "critical gerontology embraces a broad framework of political economy of aging and considers how political, socioeconomic, and related factors interact to shape and determine the experience of growing old" (p. 289). They state it is "deeply concerned with the intersection of gender and aging and views gender (along with race and class) as a pivotal variable influencing the trajectory of growing old by predetermining an individual's location in the social order" (Overbo and Minkler, 1993, pp. 289-290).

These views concur with Cox and Parsons' (1994) emphasis on empowerment and powerlessness, which they define, "as a lack of access to the resources, knowledge, and skills that are necessary to solve one's own problems, including the ability to participate effectively in social change" (p. 18). The primary goal of empowerment-oriented practice, according to Cox and Parsons, is empowerment, which is "a process through which people become strong enough to participate within, share in the control of, and influence events and institutions which affect their lives" (p. 61).

In contrast to prevailing male models of retirement that have dismissed the contributions of other roles, specifically family responsibilities, in this chapter I endorse a feminist and holistic conceptualization of retirement that focuses on empowering older women. This perspective takes into account the intersection of gender and aging and interconnections among the many roles that women occupy.

The first step in empowerment-oriented practice is assessment, which Cox and Parsons (1994) conceptualize as consciousness raising. They state that "this process considers sources of problems from personal to external (or structural) and from historical to contemporary, thus opening up the personal and political dimensions for consideration" (Cox & Parsons, 1994, pp. 46).

In the spirit of assessment and consciousness raising, in the next section, salient issues especially important to women and retirement are identified and discussed. They include structural issues, such as economic trends, as well as social psychological factors, such as caregiving and marriage. Recommendations for changes in policy and practice are presented later.

ECONOMIC ISSUES AMONG RETIRED WOMEN

In contrast to retired men, many retired women experience marked reductions in income following retirement, and they often lack pension coverage. Poverty among older women is caused by multiple factors. The most salient include: (1) life long gender inequities; (2) systematic inequities in retirement policies that discriminate against women; and (3) women's life long involvement in caregiving. As long as these gender disparities continue, retired women will continue to struggle with economic issues, especially in their later years.

Women's jobs pay less than men's do. Women's lower earnings than men's throughout their lives mean lower retirement benefits in late life. Women who receive Social Security benefits based on their own work records average $151 less a month than men receive (Older Women's League, 1990). Many female retirees receive higher benefits as spouses or as widows. These gender inequities are not likely to lessen because working women still earn less than men do. Full-time, year-round working women make about 75% of men's wages for the same or similar work (Older Women's League, 1998; Bureau of Labor Statistics, 1995; Bureau of Labor Statistics, 1997). According to the Bureau of the Census, even when men's and women's education levels are held constant, women still make less than men do, and the disparity increases with age. Behling, Kilty and Foster (1983) found that professional women, including those who never married and maintained continuous work histories, were still paid less than were their male counterparts.

Women tend to work at jobs without pensions. Regardless of women's increased involvement in the labor force 52% of working women still lack pension coverage. Less than half (48%) of these women work at jobs that provide pension coverage (OWL, 1998). Working women under the age of 30 are the least likely to have pension coverage (OWL, 1998).

In 1994, three out of four women age 65 and over received no income from employer-provided pensions. For women who did receive private pensions, their median benefit was $4,200, compared to a median benefit of $7,800 for men. Although the percentage of women participating in pension programs should increase in the future, the income disparity between men's and women's pensions will remain. In addition, more women are working part-time, as consultants and in shared jobs that are not protected by pensions. The gender differences in part-time work are noteworthy: over 26% of working women worked part-time in 1996 compared to 10% of the working men (Bureau of Labor Statistics, 1997). Federal laws permit employers to exclude from pension coverage employees who work fewer than 20 hours a week or fewer than 1,000 hours a year. About 75% of women who work part-time in the private sector lack pension coverage (OWL, 1998).

The disparities in pension coverage are exacerbated when low income groups are examined. These women have remarkably low rates of pension coverage; about 80% of women earning $10,000 or less lack pension coverage. Among those who earn between $10,000 and $14,999 the percentage is only slightly lower at 60% (OWL, 1998).

About 20% of women contribute to 401 (k) type plans. In contrast to previous assumptions, many women do invest in their retirement and save more of their earnings annually than men (OWL, 1998). At almost every income level, women contribute a higher percentage of their annual earnings to their 401 (k) type plans than men do (Department of Labor, 1994). Although more and more women are investing in their retirement, they still lack adequate resources to invest in the most lucrative retirement resources (Richardson & Kilty, 1997). In an analysis of 242 retirees (125 men and 117 women) from a variety of occupational backgrounds, Richardson and Kilty (1997) found significant gender differences indicating major differences in women's in-

volvement with diverse retirement programs. Perhaps the most interesting finding from this study was that contrary to their expectations,
retired women retained much less income after they retired than they
expected.

Women's lower pension and investment coverage relative to men's
is still explained in part by the types of jobs, specifically at small firms
or in the service sector, at which many women work that are less likely
to provide pensions. Women also tend to have more intermittent work
trajectories. They change jobs more often than men and take more
time off work for family responsibilities. Many women lose pension
coverage or vesting rights when they change jobs. This lack of pension
coverage among working women means that substantial numbers of
women depend solely on Social Security benefits during retirement
(Gonyea, 1998; Grad, 1996; OWL, 1998).

*Systematic biases in retirement policies exacerbate these gender
inequities.* Many women, for example, pay more into Social Security
than they get back. The years they worked offered them no advantage.
This is what happened to Ms. Anderson, referred to earlier in the
chapter.

Dually entitled policies under Social Security suggest that a woman
should benefit from working, but she does not if her spouse's benefits
or her husband's earnings are larger. Dual entitlement occurs when a
woman is eligible for a retirement benefit based on her own work
history and a higher benefit as a wife or widow, based on her husband's work record. When a woman qualifies for her own Social
Security benefit, she is always paid that benefit first. If her spouse's
benefit is higher, she receives an additional Social Security payment to
cover the difference. In other words, although many working women
have contributed to the Social Security system for many years, they
receive no more benefits than if they had contributed nothing. The
years that they worked provided them with no advantage.

Most women are also unaware of how devastating divorce can be
on future retirement benefits. Women who divorce prior to 10 years of
marriage are excluded from consideration for dual entitlements. Divorced women qualify for a spouse's benefit on their ex-husbands'
record only if they were married for at least 10 years and if she is
currently unmarried.

Widows encounter different problems. Because women typically
outlive their husbands, they often deplete their husband's retirement

income. Despite successful passage of the Retirement Equity Act of 1984 that directed employers to directly pay survivor benefits to widows after their spouse died, problems continue. Many couples opt not to include the survivor benefit option. Even if they do, employers usually provide only about two-fifths of what the former spouse received when he was alive (Bell & Graham, 1984; OWL, 1998).

These economic problems have dire consequences for women's retirement. One result is that women have inadequate resources to prepare as well as men can for retirement. Without an adequate income, it is impossible to invest in retirement. Income is the greatest predictor of retirement planning in various forms (Kilty & Behling, 1985). Lack of adequate preparation for retirement can have devastating consequences on women's adjustment later. In 1995, the average annual Social Security benefit for women age 65 and over was $6,971 compared to an average benefit of $9,376 for men in this age group (OWL, 1998).

Another consequence of limited income in retirement is that it restricts that types of activities in which people can participate. Entertainment is expensive these days. Retirees in poverty are unable to travel like their more affluent counterparts. They eat out less often and limit their leisure activities to those they can afford.

Many women who do retire return to work as Ms. Anderson did. Substantial numbers of female retirees return to work because they are unable to live on their retirement income. Retired women who report that their primary source of income originates from Social Security are especially likely to return to work after they retire even if they struggle with poor health.

The stresses that retired women experience from low income can not be overemphasized. Persistent financial stress has enormous psychological costs and can result in serious emotional distress, low self esteem, and high anxiety as well as major health problems.

CAREGIVING AND RETIREMENT

More women than men retire for caregiving reasons and often involuntarily (Matthews & Brown, 1987; Richardson, 1993). Unfortunately, those who retire involuntarily, against their wishes, have more problems adjusting to retirement; they tend to have lower morale, less life satisfaction, and unhappy retirements than do voluntary retirees.

They also tend to be more depressed with higher suicide rates than those who retire voluntarily (Richardson, 1993).

Several researchers have documented that when it comes to decisions about retirement women consider their family situations more often then men do (O'Rand, Henretta, and Krecker, 1992; Ruhm, 1996; Szinovacz and Ekerdt, 1995; Weaver, 1990). Hatch and Thompson (1992), who looked at various factors that predicted the decision to retire among women, found that having an ill or disabled household member who required assistance was the greatest predictor of retirement among women.

It is now well documented that compared to men, women provide more informal adult care, and higher levels of assistance (Brody, 1990). Compared to sons, daughters and often daughters-in-law provide more care. According to Matthews and Campbell (1995), approximately three-quarters of all informal caregivers are women who often experience burden, stress, and depression as a result of their caregiving responsibilities.

Emotional strains from caregiving are the most serious negative effects (Brody, 1990). These include depression, anger, anxiety, frustration, guilt, sleeplessness, demoralization, feelings of helplessness, irritability, lowered morale, and emotional exhaustion. Other problems stem from disruptions in other relationships as a result of caregiving, limited free time for oneself, inability to get out of the house, problems with meeting demands of work, and constant sleep interruptions. The stress of caregiving is greatest when family members suffer a dementia, are unable to communicate, and become uncooperative, incontinent, immobile, or excessively demanding (Brody, 1990). These situations require enormous energy, patience, and resilience from caregivers.

Hooyman and Gonyea (1995) argue that three trends will exacerbate these gender inequities in caregiving. First, the trend toward privatization of long term care services will substantially increase women's caregiving burdens. Second, the medicalization of care and shift to highly technical care at the same time that managed care pressures result in shorter stays in hospitals will complicate caregiving. More and families, specifically women, are being required to carry out this medical technical care that was formally provided by professionals. This greater complexity in home care means that caregivers must spend more time and energy away from work and at unpaid caregiving tasks at home. According to Hooyman and Gonyea (1995, p. 103), "this trend is consistent with the ideology of community care and familism, which has assumed that family care is more cost-effective and more attuned to the needs of the care receiver." As women spend more and more of their time at caregiving, which is likely to increase in the next millennium, they spend less and less time at work or become increasingly stressed. They spend fewer years vesting in pension programs, and more women will retire involuntarily.

MARRIAGE AND RETIREMENT

Patriarchal forces prevail in the timing of many women's retirements. For example, more married women tend to retire when their husbands retire than do husbands for wives (Arber and Ginn, 1995; Matthews and Brown, 1987). Campione (1987) was one of the first to demonstrate that husbands' retirements significantly impacted the timing of wives' retirements. Since this study, more and more researchers (e.g., O'Rand, Henretta, and Krecker, 1992), have shown that for many older couples, retirement is often a joint decision.

Arber and Ginn (1995) articulate that despite trends toward mutual decision-making, married men more frequently than married women pressure their spouses to retire in accordance with their wishes. Some research suggests when husbands do retire before wives, many marriages struggle with power inequities and disparate commitments to work and leisure. Mason (1987) found that many retired men disliked being home alone without their wives. Researchers who have studied couples where wives work while their husbands are retired report marital problems, specifically, increased marital strain, more spousal conflict and lower marital satisfaction (Szinovacz & Ekerdt, 1995). Many wives who continue working live in low income household in which the couples need earnings from the wife's employment (O'Rand et al., 1992). Some of these couples have dependent children to care for or the husbands are in poor health.

Recent research suggests that contrary to previous assumptions, widowhood and retirement are interconnected. For example, Ozawa and Lum (1998) found that when women retired after widowhood they were more likely to experience poverty during retirement in contrast to those women who became widowed after they retired. Until recently,

gerontologists studied widowhood and retirement separately and assumed these events were unrelated.

PSYCHOLOGICAL ISSUES

Economics and caregiving are not the only areas in which retired
men and women differ. An increasing amount of research indicates
that women's and men's adaptation to retirement differs. For example,
Szinovacz and Washo (1992) compared the effects of multiple life
transitions on retirement adjustment on men and women. They found
that as the number of life events experienced increased, women's
adaptation to retirement declined. This relationship was not significant, however, for male retirees.

Retired women are apparently more vulnerable to the accumulation
of life changes than men are. A more in-depth analysis of the types of
life events that retired men and women experience as well as the
differences in the contexts in which men and women retire will illuminate other factors that may account for these differences. They bolster
recent indications that gender differences presumably exist in psychological and social experiences during retirement.

Richardson and Kilty (1995), who examined gender differences in
mental health among retired women and men, obtained statistically
significant gender effects in the expression of symptoms of mental
health across three different time periods: (1) at preretirement; (2) six
months after retirement; and (3) one year later. They found that gender
was significantly associated with psychological anxiety, immobiliza-
tion, drinking problems and health. A gender $\times$ time interaction effect
was also observed for physical anxiety as well as psychological anxiety. These data suggest persistent gender differences across time rather
than transient or temporary responses.

RECOMMENDED INTERVENTIONS

According to Cox and Parsons (1994, p. 50), ". . . empowerment-
oriented practice may be conceptualized on a continuum of focus that
ranges over the personal, interpersonal, environmental, and political
aspects of the problem at hand." They identify four dimensions to

intervention: (1) the personal; (2) the interpersonal; (3) micro environmental and organizational; and (4) macro environmental or sociopolitical. Although the emphasis may vary from personal to political and from political to personal, depending upon the problem, all dimensions are taken into account in empowerment-oriented practice. In this section, Cox and Parsons' model is applied to women and retirement and to what changes we need to make in this area.

On the personal level, practitioners must better inform women about current retirement policies and encourage all women to carefully examine how their unique life circumstances will affect their retirements. The discrepancies, for example, that researchers have observed in women's expectations about retirement compared to what they actually encountered are disturbing and underscore the importance of preretirement planning for women. In addition, women must be aware of the potentially negative consequences to their future retirement when they take time off work to care for others. We must recognize, however, that these changes on the personal level will not eliminate impoverishment among substantial numbers of older women.

On a micro environmental and organizational level, we need better services for working and retired women that are sensitive to the diverse experiences that women encounter in work and family roles. Although many agencies that serve older adults have support groups for widows and caregivers, few offer groups specifically for retired women. Fewer still offer groups that take into account the intricate connections between work and family, between the informal and formal, and between the private and public, that are imperative to consider if we expect to successfully assist older women with their problems. Both preretirement and postretirement groups that take into account these intersections and connections are needed to help women decide when and how they will retire.

Several changes must occur on the macro environmental or sociopolitical level if retired women ever expect to achieve parity with retired men. First, and, most importantly, *we must eradicate gender and ethnic differences in wages that are discriminatory and unjust.* The gender inequities that begin early in women's careers are problematic. Second, and related to the previous recommendation, is that *women who work in female-dominated professions should receive comparable wages.* Third, *women need compensation for caregiving.* Some of the suggestions that Hooyman and Gonyea (1995) recommend include: modifying the definition of work to incorporate unpaid labor in the home and community; providing credit for years lost resulting from caregiving; financing paid caregiving over the family life cycle through a social insurance approach; and providing direct financial support for caregiving. Fourth, *we must eliminate pension policies that require women to pay more into the system or pay women lower benefits because they live longer.* Fifth, *Social Security rules should not penalize married working women when their husbands' benefits are higher.*

Reforms in Social Security and Medicare programs are inevitable. Recent arguments for increased privatization have ominous implications for older women. Gonyea (1998) explains, for example, how Personal Savings Accounts for the majority of women will be smaller because women's wages are lower, their work trajectories are more disordered, they are more likely to work part-time, they live longer than men, and they tend to invest in low risk funds.

Smeeding (1998) recommends we adopt a nonpoverty standard of living for every older American. He suggests that one way to accomplish this is by restructuring both minimum social retirement benefits and income-tested benefits so that poverty is eradicated for all older women. Compared to other countries, the United States has one of the lowest income support systems. By raising the percentage of median income to that which is more comparable to other countries, such as Canada where it is 54-59% or Sweden where it is even higher (66-72%), we could eliminate poverty for most older women in the United States.

CONCLUSION

When retired women seek help practitioners may "fluctuate" their emphasis from the personal to the political depending upon the circumstances. For example, in the case of Ms. Anderson, a widow who started working for economic reasons after her husband died, several issues ranging from personal to political emerged. On the one hand, she required intervention on an individual level such as education and training that would improve her marketability in the labor market. She also needed financial counseling to help her better understand her Social Security entitlements and how to better invest in her future.

From a sociopolitical perspective, discriminatory retirement policies that neglected to take into account the many years she spent caring for others also contributed to her impoverishment during retirement. Ms. Anderson's situation was both personal and political.

These issues are complex and multidimensional. They involve variegated interactions in many roles, especially in work and family domains. As a result, interventions for retired women must transpire on multiple levels.

Innovative conceptualizations of retirement that appreciate and consider the diverse paths that many women's lives take will deepen our understanding of older women's lives. Theories of retirement that incorporate the multiple roles that women occupy and recognize interactions between work and family, paid and unpaid work, public and private will advance our knowledge of retired women. Similarly, interventions that seek to empower older women while increasing the control and influences they have over their personal and public lives will help more female retirees. Practice strategies that understand the interplay and interactions between the personal choices women make about their jobs, their marriages, and their families and systemic forces that affect these choices will more successfully emancipate women from involuntary retirement, marital strains, and economic hardship. When retirement policies consider the many hours of unpaid work that women spend caretaking, we will move closer to freeing so many older women from financial stress and impoverishment. Responsible societies take care of their people and support them with services and programs that empower and fortify.

The increasing heterogeneity among older persons requires radical reforms in retirement policies and practices as well as fundamental changes in sex roles. Parity with men in late life will only happen when we change what we expect of women at work and at home and implement progressive policies on behalf of older women. Only then will "Successful Aging" become reality for all older persons regardless of gender, ethnicity, or marital status.

REFERENCES

Arber, S. & Ginn, J. (1995). Choice and constraint in the retirement of older married women. In S. Arber & J. Ginn (Eds.). *Connecting Gender & Ageing* (pp. 69-86). Philadelphia: Open University Press.

Atchley, R. (1977). *Social forces and aging* (Second edition). Belmont, CA: Wadsworth Publishing Company.

Atchley, R. (1988). *Social forces and aging* (Fifth edition). Belmont, CA: Wadsworth Publishing Company.

Atchley, R. (1993). Critical perspectives on retirement. In T. Cole, W.A. Achenbaum, P. Jakobi, R. Kastenbaum (Eds.). *Voices and visions of aging: Toward a critical gerontology* (pp. 3-19). New York: Springer Publishing Company.

Best, S. & Kellner, D. (1991). *Postmodern theory: Critical interrogations.* New York: Guilford Press.

Behling, J., Kilty, K. & Foster, A. (1983). Scarce resources for retirement planning: A dilemma for professional women. *Journal of Gerontological Social Work, 5,* 49-60.

Bell, D. & Graham, A. (1984). Surviving spouse's benefits in private pension plans. *Monthly Labor Review,* 23-31.

Brody, E. (1990). *Women in the middle: Their parent-care years.* New York: Springer Publishing Company.

Bureau of Labor Statistics. (1995).*Women in the workforce: An overview.* Prepared by Diane E. Herz and Barbara H. Wooton. Washington, DC: Department of Labor.

Bureau of Labor Statistics. (1997). *Employment and Earnings, 44,* No. 1. Washington, DC: U.S. Government Printing Office.

Campione, W. A. (1987). The married woman's retirement decision: A methodological comparison. *Journal of Gerontology, 42,* 381-386.

Caputo, R.K. (1997). Psychological, attitudinal, and socio-demographic correlates of economic well-being of mature women. *Journal of Women & Aging, 9,* 37-53.

Cox, E. O. & Parsons, R. J. (1994). *Empowerment-oriented social work practice with the elderly.* Belmont, CA: Wadsworth Publishing Company.

Department of Labor. (1994). *Pension and health benefits of American workers: New findings from the April 1993 Current Population Survey.* Washington, DC; Department of Labor.

Devlin, S. & Arye, L. (1997). The social security debate: A financial crisis or a new retirement paradigm? *Generations, 21,* 27-33.

Gonyea, J.G. (1998). Social insecurity: The debate regarding privatization and risk. In J. Gonyea (Ed.). *Resecuring Social Security and Medicare: Understanding privatization and risk.* Washington, DC: The Gerontological Society of America.

Grad, S. (1996). *Income of population 55 and older,* 1994. Washington, DC: Social Security Administration.

Habermas, J. (1976). *Communications and the evolution of society.* Boston: Beacon Press.

Hatch, L. R. & Thompson, A. (1992). Family responsibilities and women's retirement. In M. Szinovacz, D. Ekerdt, and B. Vinick (Eds.). *Families and retirement* (pp. 99-113). Newbury Park, CA: Sage Publications.

Held, D. (1980). *Introduction to critical theory.* Berkeley and Los Angeles University of California Press.

Hess, B. & Markson, E.W. (1995). Poverty. In George L. Maddox (Ed.), *Encyclopedia of aging* (Second edition.). (pp. 748-751). New York: Springer Publishing Company.

Hooyman, N.R. & Gonyea, J. (1995). *Feminist perspectives on family care.* Thousand Oaks, CA: Sage Publications.

Horkheimer, M. & Adorno, T. (1972). *Dialectic of enlightenment*. New York: Seabury Press.

Kilty, K.M. & Behling, J.H. (1985). Predicting retirement intentions and attitudes of professional workers. *Journal of Gerontology, 40*, 219-227.

Leavitt, T. (1996). Labor force characteristics of Older Americans. In W. Crown (Ed.). *Handbook of employment and the elderly*. (pp. 15-56). Westport, Conn: Greenwood Press.

Mason, J. (1987). A bed of roses? Women, marriage and inequality in later life. In P. Allatt, T. Keil, A. Bryman, and B. By the way (Eds.). *Women and the life cycle: Transitions and turning points*. London: Macmillan.

Matthews, A. & Campbell, L. (1995). Gender roles, employment and informal care. In S. Arber & J. Ginn (Eds.). *Connecting Gender and Ageing* (pp. 129-143). Philadelphia: Open University Press.

Matthews, S. & Brown, D. (1987). Retirement as a crucial life event: The differential experiences of women and men. *Research on Aging, 9*, 548-551.

Moody, H. (1988). Toward a critical gerontology: The contribution of the humanities to theories of aging. In J. Birren & V. Bengston (Eds.) *Emergent theories of aging* (pp. 19-40). New York: Springer Publishing Company.

Older Women's League (1990). *Heading for hardship: Retirement income for American women in the next century*. Washington, DC: Author.

Older Women's League (1998). *Women, work, and pensions: Improving the odds for a secure retirement*. Washington, DC: Author.

O'Rand, A., Henretta, J. & Krecker, M. (1992). Family pathways to retirement. In M. Szinovacz, D. Ekerdt, and B. Vinick (Eds.) *Families and Retirement* (pp. 81-98). Newbury Park, CA: Sage Publications.

Ovrebo, B. & Minkler, M. (1993). The lives of older women: Perspectives from political economy and the humanities. In T. Cole, W. Achenbaum, P. Jakobi, and R. Kastenbaum (Eds.). *Voices and visions of aging: Toward a critical gerontology* (pp. 289-308). New York: Springer Publishing Company.

Ozawa & Lum (1998). Marital status and change in income status 10 years after retirement. *Social Work Research, 22*, 116-128.

Richardson, V.E. (1993) *Retirement Counseling*. New York: Springer Publishing Company.

Richardson, V. E. & Kilty, K.M. (1995). Gender differences in mental health before and after retirement: A longitudinal analysis. *Journal of Women & Aging, 7*, 19-35.

Richardson, V.E. & Kilty, K.M. (1997). A critical analysis of expected and actual finances among retired women and men. *Journal of Poverty, 1*, 19-47.

Ruhm, C.J. (1996). Gender differences in employment behavior during late middle age. *Journal of Gerontology: Social Sciences, 51B*, S11-S17.

Smeeding, T.M. (1998). Reshuffling responsibility in old age: The United States in a comparative perspective. In J. Gonyea (Ed.). *Resecuring Social Security and Medicare: Understanding privatization and risk*. Washington, DC: The Gerontological Society of America.

Szinovacz, M. & Ekerdt, D. (1995). Families and retirement. In R. Blieszner &

V. Hilkevitch Bedford (Eds.). *Handbook of aging and the family* (pp. 376-400). Westport, Connecticut: Greenwood Press.

Szinovacz, M. & Washo, C. (1992). Gender differences in exposure to life events and adaptation to retirement. *Journal of Gerontology, 47*, S191-S196.

Weaver, D. A. (1994). The work and retirement decisions of older women: A literature review. *Social Security Bulletin, 57*, 3-24.

Older Women, Their Children, and Grandchildren: A Feminist Perspective on Family Relationships

Karen A. Roberto, PhD
Katherine R. Allen, PhD
Rosemary Blieszner, PhD

SUMMARY. Using gerontological and feminist frameworks, we explored the relationships older women have with their children and grandchildren. In-depth, qualitative interviews were conducted with 34 women, ranging in age from 55 to 88. From our analyses of the women's perceptions of their family relationships, two themes were prevalent: the centrality of children and the peripherality of grandchildren in their everyday lives. The women had varying degrees of involvement with their children and grandchildren, and these relationships contributed to their sense of self and family. Their relationships were not stagnant, but were continually reshaped as both the women and their family members proceeded through the life course. *[Article copies available for a fee from The Haworth Document Delivery Service: 1-800-342-9678. E-mail address: getinfo@haworthpressinc.com]*

KEYWORDS. Adult children; grandchildren; feminist gerontology; older women

This project was supported by an ASPIRES grant awarded to the authors by Virginia Polytechnic Institute and State University. An earlier version of this paper was presented at the Annual Meeting of the Southern Gerontological Society, Chattanooga, TN, April, 1998.

[Haworth co-indexing entry note]: "Older Women, Their Children, and Grandchildren: A Feminist Perspective on Family Relationships." Roberto, Karen A., Katherine R. Allen, and Rosemary Blieszner. Co-published simultaneously in *Journal of Women & Aging* (The Haworth Press, Inc.) Vol. 11, No. 2/3, 1999, pp. 67-84; and: *Fundamentals of Feminist Gerontology* (ed: J. Dianne Garner) The Haworth Press, Inc., 1999, pp. 67-84. Single or multiple copies of this article are available for a fee from The Haworth Document Delivery Service [1-800-342-9678, 9:00 a.m. - 5:00 p.m. (EST). E-mail address: getinfo@haworthpressinc.com].

Family relationships are a central aspect of women's lives. The literature on families in later life provides an understanding of the structural and relational factors that characterize associations between older women and their individual family members (Roberto, 1996). Less is known, however, about dynamics that occur within families that influence the quality, meaning, and maintenance of these relationships. In this paper, we focused our attention on two independent, yet interrelated, relationships in the lives of most older women–those with their children and grandchildren.

About 80% of older women have living children. Regardless of geographic proximity, older women report having frequent contact with their children. A reciprocal relationship often exists between parents and their children, particularly when the parents' health is intact. Older mothers and their adult children frequently report a mutual exchange of instrumental and emotional support and most often assess their interactions as positive (Kulis, 1992; Logan & Spitze, 1996). These relationships, of course, are not without conflict. In several recent studies, mothers and their adult children also describe problems and dissatisfactions within their relationships (Blieszner, Usita, & Mancini, 1996; Henwood, 1993). Difficulties ranged from minor conflicts and disagreements that had a limited impact on relationship satisfaction to more pervasive issues that continually strained their relationships.

Of women who have adult children, about 94% have grandchildren. Grandmothers' direct involvement with their grandchildren depends on a variety of factors. For example, older women with better physical and mental health play a more active role in the lives of their grandchildren than those who must contend with daily health problems (Hodgson, 1992; Kivett, 1991; Troll, 1985). Some researchers suggest that interactions and perceived closeness between grandparents and grandchildren decline with the increased age of the grandchild (Barranti, 1985; Clingempeel, Coylar, Brand, & Hetherington, 1992; Thompson & Walker, 1987). Others, however, report closer and more meaningful relationship with increases in the age of the grandchild (Cherlin & Furstenberg, 1986; Hodgson, 1992; Roberto & Stroes, 1992). Geographical distance from grandchildren has a negative effect upon the frequency of association that heightens the ambiguity in the grandparent's role and its symbolic rather than functional nature (Matthews, 1984). Other variables influencing grandmother-grandchild interactions include relationships with intervening generations (Barranti, 1985; Wentowski, 1985) and the marital instability of the middle generation (Johnson, 1988).

In this paper, we employ gerontological and feminist frameworks for exploring the relationships older women have with their children and grandchildren. Traditional theories of individual psychosocial development highlight the challenges individuals face as they proceed through the life cycle. In each developmental stage, individuals strive to achieve a creative balance between two opposing tensions using their own instinctive energies and a widening radius of interpersonal relations (Erikson, Erikson, & Kivnick, 1989/1994). Although individuals face a focal challenge at each stage of the life cycle, they also engage in the anticipation of future challenges, reexperience tensions that were inadequately integrated at an earlier stage of life, and reexamine those events that were appropriately integrated in the past but are no longer adequate explanations or solutions in their current stage of life. How individuals respond to these challenges and develop a sense of well-being is strongly influenced by their perceptions of themselves, their interactions with others, and societal norms.

Gilligan (1982) pointed out the limitations of the early life stage models and contended that they do not capture the complexity of women's lives. She suggested that the tasks frequently associated with adulthood, such as the development of identity, intimacy, generativity, and integrity, do not occur as discrete processual events in the lives of women but instead are fused throughout the life course. Women often come to know themselves as they are known through their relationships with others. Many women define their lives in terms of their family (Baber & Allen, 1992). Relationships serve as sources of their happiness and despair. By integrating a feminist perspective into the conceptualization of life span development, we acknowledge the importance of women's family relationships and seek better understanding of the meaning and influence of adult children and grandchildren in their lives.

METHODS

Sample Selection Process

Interviewers from the Center for Survey Research at Virginia Tech administered a telephone survey to individuals 55 years of age and older living within a 13 city/county area in southwest Virginia. The brief screening survey was designed to identify persons with grandchildren age 16 and over who would be willing to participate in an in-home interview. The sampling frame consisted of 600 age-targeted households drawn from a comprehensive database of households with listed telephone numbers. Sixty-three households reported no individuals age 55 or older and an additional 114 households reported no grandchildren age 16 or older. Of the remaining 283 households, 92 individuals completed the interview, and 71 gave permission to be contacted for an in-depth interview. Of these, 34 women and 11 men agreed to a personal interview.

In-depth interviews were conducted in the women's homes by the authors and three research associates. The interviews ranged from one to three hours in length; they were taped recorded and transcribed verbatim. The women described their family relationships in detail, including intergenerational and lateral kin relationships with people related by blood, marriage, and adoption. They also discussed "chosen kin," or those whom they felt were "like family" but with whom they had no legal tie. As interviewers, we listened for and probed about diversity in family structure, relationship processes, and interpersonal connections and tensions among family members. We also asked about closeness and support within the family, expectations for their children and grandchildren's lives, the meaning of family in their lives, and advice they would give future grandparents.

Background Characteristics of the Women

The women ranged in age from 57 to 88 with a mean age of 72.4 years (S.D. = 7.83). Of these, 82% (28) were White and 15% (5) were African American, reflecting the population from which they came. Most of the women either were currently married (41%) or widowed (44%). The women had an averaged 13.1 years (S.D. = 3.1) of formal education. Thirty-four indicated that they were homemakers or retired and 11 were currently employed. Their average monthly income ranged from less than $500 to more than $2,500 per month. Most of the women rated their health as fair (26.5%) or good (47.0%).

One woman reported having no biological children or grandchildren, but she had a stepdaughter and step-grandchildren. The other women said they had from one to six children with an average of 2.6. Their children ranged in age from 24 to 58. They had between one and 14 grandchildren, with an average of 4.4. The grandchildren ranged from newborns to more than 45 years of age. Many of these women also had stepchildren and step-grandchildren.

Data Analysis Process

Based on multiple readings of the women's transcripts and reflective process notes written by the interviewers after each interview, we used an open coding process to generate a comprehensive understanding of themes and patterns in the data (Bogdan & Biklen, 1998; Strauss & Corbin, 1990). We applied the coding scheme to the transcripts to identify ways in which older women develop and maintain their relationships with their children and grandchildren and the influences of individual, family, and social change on these relationships and their personal well-being.

The coding scheme was developed as we completed six full readings of the 45 transcripts. After verifying and refining the coding scheme, we read each coded transcript aloud in team meetings, a process that allowed us to reach 100% agreement on identifying themes. The data reported in this paper are a complete representation of one full coding category, "centrality of parenting roles," in which we developed a typology of responses.

RESULTS AND DISCUSSION

From our analyses of the interviews, we gleaned two overarching insights about the women and their relationships with their children and grandchildren. What first became apparent was the centrality of children in the women's everyday lives. Regardless of the number of children, their geographic proximity, or how close the mothers felt to them, both previous and current actions of and interactions with their children contributed to the women's perceptions of themselves and shaped their ideas about family life. In contrast to the powerful influence of their children, our second finding provides support for Johnson's (1988) empirical observation of a the peripherality of grandchildren in the lives of older adults. We use examples from the transcripts to illustrate each of these findings and to show how the women sustain their relationships with children and grandchildren.[1]

---

1. Pseudonyms are used throughout this paper to protect the identity of the women.

Centrality of Children

Although it is not surprising that we found children to be an influential presence in the lives of the older women, recognizing the similarities and differences in the ways the women interpreted their interactions with their children gives new insights into the mother-child relationship in later life. The women's perceptions of their experiences, sense of self, and interpretations of their children's actions and interactions merged as they described their families. Three distinct depictions of late life motherhood emerged from our analysis of the transcribed data.

Children are everything. For 12 of the 34 women, their relationships with their children were clearly central to their lives. Usually, frequent contact, active parenting, and shared family and recreational activities characterized these relationships. The relationship between Cora and her three children provide an example. Cora is 66 years-old, White, and married. She and her husband had just returned from a week-long vacation with their middle son. When asked to describe her relationship with her three children, she responded:

> We just have a wonderful relationship with all of them. And we realize that we're very fortunate that we're close. We're in touch with them just–there's never a week that goes by that I'm not in touch with all three of them, and quite often on a daily basis . . . we always have an idea of where everybody is and what's going on. So we try to give everybody all the space they want, but we're pretty important to each other. We always celebrate birthdays together and holidays.

For Cora, as for several other of the women, the needs of their children outweighed personal desires and traditional life stage expectations. For example, Cora's oldest son is divorced. His former wife suffers from a mental illness and Cora has cared for his 16-year-old daughter for most of the girl's life. When discussing her situation, she commented:

> So although it cramped my style to change my daily routine and do what she needed, I still managed to do it. And I was going to school at the time–I had gone back to school and it just always seemed to work that when I had a special project or a deadline or

something, it would end up the time that I had her. And lots of time I just had to let things go or reschedule or whatever. But I considered her the priority and managed to get everything done.

Cora's granddaughter has lived with her for the past several years. Her son works out of town but comes to stay with them most weekends. In addition, Cora's daughter recently separated from her husband, and she is providing child care several days a week for her 2-year-old grandson.

The women often interpreted their feelings about themselves and their relationships with others through the actions and reactions of their children. For example, when Cora was asked, "What's the best thing about being a grandmother?" she responded:

> Well, I think seeing the fulfillment in my children that they are having a measure of success with their children and I know how good it feels to be a parent, and I see my children have the same fulfillment, same measure of fulfillment in their children.

The role of mother and the women's interaction with their children defined and gave meaning to their lives. It was through their experiences with their children that they continued to grow and find satisfaction in their later years. A comment made by Winnie, a 56 year-old never married African American woman with two children, epitomized the importance of motherhood at this stage of the women's lives:

> My children are my heart, cause I don't have a husband and I don't have a social life as of now, I don't care to have one. So my children are my life. That's the way I feel about it.

Mothers whose children exerted a strong presence in their lives most often spoke positively about themselves and their relationships with their children. However, for a few of these women, their relationships with their children were strained. The responses of these women suggested that they were emotionally estranged from some or all of their children. This distance, or lack of cohesion in their relationships with their children, did not mean that the relationship was irrelevant in their lives. Rather, it appeared to consume their thoughts and energy.

Ila's relationship with her son and daughter illustrates this type of mother-child interaction. Ila is 67 years-old, White, and married, although she has not lived with her husband for more than five years. She says she feels close to her children yet she struggles to understand what they want from her. For example, she discussed sending a letter to her children asking them to help her understand the difficulties in their family and what she could do to alleviate them. As she explained, she was taken aback by the response of her son:

> I thought there's never been anything in my life that I've tackled that I haven't done and done well. And I had a pretty good feeling that I could handle my life. And then I went out to see [my son]. He said, "We are not the same kind of people. That I was too watery and too emotional. And that he loved me but he didn't like who I was." This was almost unbelievable to me because he is a very loving, sweet-natured, neat person. And he's never, that I know of, had a grudge against anybody or been unreasonable in his thinking or actions with other person. It wowed me, it really wowed me. So I just figure, when he wants to be in touch with me. He calls me about once a month and as soon as he gets on the phone he says, "Well I'm going to let you go now." We don't pass any information.

When relationships with their children did not "fit" within their personal construction of family, some women struggled to define themselves and often questioned their abilities as an individual. This was particularly evident in situations like Ila's where the women perceived conflicts with more than one family member. For example, when asked about her personal strengths, Ila responded:

> I'm very confused right now about what my strengths are. I really always thought I was a good person and that I could do as well, if not better, than any other person. And it was an abrupt change when I suddenly found out that my husband of 40 years didn't like me. My son didn't like me. It's been very painful. I mean, it causes me a lot of thought about it, and I suppose it'll all, in time, wear out. But I am getting older, and I don't remember as well as I did.

In summary, relationships with adult children were the essence of life for the older women. The nature of these relationships shaped how the women thought about themselves both as individuals and as parents. Positive relationships allowed the women to continue in a parenting role, looking out for their children and, at times, caring for grandchildren. The women sometimes permitted strained relationships to cast doubts upon their selfhood as they pondered changes in their parental role and their relationships with their children.

Children are important, but. . . . Sixteen of the 34 women also firmly acknowledged the importance of their children, but differed from the first group of women in that their lives did not totally revolve around their children. Rather, the mother-child relationship was but one of several relationships that added meaning to their lives. These women often described having close and active relationships with siblings and friends. The women were very satisfied with their lives and what they were contributing as elder members of their communities. They talked with much enthusiasm about their social activities, church work, and personal interests. In addition to their own involvement with people and activities, they also recognized that their children had their own lives, separate from their family of origin. Comments from Zelda, a 74 year-old White woman in her second marriage, captured this sentiment as she described one of her three biological children.

> My youngest daughter's just as caring and good as she can be . . . The fact that their child, that her and her husband–both of them, their child is their life. They never do much of anything that's not with or for the child. I don't suppose they do anyway.

The women appeared to have a sense of pride about whom they were, both as individuals and as parents. They were very familiar with their children's lives and were pleased with their children's accomplishments. When they were asked to describe "in a nutshell" what family meant to them, they consistently responded "everything" or "the world." As illustrated in by the following examples, children were a significant part of the women's lives.

> Rita (age 56, African American, married, five children): We are a close knit family. And they mean a lot to me, you know. They mean a lot. I just thank God we raised them good . . . Like I said, we raised 'em the best we could and if they was here, they'd tell

you the same thing, that Mom and Dad did a good job raising'em.

Kitty (age 70, White, divorced, three children): They're the
world to me. They are my world. And I just adore them so, you
know, and I depend on them too. And, like, I can feel like I can
call them and talk anything over with them, with all three of
them.

Although the women had regular contact with their children and
perceived their relationships as close, they avoided depending solely
on their children for support. Several women said that they would turn
to their siblings, friends, neighbors, or formal services for help rather
than their children. Others relied on their children, but tried not to
impose too much on them. For example, Lynn, a 72 year-old White
widow with three children, acknowledged that she currently depends
on her daughter more for both physical and emotional support because
she is experiencing some health problems. However, she named a
person in the community as the person she would call for help and
assistance.

Interviewer: The two that really you call on would be [daughter]
and [granddaughter], the most, because they are around?

Lynn: Well, let me say no. The other person I would really call
on the most is a Black gentleman here in town whose name is
Hank . . . I call on Hank FREQUENTLY. I mean, he came over
and picked up my vacuum cleaner and took it to the repair shop
and he will go back and get it and he comes over occasionally
and hauls my garbage out. Oh, he is wonderful and he is one of
my best friends . . . I don't know what I would do without him.

In summary, most of these women perceived having a high level of
involvement in their children's lives. They were cognizant of changes
that took place in their relationships over time, and in fact, often
alluded to their necessity. In some respects, the women appeared to
view developing and maintaining a sense of independence well as
family connectivenes as a measure of personal success.

Children are a part of life. Children did not play a very active role in
the lives of six women in our sample. These women viewed their lives

as independent of their children. They often had limited contact with their children, even when they lived in the same town. This distance did not appear to disturb the women. In fact, they often remarked that they did not want to bother their children nor did they want their children interfering with their lives.

One example of this type of relationship comes from our interview with Nell, a 68 year-old White widow who works part-time and volunteers at the local museum and her church. She has one child, a son, who lives in the same town; she sees him once or twice a week. When asked who among her family members she felt closest to, Nell named her son. She went on to say:

> We do share. I try not to interfere in his life in any way, but I also try to support whatever is going on. At the same time I feel like if I have any needs I can call on him . . . I broke my leg a few years ago. I was walking at 5:00 in the morning and I had to go and wake someone up for help. And of course they called him and he came and got me to the hospital and this kind of thing, but you know–if there's a need, he comes, but I try not to call him for silly things. But I feel physically well and can do almost anything I need to do anyway.

Women who had more than one child were quick to point out inherent differences among their children. The women often prefaced their description of the relationship with a particular child with a brief statement about his or her personality. For example, when asked about her four children, Patsy, a 73 year-old White woman who was divorced, began her discussion of her oldest daughter by saying:

> She's always been–her personality is more distant. Well, even when she was growing up she never was confidential or anything. She always had her friends and separate, kind of, from the family. As she grew up, she never wanted to do anything as a family.

There was an underlying sense of tension or conflict in these women's relationships with their children. Sometimes, the problems were overtly discussed. For example, two mothers expressed disappointment that their children did not take advantage of opportunities to advance their education. Past problems with alcohol also were a source of contention for two of the mothers. More frequently, the women made general statements alluding to friction between themselves and their children. As illustrated by Patsy's following comments, differences appeared easier for the women to manage or accept when they had other children with whom they shared a closer relationship and when they attributed the differences between them and their children to the life-long traits of their children.

> He [son] respects what I want. And when I have odd ideas or odd ways of wantin' to do something, he doesn't put me down for it. It's "I respect you enough to where you have the right to do what you want to." Where I don't feel that so much with my other kids. They're always trying to control or to get you to do what they want you to do. Where [son] wants me to do what I want to do.

Overall, children were a part of these women's lives to the extent that they were bound by expected family ties. Some women had frequent interactions with their children whereas others saw them only for special occasions such as holidays and birthdays. They spoke matter-of-factly about their children and their involvement in their lives.

Peripherality of Grandchildren

The women's descriptions of their relationships with grandchildren suggested that although these relationships were meaningful, they were peripheral to their everyday lives. The one exception was for the grandmothers who were rearing or providing temporary child care for one or more of their grandchildren. These women saw themselves as both grandmother and mother for their grandchildren, switching back and forth depending on the presence or absence of their children and the needs of their children. In Cora's situation, she relinquished the parenting role for her granddaughter when major decisions were to be made and when her son was at home with his daughter. She explained it this way:

> There are times when I almost feel like I'm her mother, although she's had a relationship with her father that I have not had total responsibility for her. Ultimately we get back to him when there's a situation that needs to be dealt with.

Working with Abused Older Women
from a Feminist Perspective

Linda Vinton, PhD

SUMMARY. Domestic violence in older families is often referred to not as family violence but as elder abuse. This chapter will begin by discussing how perceptions of this type of violence impact informal and formal interventions. The prevalence and etiology of domestic violence are described, along with how the joint forces of ageism and sexism affect older female victims. National, state, and local efforts to prevent and remediate the abuse of older women are also covered. In conclusion, the author presents implications for working with groups and individual abused older women from a feminist perspective. *[Article copies available for a fee from The Haworth Document Delivery Service: 1-800-342-9678. E-mail address: getinfo@haworthpressinc.com]*

KEYWORDS. Elder abuse, domestic violence, older women, feminist practice

Although violence within families has long been documented, remarkably, it was not until recent times that such behavior was viewed as warranting the general public's attention. During the 1950s and 1960s in the U.S., the prevalence and harmful consequences of child abuse and neglect were publicized, and during the 1970s, the widespread abuse of women became a focus. Responses to these forms of domestic violence included legal remedies and safeguards, protective and social services, educational campaigns, and temporary housing for

[Haworth co-indexing entry note]: "Working with Abused Older Women from a Feminist Perspective." Vinton, Linda. Co-published simultaneously in *Journal of Women & Aging* (The Haworth Press, Inc.) Vol. 11, No. 2/3, 1999, pp. 85-100; and: *Fundamentals of Feminist Gerontology* (ed: J. Dianne Garner) The Haworth Press, Inc., 1999, pp. 85-100. Single or multiple copies of this article are available for a fee from The Haworth Document Delivery Service [1-800-342-9678, 9:00 a.m. - 5:00 p.m. (EST). E-mail address: getinfo@haworthpressinc.com].

victims. While we cannot agree as a society on how to prevent and remediate abusive behavior, nor on the extent that public institutions should be involved, there is wide scale acknowledgment that family violence is a social problem.

One of the last types of maltreatment between intimates to gain our attention has been elder abuse. The term "granny bashing" was coined by the British press during the 1970s, and in 1979 and 1980, the House Select Committee on Aging heard testimony about the phenomena of elder abuse and neglect in the U.S. Legislation surrounding reporting and investigating elder maltreatment has been primarily modeled after child protective statutes; however, not all states mandate the reporting of elder abuse (Ono, 1997).

This chapter will begin by discussing how the public, professional helpers, and women themselves view older abuse victims and how labels impact how victims' situations are assessed and treated. Next, the prevalence of domestic violence in later life will be presented, along with its etiology. How the joint forces of ageism and sexism affect older women who are victimized will be highlighted. National, state, and local efforts to prevent and remediate the abuse of older women will be covered. In conclusion, the author will discuss implications for working with groups and individual abused older women from a feminist perspective.

IS SHE AN ABUSED WOMAN OR ELDER?

Perhaps an appropriate subtitle would be–And why can't she be both? Although a false dichotomy, whether an older woman who has been maltreated by a family member or intimate is seen as an abused woman or an abused elder matters (Vinton, 1991). I will relate a story from my own work to illustrate how labeling a situation can make a difference in how one goes about intervening with victims of abuse. In 1980 I worked as the coordinator of a battered women's shelter. My next job was in an Adult Services unit at a public welfare agency following the passage of adult protective services/elder abuse legislation. While working at this job, I also volunteered at a domestic violence shelter. Despite seeing older women that had been abused by their partners and other family members while doing adult protective services, I never viewed these clients as "battered women" who could possibly benefit from the same approach and types of services that the shelter clients were offered. Rather, I viewed my older female clients that had been maltreated by family members as elderly persons in need of "aging services." Most often this meant periodic home visits and homemaking services.

Linda Osmundson (1997), in her article, "Watching Our Words," states that by categorizing individuals we can seriously risk the safety of victims of abuse. She writes that, "As women (and a few men) age, they become more sympathetic in the eyes of friends, neighbors, medical systems, and places of worship if they appear vulnerable. When those who appear vulnerable are abused, it is called "elder abuse"–a term more palatable than domestic violence, because it presumes the same "innocence" the system accords to children who are abused" (p. 10). Osmundson further points out that in some states, unless the older woman is "frail," apart from law enforcement, she may not be eligible to receive services from state agencies.

This is a catch-22 situation for the older woman–on the one hand, she may be eligible for adult protective and supportive services if she is of a certain age and frail; on the other, as a victim of elder abuse, she may be served in a manner quite different from younger women who experience domestic violence. For instance, she may not be told about or given access to interventions that have been found to work well with battered women (e.g., group support). In addition, because of our dichotomous thinking (a woman can be a battered woman or an abused elder but not both), many elderly women do not perceive themselves to be battered women, and thus, do not seek services for victims of domestic violence. Seaver (1996) has concluded that, "older abused women need to be seen for who they are, not who we imagine or need them to be, if they are to be adequately served by any system" (p. 3).

HOW FREQUENT
IS DOMESTIC VIOLENCE IN LATER LIFE?

First the good news: although many nationwide studies of family violence have been limited by the lack of survey respondents over the age of 65 or 70, researchers have consistently found that spouse abuse and age are negatively correlated–as age increases, the rate of marital violence decreases (Stark, Flitcraft, Zuckerman, Gray, Robinson, & Frazier, 1981; Straus, Gelles, & Steinmetz, 1980). National Family

Violence Survey data were examined by Suitor, Pillemer, and Straus (1990) in order to examine marital violence across the life course. These authors found that the direction and strength of the relationship between marital violence and age were similar for the 1975 and 1985 National Family Violence Surveys. Both indicated a statistically significant decrease in the rate of marital violence reported by husbands and wives across age groups (18-29, 30-39, 40-49, 50-65).

The results also indicated that age continued to be related to marital violence even when the effects of three factors–marital conflict, verbal aggression, and the husband's drinking behavior–were taken into consideration. Interestingly, although some have suggested that older persons succumb more to societal pressure to conform to norms (in this case, to accept marital violence as normative or be reluctant to label it as spouse abuse), when respondents were asked in the National Family Violence Surveys about their attitudes toward marital violence, no relationship was found between age and attitudes for either men or women.

Now the bad news: in the first large-scale random sample survey of elder abuse, Pillemer and Finkelhor (1988) determined the rate of abuse for persons aged 65 and over who were living only with a spouse to be 41 per 1,000 couples. In terms of abuse, 58% of the perpetrators were spouses, as compared to adult children who constituted 24% of the abusers. The authors point out that people are most likely to be abused by persons with whom they live, and substantially more older persons, especially men, live with their spouses. Among reported cases of elder abuse, however, adult children are more likely to be named as the perpetrators. In a study of reported cases in 18 states, Tatara (1993) found that more than twice as many adult children (32.5%) were suspected of abuse than spouses (14.4%). This may be a function of the types of situations that are likely to come to the attention of health and social services professionals, as well as other reporters. Spouse abuse may be more likely to remain hidden.

DYNAMICS OF DOMESTIC VIOLENCE ACROSS THE LIFESPAN

Schechter (1987) defines domestic violence as "a pattern of coercive control that one family member exercises over another. Abusers use physical and sexual violence, threats, emotional insults, and economic deprivation as a way to dominate their victims and get their way." In a chapter on family violence theories, Yllö (1997) describes microtheories that attempt to explain domestic violence by focusing on the behaviors of specific individuals and macrotheories that take a sociocultural view of family abuse. Feminist theories blend these perspectives by treating interpersonal behaviors–in this case, abusive and manipulative behaviors, as manifestations of a social context that includes gender inequality of power and cultural acceptance of the control and domination of women by men. Throughout the life course, we see incest perpetrated primarily on young girls and female adolescents by their fathers and stepfathers, the battering of girlfriends and wives in disproportionate numbers, and a particularly high rate of physical abuse of older women by sons in light of the fact that daughters are far more likely to spend more time interacting with their mothers (Pillemer, 1985). While there is some debate over whether to view older women who are frail and have been maltreated by a caregiver as victims of family violence, in a significant number of such cases, the key components are power and control (Brandl & Wisconsin Coalition Against Domestic Violence, 1997; Brandl & Raymond, 1997).

In their handbook on developing services for older abused women, the Wisconsin Coalition Against Domestic Violence (1997) gives common scenarios of domestic violence in later life. First, victims tend to have internalized messages that they are to blame for the abuser's violence. Second, victims may fear retaliation and the consequences of making their situations known to others. Isolation may further stymie such disclosure. Finkelhor (1983) states that oftentimes abusers manipulate the psyches of their victims by using psychological abuse, exploitation, and verbal threats in addition to physical abuse. Third, the potential loss of income and assets may be a barrier to living violence free. Fourth, the woman's emotional and/or physical health may affect her decision making. And fifth, the social context may be influential in encouraging older women to maintain the status quo. Friends and relatives who may share generational values that suggest women are responsible for relationships and should self-sacrifice, that stigmatize assertive behaviors and separation and divorce, might not support older women in taking action to stop family violence. And although some adult children do encourage their mothers to take steps to improve their lives, others may create obstacles by making their mothers feel guilty or ineffectual.

THE OPPRESSION OF OLDER WOMEN

Pauline Bart (1975) has said, "This is not a good society in which to grow old or to be a woman, and the combination of the two makes for a poignant situation." Perhaps the word poignant makes this an understatement. While there are cultures that revere older women, in general, as American women age, they face ageist and sexist constructions about women past midlife that limit their social, economic, legal, and political opportunities (Aitken & Griffin, 1996; Rosenthal, 1990). Put bluntly, Markson (1992) states, "Once past menopause, females are more likely to be both denigrated and feared than their male counterparts" (p. 1). She goes on to point to numerous popular images of older women as ugly, absurd, menacing, or dependent.

In her essay, "The Double Standard of Aging," Susan Sontag (1975) suggests that while the prestige of youth affects women and men alike, getting old is more profoundly wounding for women. The special severity derives from another form of oppression–beautyism. While the perception that aged people are not physically attractive underlies ageist attitudes, our society defines physical attractiveness for women in terms of particularly youthful ideals, and the value of women is more intertwined with their looks than men's. Status or rewards for women are also more often dependent on affiliations with men than vice versa. Itzin (1984) suggests that ageist and sexist forces give out the message that women have two functions–one domestic and the other sexual, each involving availability and services to men. According to this view, older women may face sexual disqualification and redundancy because they are past their childbearing/rearing years.

Other common age related stereotypes are that old people are dependent and incompetent. Dependence can be viewed from different perspectives, including economic and social dependence. In a feminist critique of how Americans have traditionally defined "productive aging," Holstein (1992) posits that the narrow, work-oriented meaning of the term "productive" runs counter to the humanistic view that the worth of older people should be grounded on the principles of dignity and respect for all people. An econometric versus social definition of a productive aging society has particularly negative consequences for older women since they face disproportional economic impoverishment. Nearly three-fourths of the elderly poor are women. According to Harrington Meyer (1996), retirement income is ". . . significantly gendered in that it reflects the influence of the waged labor force; a gendered conception of work; and a view of marriage and family life as permanent" (p. 465).

In an article titled, "The Competent Older Woman," Boellhoff Giesen and Datan (1980) propose that society tends to take the opposite view and stereotypes older women as dependent, passive, and lacking in competence. These authors state that such thinking is based on a misconception that older women have not acquired the same levels of competence as older men (again, as may be related econometric definitions of productive aging) and that with increasing age comes a decrease in everyday problem-solving ability (an ageist assumption).

Some of the consequences of ageist and sexist attitudes for older women are invisibility and lack of credibility. In our society, older women as a group and as individuals can be safely ignored because their voice cannot be heard. Recent efforts to join gerontological and feminist theory (Reinharz, 1986) and to conduct gender-specific research in gerontology (Markson, 1992), however, are helping to give a voice to middle-aged and older women's issues. The expansion of the battered women's movement to include the cause of abused older women is also making a difference in this regard.

NATIONAL, STATE, AND LOCAL EFFORTS TO PREVENT AND REMEDIATE THE ABUSE OF OLDER WOMEN

Among the states, Wisconsin was one of the earliest to bring attention to the abuse of older women and since the 1980s, has been a leader in the development of educational materials and specially targeted services. Importantly, the Wisconsin Bureau on Aging and Wisconsin Coalition Against Domestic Violence have worked closely together for more than a decade. It was, no doubt, helpful that during the 1980s, Wisconsin's Director of the Bureau on Aging, Donna McDowell, had a raised consciousness and talked about the abuse of older women and the need for statewide advocacy (McDowell, 1988). Moreover, an early study of domestic violence shelter programming took place under her leadership (McKibben, 1988) and positions were created within the Bureau on Aging (and jointly with the Wisconsin Coalition Against Domestic Violence) to address the concerns of older battered women.

Another woman in a position to bring attention to how domestic violence affects older women was Maxine Forman, Manager of the Women's Initiative section of the American Association of Retired Persons (AARP). Having been involved in the work of a domestic violence shelter earlier in her career and having read an article on abused older women, she became interested in bringing people to Washington, D.C., for a discourse on the subject. The result was the 1992 AARP sponsored forum titled "Abused Elders or Older Battered Women?" that brought together aging service providers and the domestic violence community. Alarmingly, when the AARP publicized the meeting in their newsletter, more than 500 older women wrote the Women's Initiative about their own situations, often detailing long years of emotional and physical abuse at the hands of family members.

A report from the forum (AARP, 1993) listed numerous recommendations with respect to community based services for abused older women. Some of these included: (1) ensuring that appropriate, accessible, safe shelters and other services were available that take into account the needs of older women; (2) sensitizing and educating all service providers, including the medical and legal professions, counselors, and religious leaders about sexism, racism, and ageism; (3) instituting cross-training, coordination, and coalition-building between the elder abuse and domestic violence communities; (4) providing support and social services by creating a comprehensive, integrated support and intervention system; (5) reaching out to older women by disseminating information about domestic violence through senior centers and home services, health clinics and physicians, civic association, and public benefits officers; and (6) providing victim advocates and creating sister-to-sister "buddy" programs between recently battered and formerly battered women (pp. 23-24).

With support from the AARP's Women Initiative, a survey was conducted in 1993 of 53 statewide domestic abuse coalitions, 50 state offices on domestic violence, 54 state offices on aging, 56 offices of attorneys general, and 27 participants of the "Abused Elders or Older Battered Women" forum (AARP, 1994). The purpose of the survey was to ascertain if statewide statistics were being kept on the number of older battered women receiving services and if specialized programming was available through these offices. Primarily, state offices on domestic violence (12 of the 27 agencies that responded) kept statistics, followed by domestic violence coalitions and state offices on aging. Although the response rate was low for the survey, it was tentatively concluded that older battered women were an undeserved population after finding only 15 specialized programs in four states.

Research on the use of domestic violence shelters to meet the needs of older battered women since that time has been only somewhat more hopeful. In a look at Florida's shelters, Vinton (1992) reported that less than one percent of the women served were age 60 and over, despite the fact that the percentage of older persons in the counties where shelters were located ranged from 11 to 45 percent. In a follow-up study of Florida's shelters (Vinton, Altholz, & Lobell, 1997), it was found that the number of shelters with special programming had increased from two or 8% to five or 22% over a five-year period, and that the percentage of older staff members, volunteers, and board members of domestic violence shelters had also increased.

Most recently in a nationwide study, Vinton (1998) reported that 61 of 428 respondent shelters offered some type of special programming for older women. This programming primarily consisted of outreach or individual interventions. Many of the shelters reported the lack of funds as an obstacle to providing specially targeted services or outreach. With the exception of six demonstration projects funded by the Administration on Aging in 1994-1996 and some limited state funding, there have been scant funds available to specially target older female victims of domestic violence.

A FEMINIST APPROACH
TO HELPING OLDER ABUSED WOMEN

Countering Sexist and Ageist Beliefs Among Helpers

Perceiving the abuse of older women as a women's issue is a starting point for feminist practice with older women victims. Although many of us like to believe helping professionals have a heightened sense of awareness when it comes to the dynamics and effects of sexism and ageism, such individuals are not immune to stereotypes. We must be able to see older women as women, with the common connections that women have. We must be able to hear what older women tell us and understand how the forces of oppression not only affect victims of domestic abuse, but helpers as well.

In a literature review on the subject of counselor bias, Eisenberg

(1979) discusses the many studies that show that the attitudes of counselors, social workers, psychologists, medical professionals, and other helpers, reflect those of society at large when it comes to stereotyping. As a social work educator, I have used one particular study in the classroom that I feel is provocative and helps students to see their own vulnerability to ageism and sexism. Kurtz, Johnson, and Rice (1989) designed an experiment that had students view a series of videotaped vignettes depicting doctor-patient interactions. As many conditions were held constant as possible (physician's manner and behavior, setting, patient complaint, dialogue) while the sex, age, race, social class/occupation, income, and physical attractiveness (as agreed on by a panel) of the patient varied across the vignettes.

Patient I was a young, attractive African American woman who was attending college and struggling with money. She was articulate in describing her symptoms. Patient II was also young, attractive, and a college student, but she was white and had poor verbal skills. Patient III was a middle-aged white man who was a judge. Although he had trouble articulating, he appeared confident when discussing his symptoms. Patient IV was a middle-aged, white woman. Her appearance was described as ordinary. Unlike Patient's II and III, she was very articulate and an explicit source of information about her symptoms. Patient V was an elderly, white man who was assertive with the physician and had a grasp on his condition, but who turned to his wife for clarification during the interview. After watching all of the vignettes, the master's level social work students in the sample were asked to check which characteristics from a list of 10 positive and 10 negative characteristics applied to each patient. They were also asked to indicate the probability of successfully helping each patient in the resolution of his/her complaint, and to rank order the patients in terms of liking to work with them, and the degree to which they felt the patients would cooperate with treatment.

As you may have already surmised, the middle-aged woman and man were assigned the "most favored" status by the lowest percentage of students, followed by the elderly man. The elderly man had the distinction of being the "least favored" patient by the highest proportion of students (35%). Stereotypic thinking was shown by assigning characteristics such as "is dependent," "is a complainer," and "probably needs psychological help" most frequently to the middle-aged woman and "is rigid" to the older man. Despite the fact that the young, white woman (Patient II) was inarticulate and the middle-aged woman was an explicit source of information, three-fourths of the sample viewed the younger woman as "a reliable source of information" and "intelligent"; whereas less than half assigned these same characteristics to the middle-aged woman.

These results may be explained to some extent by the students' own demographics (primarily under age 30, female, and white). If individuals tend to idealize people most like themselves and to stereotype others, as the students did in this experiment, this leaves older women in a precarious position. Women aged 50 and over are not well-represented among law enforcement officers, medical doctors, and domestic violence shelter staff. And while they are better represented among private counselors, social service, and mental health agency staff, the percentage is probably still not proportionate to their numbers. Furthermore, if we consider representation by minority women among these professionals, a greater disproportion will be seen.

For more than two decades, there have been repeated calls to integrate content on women's issues, and specifically, older women's issues, from a feminist perspective, into educational and training curricula for helping professionals (Abramovitz, Hopkins, Olds, & Waring, 1982; Cavallaro, 1991; Kravetz, 1982; Thompson, 1988). Underlying such recommendations is the belief that the integration of feminist principles and commitments will promote humanistic practice (Bricker-Jenkins, 1991). While there is no unified feminist perspective, Kravetz and Jones (1991) suggest that a basic tenet of feminist thinking is that the forces of oppression such as sexism, are institutionalized, thus inextricably linking personal and sociopolitical transformations. According to this view, a woman's situation exists within a social context that fosters the inequality of women, powerlessness, and dependency, and these factors relate to individual problems and the victimization of women.

It would be glib to simply end here with the recommendation that helping professionals be educated or trained about older women's issues from a feminist perspective. Bedard and Hartung (1991) state that when students are required to learn about women's issues, the classroom may be transformed into one in which the balance of attention shifts from those students who are interested and sympathetic to studying women to those who are reluctant or even hostile. Some educators believe resistance is positive because it means those that need to hear about views different than their own have listened and reacted (Rothenberg, 1989), but others have found that with certain groups, consciousness-raising can be an emotionally draining and intellectually disappointing experience. It is not only difficult to promote self-reflection among passive students but those who believe they are egalitarian humanists as well.

Some guidelines are to not avoid the issues when educating groups about older women's issues. Material that provokes is needed by all students–even those with heightened awareness of women's issues, to keep them interested and continually examining their own beliefs and practices. Deal openly with issues of the domination of women by using the circumstances at hand as an example if emotions and behaviors get out of control while discussing women's issues, oppression, and feminism. Finally, do not assume there is only one kind of feminist belief system or approach; rather, discuss "What is feminism?" "Am I a feminist?" "What does it mean to me? Us? Women we work with and advocate for?" (Hanmer & Statham, 1989).

Specialized training materials have been developed that focus on older women. Among them are the BIHA Women in Action's manual titled *Ageism and Battering for Women of Color* and the National Coalition Against Domestic Violence's special edition of *Voice* (Fall 1997) which is devoted to older battered women. Several state coalitions also offer training guides such as the Wisconsin Coalition Against Domestic Violence (*Developing Services for Older Abused Women: A Guide for Domestic Abuse Programs*) and Florida Coalition Against Domestic Violence (*The Florida Older Battered Project: Training and Information Packet*).

Working with Abused Older Woman at the Agency and Individual Level

Feminist practice is derived from a rights and strengths perspective. The importance of women having control over their everyday lives and bodies is stressed (Kravetz & Jones, 1991), along with their right to choose their lifestyle (Brandl & WCADV, 1997). It is assumed that most all women have skills that can help them live violence-free lives and that such capacities can be validated through support and bolstered by resources. Some general techniques of feminist practice include "finding language to describe and talk about women and their oppression which is understandable and addresses their circumstances" and "assuming client oppression and lack of choices [but] exploring choices and challenging where there appear to be none" (Hanmer & Statham, p. 130).

Agencies and practitioners can create a welcoming atmosphere for older women by altering the physical environment in which they might typically work. By meeting with women in their homes or places close to where they live, their receptivity to using services and resources may increase. Health problems, as well as changes in hearing, vision, and mobility, can make it difficult to get to and manipulate the physical layout of offices, shelters, and meeting places. Making transportation, important parts of the environment (e.g., chair, walkway, main office, bathrooms, private area), and reading materials accessible is a start, but comfort should also be a goal.

A socially supportive environment is another aspect of programming for older women that can be empowering. The Manager of the Older Abused Women's Program at the Milwaukee Women's Center (Seaver, 1996) has stated that the most visible impact of her program was on the 45 women that attended their support group. Validation refers to affirming an individual's subjective experience of reality. Since we know that the dynamics of oppression and domestic violence against women include discounting or marginalizing women's concerns, group support plays a crucial role in letting women know that they are believed, that their lives matter, and that they are not alone. Peer or professional facilitators may also share their perceptions and assessments as part of the validation process (Bricker-Jenkins, 1991). Brandl and the Wisconsin Coalition Against Domestic Violence (1997) offer the following advice in developing support groups for older abused women: (1) consider naming the group in such a way that does not only focus on the dynamics of domestic violence but instead what the group aims to do such as promote safety, well-being, and support; (2) find a community-based sponsor that is familiar as an aging services organization; (3) have at least one facilitator that is an older woman; and (4) count on women themselves to advertise the group or local media rather than mass communication.

Many of the same strategies that have been found to be effective in working individually with younger abused women work well with older women. Brandl and Raymond (1997) list the elements of an empowerment model as:

- Empathic listening;
- Making time to properly document;
- Providing information about domestic abuse in later life;
- Offering options and choices;
- Working with domestic abuse and elder abuse specialists;
- Encouraging planning for safety and support;
- Referring to local resources. (p. 65)

While older abused women may be more likely to need a different complement of services than younger women due to physical or cognitive impairment, we cannot ignore the complexity of their needs. Victims of elder abuse are often victims of domestic violence. In turn, we need to view domestic violence services and resources as aging services and resources, thus borrowing from the domestic violence shelter movement that has long promoted feminist principles.

REFERENCES

Abramovitz, M., Hopkins, T. J., Olds, V., & Waring, M. (1982). Integrating content on women into the social policy curriculum: A continuum model. *Journal of Education for Social Work, 18*(1), 29-34.

Aitken, L., & Griffin, G. (1996). *Gender issues in elder abuse.* Thousand Oaks, CA: Sage.

American Association of Retired Persons (1993). *Abused elders or older battered women? Report on the AARP forum.* Washington, DC: Author.

American Association of Retired Persons (1994, January). *Survey of services for older battered women: Final report.* Washington, DC: Author.

Bart, P. (1975). Emotional and social status of older women. In *No longer young: The older woman in America* (pp. 3-21). Ann Arbor, MI: Institute of Gerontology, University of Michigan.

Bedard, M., & Hartung, B. (1991). "Blackboard jungle" revisited. *Thought & Action, VII,* 1, 7-20.

Boellhoff Giesen, C., & Datan, N. (1980). The competent older woman. In N. Datan & N. Lohmann (Eds.), *Transitions in aging* (57-72). NY: Academic Press.

Brandl, B., & Raymond, J. (1997). Unrecognized elder abuse victims. *Journal of Case Management, 6*(2), 62-68.

Brandl, B., & Wisconsin Coalition Against Domestic Violence. (1997). *Developing services for older abused women: A guide for domestic abuse programs.* Madison, WI: Author.

Bricker-Jenkins, M. (1991). The propositions and assumptions of feminist social work practice. In *Feminist social work practice in clinical settings* (pp. 271-303). Newbury Park, CA: Sage.

Cavallaro, M. L. (1991). Curriculum guidelines and strategies on counseling older women for incorporation into gerontology and counseling coursework. *Educational Gerontology, 17*, 157-166.

Eisenberg, J. M. (1979). Sociologic influences on decision-making by clinicians. *Annals of Internal Medicine, 90*, 957-964.

Finkelhor, D. (1983). Common features of family abuse. In D. Finkelhor, R. J. Gelles, G. T. Hotaling, & M. S. Straus (Eds.), *The dark side of families: Current family violence research* (pp. 17-30). Beverly Hills, CA: Sage.

Hanmer, J., & Statham, D. (1989). *Women and social work: Towards a woman-centered practice.* Chicago, IL: Lyceum.

Harrington Meyer, M. (1996). Family status and poverty among older women: The gendered distribution of retirement income in the United States." In J. Quadagno & D. Street, *Aging for the twenty-first century* (pp. 464-479). NY: St. Martin's Press.

Holstein, M. (1992). Productive aging: A feminist critique. *Journal of Aging & Social Policy, 4*(3/4), 17-34.

Itzin, C. (1984). The double jeopardy of ageism and sexism: Medical images of women. In D. B. Bromley (Ed.), *Gerontology: Social and behavioural perspectives* (pp. 170-183). London: Croom Helm.

Kravetz, D. (1982). An overview of content on women for the social work curriculum. *Journal of Education for Social Work, 18*(2), 42-49.

Kravetz, D., & Jones, L. E. (1991). Supporting practice in feminist service agencies. In M. Bricker-Jenkins, N. R. Hooyman, & N. Gottlieb (Eds.), *Feminist social work practice in clinical settings* (pp. 223-249). Newbury Park: Sage.

Kurtz, M. E., Johnson, S. M., & Rice, S. (1989). Students' clinical assessments: Are they affected by stereotyping? *Journal of Social Work Education, 25*(1), 3-12.

Markson, E. W. (1992). On behalf of older women: An apologia and review. *AGHE Exchange, 15*(3), 1-3.

McDowell, D. (1988, May). *Aging America: The images of abuse.* Keynote presentation at A National Conference on Elder Abuse: Linking Systems and community services, Milwaukee, WI.

McKibben, M. (1988). *Programming issues regarding older battered women.* Unpublished report, Madison, WI: Wisconsin Bureau on Aging.

Ono, J. E. (1997). Opening the closet door: Exposing elder abuse. *Voice: The Journal of the Battered Women's Movement, 1*, 6-7.

Osmundson, L. A. (1997). Watching our words. *Voice: The Journal of the Battered Women's Movement, 1*, 10.

Pillemer, K. (1985). *Physical abuse of the elderly.* Unpublished doctoral dissertation, Brandeis University, Boston.

Pillemer, K., & Finkelhor, D. (1988). The prevalence of elder abuse: A random sample survey. *The Gerontologist, 28*(1), 51-57.

Reinharz, S. (1986). Friends or foes: Gerontological and feminist theory. *Women's Studies International Forum, 9*(5,6), 222-241.

Rosenthal, E. R. (1990). Women and varieties of ageism. In E. R. Rosenthal (Ed.), *Women, aging and ageism* (pp. 1-6). Binghamton, NY: Harrington Park Press.

Rothenberg, P. (1989). The hand that pushes the rock. *The Women's Review of Books, 5*, 18-19.

Schechter, S. (1987). *Guidelines for mental health workers*. Denver, CO: National Coalition Against Domestic Violence.

Seaver, C. (1996). Muted lives: Older battered women. *Journal of Elder Abuse & Neglect, 8*(2), 3-21.

Sontag, S. (1975). The double standard of aging. In *No longer young: The older woman in America* (pp. 31-39). Ann Arbor, MI: Institute of Gerontology.

Stark, E., Flitcraft, A., Zuckerman, D., Grey, A., Robison, J., & Frazier, W. (1981). *Wife abuse in the medical setting: An introduction for health personnel*. (Domestic Violence Monograph Series. No. 7). Rockville, MD: National Clearinghouse on Domestic Violence.

Straus, M. A., Gelles, R. J., & Steinmetz, S. K. (1980). *Behind closed doors: Violence in the American family*. NY: Anchor/Doubleday.

Suitor, J. J., Pillemer, K., & Straus, M. (1990). The National Family Violence Surveys. In M. Straus and R. Gelles (Eds.), *Physical violence in American families* (pp. 305-317). New Brunswick, NJ: Transaction.

Tatara, T. (1993). Understanding the nature and scope of domestic elder abuse with the use of state aggregate data: Summaries of the key findings of a national survey of state APS and aging services. *Journal of Elder Abuse & Neglect, 5*(4), 35-57.

Thompson, L. (1988). Feminist resources for applied family studies. *Family Relations, 37*, 99-104.

Vinton, L. (1991). Abused older women: Battered women or abused elders? *Journal of Women & Aging, 3*(3), 5-19.

Vinton, L. (1992). Battered women's shelters and older women: The Florida experience. *Journal of Family Violence, 7*(1), 63-72.

Vinton, L. (1998). A nationwide survey of domestic violence shelter programming for older women. *Violence Against Women, 4*(5), 559-571.

Vinton, L., Altholz, J. A., & Lobell, T. (1997). A five year follow up study of domestic violence programming for battered older women. *Journal of Women & Aging, 9*(1/2), 3-15.

Yllö, K. (1997). Theories and methodology: Investigating the problem of family violence. In O. W. Barnett, C. L. Miller-Perrin, & R. D. Perrin, *Family violence across the lifespan: An introduction*. Thousand Oaks, CA: Sage.

Working with Terminally Ill Older Women: Can a Feminist Perspective Add New Insight and Direction?

N. Jane McCandless, PhD
Francis P. Conner, ACSW

SUMMARY. While sexism and ageism in the health care system have been systematically documented, nowhere is the treatment of aging women more androcentric than in the care for the terminally ill. In fact, a terminally ill older woman is too often disadvantaged by a health care system which excludes her from decision-making and renders her powerless. In response, we propose a feminist approach to health care for terminally ill older women and argue that it is this approach which will not only put knowledge and power into the hands of women, but will change the fundamental ways in which women approach death. *[Article copies available for a fee from The Haworth Document Delivery Service: 1-800-342-9678. E-mail address: getinfo@haworthpressinc.com]*

KEYWORDS. Aging, women, aging women, elderly women, older women death, dying, illness, terminal illness feminism, feminist, feminist health care, health care, medical care

Though discriminatory practices in the health care system have been systematically documented, the feminist movement has focused almost exclusively on health issues of importance to younger women and placed little emphasis upon health issues of relevance to older women.

[Haworth co-indexing entry note]: "Working with Terminally Ill Older Women: Can a Feminist Perspective Add New Insight and Direction?" McCandless, N. Jane, and Francis P. Conner. Co-published simultaneously in *Journal of Women & Aging* (The Haworth Press, Inc.) Vol. 11, No. 2/3, 1999, pp. 101-114; and: *Fundamentals of Feminist Gerontology* (ed: J. Dianne Garner) The Haworth Press, Inc., 1999, pp. 101-114. Single or multiple copies of this article are available for a fee from The Haworth Document Delivery Service [1-800-342-9678, 9:00 a.m. - 5:00 p.m. (EST). E-mail address: getinfo@haworthpressinc.com].

While it would seem reasonable that "women, as the majority of consumers and workers, paid and unpaid, should have the major voice in health and medical care," the reality is quite different (Boston Women's Health Book Collective, 1984, p. 556). One of the most disturbing trends in the medical institution is that "practitioners of health care have tended to view women largely in terms of their reproductive organs and capacities" (Sapiro, 1994, p. 150). Furthermore, "women's medical complaints are treated less seriously than men's, and women's symptoms are more often attributed to psychogenic rather than organic causes" (Basow, 1992, p. 201). Other long-standing contentions are that women are systematically excluded from medical research, are too often treated with prescription drugs, and are subjected to unnecessary surgeries. Just as astounding is "the practice of charging women substantially more for individual coverage because of the 'extra costs' incurred by their use of obstetrical care, primary care, and mental health care" (Baylis and Nelson, 1997, p. 1841).

The sexist treatment of women in the health care system is, however, of major concern to all women, especially older women. Since women live longer than men, a pattern of seeking health care continues to increase across the life span as "patterns of illness and disability for women logically follow from their greater longevity" (Logue, 1991, p. 99).

Authors have sometimes noted that being both female and older presents new challenges in one's effort to maintain good health. One of the most consistent arguments is that sexism in the health care system continues across a woman's life span. For example, given the fact that natural life events in the younger years, such as menstruation and childbirth, are medicalized, it is not surprising to find that normal later life events, such as menopause, are also medicalized. Like younger women, older women's complaints of medical problems are not taken as seriously or treated as aggressively as those of men. Older women are also more likely to be treated with the overprescribing of drugs, almost two and one-half times as often as older men, and are often subjected to unnecessary surgeries. We must also continue to consider the financial burdens of health care, which affect women at all ages, but older women even more severely. As stated by Belgrave (1993, p. 195) "elderly women are more likely than either younger women or aged men to be poor, and, because of their poverty, likely to be in worse health than others."

Still, little attention has been given to issues surrounding a terminal illness later in life, and thus terminally ill older women have been too often excluded from these discussions. Perhaps part of the explanation for the exclusion of discussions on terminal illness among older women lies in our reluctance to deal with issues surrounding death. No doubt, we live in a death denying society. In fact, it has been said that in the nineteenth century "sex" was the taboo and "death" was openly talked about. In the present, the reverse is true. Though there has been a nation-wide growth in death education courses, at both the high school and college levels, since the publication of Kubler-Ross' *On Death and Dying* in 1961, it can still be safely stated that ours is a death-denying society (Wass, Berardo, Neimeyer, 1988, p. 397-399). Perhaps, too, part of the explanation lies in ageism. Ageist attitudes, while not always overt, can blind an author or researcher to the point that the issue of age is only an afterthought, thrown into the discussion as an appendix. Just as women have been excluded from medical research, issues of concern to aging women are just now rising to the level of recognition.

We cannot continue to ignore the plight of the terminally ill older woman. As stated by Logue (1991, p. 97) "advances in medical technology can now delay the moment of death for almost everyone, making the timing and circumstances of death more a matter of deliberate decision than ever before in human history." Issues surrounding terminal illness, including one's right to refuse life-sustaining treatment and one's right to die are at the forefront of social concerns. We have already pointed to the fact that women continue to outlive men, and are more likely to confront a multiple of chronic illnesses, diseases, and disabilities due to their longevity. Thus, "death control issues (are) particularly salient for women" (Logue, 1991, p. 99).

Unfortunately, terminally ill older women find themselves in a health care system that limits their access to information and their ability to make their own choices. Too often terminally ill older women must attempt to deal with their illness in a system where "the medical division of labor is dictated by men and the key functions of diagnosis, prescription and treatment are controlled by men" (Levitt, 1997, p. 395). In response, "there is an emerging call for a feminist approach to health promotion for aging women, an approach which would address the current gender, class, race, and age biases in health promotion practice, research, and policy" (Ward-Griffin and Ploeg, 1997, p. 280).

As we begin to consider whether a feminist perspective can offer new ways of responding to older women who are terminally ill, we must determine just what feminist health care might entail.

> It is far easier to summarize the feminist critique of current medical practice than to define and clearly delineate feminist health care goals and principles . . . Whilst all feminists agree that current health care services for women are unsatisfactory, different groups of feminists hold alternate views of the basic causes of women's negative health care experiences and consequently put forth somewhat different solutions to this problem. (Foster, 1989, p. 340)

While it may be difficult to suggest a definitive set of feminist health care goals and practices, authors have noted general goals and strategies. Lips (1993, p. 248) suggests that a feminist approach to health care "is one that puts as much knowledge and power as possible in the hands of the patient, rather than treating the patient as a passive responder to physician recommendations." Renzetti and Curran (1995, p. 457), using the works of Withorn (1985) and Ruzek (1987), suggest that a feminist health care movement includes the principles of self-help, education, alternative services, and political practice. Peggy Foster (1989, p. 340-341) concentrated on the goals and strategies of a feminist approach to health care from a reformist/ liberal and socialist feminist perspective, and underlined the key principles of: (a) sharing knowledge to allow the patient more control; (b) an environment which is open, egalitarian, and democratic; (c) an approach that is holistic; (d) an interaction between patient and physician which is guided by empathy; and (e) care which is accessible to all women.

We suggest that there are indeed a few very broad principles within the feminist approach to health care. Included among these principles are (a) education, (b) empowerment, (c) egalitarian and supportive environments, and (d) inclusion and accessibility for all women. By educating terminally ill older women we create a knowledge base from which they can operate. By introducing the concept of empowerment we allow terminally ill older women to meet their own needs in light of their personal circumstances. When we recognize the fundamental power relationships and the barriers which affect women's choices, we ultimately begin to eradicate those conditions which impede choice. That is, a feminist framework is one alternative which can successfully identify concerns of women, implement strategies for resolution, and create for women a sense of empowerment.

EDUCATION

One criticism of the traditional health care system is its general disregard for the dissemination of information regarding health issues which are of concern to women. "Only in recent years has there even been formal endorsement of health promotion and disease prevention efforts for older women by medical and public health officials" (Sharpe, 1995, p. 16). Yet education and access to information is an essential component for changing the ways in which terminally ill older women experience health care. Without education or information, women are denied a fundamental resource when faced with making choices. What then can be said about the necessary information for older women who are terminally ill?

With the advent of improved diagnostic and life-prolonging technology, the physician no longer controls all the information about the patient's illness, treatment, and prognosis. For each patient, the amount of information required to make an accurate diagnosis, prescribe appropriate treatment, and predict outcomes is nearly impossible to assimilate. Yet, one of the choices medical personnel must make when a patient has a terminal diagnosis is whether or not to tell the truth about the illness. Physicians often fail terminally ill women by not providing full and accurate information about the condition in terms that can be understood, or worse, by deciding that the information will not be shared at all (Schneidman, 1973).

Physicians also make educated guesses as to how well a terminally ill older woman will deal with her illness. Physicians sometimes overestimate the ability of male patients, and underestimate the ability of female patients, to tolerate pain. This, in turn, may mean that female patients are more likely to get strong doses of painkiller early in the disease process, on the assumption that women do not tolerate pain as well as men. Other times physicians attribute psychogenic causes to a woman's pain during her illness or associate chronic symptoms with the belief that aging and disease are synonymous. Because women's symptoms are often attributed to psychogenic causes, psychotropic drugs, such as sedatives and tranquilizers, are often overprescribed. This is particularly dangerous, as physicians are not always aware, and thus women cannot be warned, of the potential risks and negative side effects of prescription drugs. Most recently the diet drugs Redux and Pondimim, also known as Fen-phen, were "recalled at the request of the U.S. Food and Drug Administration following reports of heart valve abnormalities in 32 percent of users. . . . The recall, which turned what had been a trickle of litigation into a flood, could lead to one of the biggest mass tort battles ever" (Hansen, 1998, p. 24).

It is vitally important that the terminally ill older woman have clear and complete information, which includes, first and foremost, her diagnosis and prognosis. Granted this may be a challenge for physicians as women have historically been excluded from medical research. As stated by Berney (1990, p. 24-26) "large studies of women are uncommon. Researchers often deliberately exclude women, and even female animals, from their studies." We might further add that the health problems of special concern to women have received much less research attention. Nonetheless, if the terminally ill older woman does not have clear and complete information then all decisions she makes are flawed from the start. While it is conceivable that a physician will be reluctant to tell a woman how long she has to live, not telling the patient that her illness is terminal, however well-intentioned, has the effect of disempowering her.

The first step towards education then requires detailed information about the normal and natural progression of the disease, both with treatment, and without treatment. "Health professionals need to have a clear understanding that the client is, in fact, the elderly person (and) to communicate clearly and directly with that individual is the appropriate ethical action" (Bata and Power, 1995, p. 150). Educating a terminally ill older woman also requires thorough explanation and information on such issues as the right to refuse life prolonging treatment, living wills, durable powers of attorney, and Hospice.

The right to refuse life sustaining treatment is now legally entrenched in our society and the law requires that health care providers inform patients of their right to refuse treatment (Logue, 1991). Living wills are documents allowing the person to refuse life-prolonging treatment or extraordinary measures to keep one alive. The durable power of attorney for medical purposes allows the patient to choose someone to act for her if and when she is unable to act for herself. The person with the power of attorney, acting in accordance with the patient's wishes, can decide whether or not extraordinary measures, including life support, will be used to prolong her dying. Hospice is an alternative to physician-hospital controlled dying. In a study by Rinaldi and Kearl (1989), about one-third of the respondents said the Hospice movement was a reaction by women health care workers to the male-dominated medical establishment (Kearl, 1989).

While Hospices are not committed to the principles of feminism, Hospices do offer a positive option for terminally ill older women. Ideally, Hospice staff operate in an open awareness context, and encourage patients to exercise their own choices and be responsible for their own death. Hospice care is intended to be holistic, emphasizing physical comfort and pain control, but also offering emotional and spiritual support and counseling. Interestingly enough, Hospice care is provided regardless of an individual's ability to pay and therefore is accessible to poor women as well as others.

EMPOWERMENT

Empowerment refers to the ability to meet our needs, solve our problems, and organize the resources necessary to take control of our lives. So, how do we begin to empower terminally ill older women?

We have already discussed the importance of education. Knowledge is a prerequisite to empowerment. But empowerment is also dependent upon choice. Just as knowledge about birth control and reproductive rights extends into our choice of giving birth, by the same token, knowledge about death and dying extends into our choice of how to die.

Unfortunately, formal agents within the health care system more often honor the choices of men than those of women, even when such choices have the effect of shortening their lives. Miles and August (1990) examined gender patterns in "right to die" cases. From a sample of persons who became dependent upon life support, but did not have advanced directives, the authors found four gender differences in the appellate courts when attempting to "construct the patient's own preference for medical care from the memories and insights of family and friends" (p. 86).

The first difference is the courts' view that a man's opinions are rational and a woman's remarks are unreflective, emotional, or immature. Second, women's moral agency in relation to medical decisions is often not recognized. Third, courts apply evidentiary standards differently to evidence about men's and women's preferences. Fourth, life-support dependent men are seen as subjected to medical assault; women are seen as vulnerable to medical neglect. (Miles and August, 1990, p. 87)

Even in cases when women left advanced directives, "a higher burden of proof was placed on bearers of the woman's directive than on the man's family" (Miles and August, 1990, p. 91).

A feminist perspective can emphasize the issue of choice in the realm of terminal illness as it has in the realm of reproductive rights. Such an approach can also help others understand that choices must be offered to women without assuming that their choices are irrational and illogical, or dependent upon a family consensus. Implicit in the issue of choice is being treated as a rational adult who has the ability and the right to make her own choices. It follows, then, that terminally ill women should be allowed and encouraged to make their own choices which meet their self-defined needs and problems. Terminally ill older women also need logistical support–the means to carry out their choices. If, for example, a terminally ill older woman is physically unable to act on her choices, then others must do so for her; to not do so is to take away her choice. The right to die is of little use if the patient is not able to carry out her choice.

EGALITARIAN AND SUPPORTIVE ENVIRONMENT

As stated by Anderson (1996, p. 698), an important theme within the literature is that "empowerment is an outcome of changes in fundamental structures and relations of power, rather than through individual actions alone." Thus, attention must be given to the environment in which health care is to be delivered.

We live in a society where sexist and ageist stereotypes prevail and are deeply entrenched within our social institutions. From the moment of birth we are socialized to engage in gender appropriate behaviors and expected to adopt gender appropriate attitudes. The end result is that males and females are clearly differentiated, as males are assigned instrumental roles and women are assigned expressive roles. By a very young age we learn that males are those who are intellectually, behaviorally, and emotionally suited for the status of physician, while females are better suited for the status of nurse. It is during the same socialization process that the stereotypes which negatively impact the elderly are also being transmitted. Interestingly, the stereotypes about the elderly are similar in content to those about women. Young is opposite of old; youth is more highly valued than age; and it is youth who most appropriately should maintain control in our society. Thus as males are competent, independent, and leaderlike, so too are the young. And as women are dependent, emotional, and incompetent, so too are the elderly.

As a result of this socialization process, the physician-patient relationship in the health care environment is not commonly egalitarian. "Feminist critiques of the interaction between male physicians and female patients describe it as a paternalistic encounter that incorporates both benevolence and social control" (Sharpe, 1995, p. 10). Even more disturbing is when the patient-physician interaction includes family members, a common scenario "involves health professionals and family members in a third-person discussion of the older woman in her presence" (Sharpe, 1995, p. 13). As Bata and Power (1995, p. 149) stated "to most elderly persons and their families, a health provider is a formidable person."

It is not surprising to find that physicians are often sexist when it comes to prescribing procedures which can prolong life. "Despite the facts that diseases of the heart are the leading cause of death for both genders and that women have been found to have higher mortality rates than men 48 months after myocardial infarction (MI), women are less likely than men to be referred for cardiac catheterization and coronary bypass surgery" (Belgrave, 1993, p. 183). On the other hand, physicians sometimes expect women to accept aggressive treatment and so prescribe intrusive and unnecessary procedures, even when the prognosis is grave. This, of course, is not a new trend. Hysterectomies remain the second most frequently performed major surgical procedure in this country, and "every year deprives hundreds of thousands of women of normal sexual responses" (Schumacher, 1990, p. 49). Yet, only 10.5 percent of all hysterectomies performed in the U.S. between 1970 and 1984 were necessary and medically indicated (Schumacher, 1990, p. 54). The interesting twist is, if the aggressive treatment fails to reverse the disease, terminally ill women are often viewed by their physicians as failures of the medical treatment, a process commonly referred to as "blaming the victim."

This being so, medical staff tend to see some patients as "good," and some patients as "bad," depending primarily on how they respond to a physician's efforts to control their illness. "Good" patients are those who follow instructions, those who do not ask too many questions, and those who allow others to make choices for them. The "good" patient adopts the "closed awareness" context of the medical staff and her frightened family (Glaser and Strauss, 1965). "Bad" patients do not accept the doctor's advice without question and prefer to control their own treatment. A "bad" patient exercises choice and adopts the "open awareness" context, talking about her illness as well as the fact that she is dying (Glaser and Strauss, 1965).

If health care providers are to afford older women the opportunity to exercise choice, an egalitarian setting is an essential element. First and foremost, health care providers must examine their own sexist and ageist attitudes and behaviors. Health care providers must recognize their socialization process and come to understand how stereotypes negatively impact the lives of older women and limit their choices. It would, of course, be optimal if such recognition were to occur early in a health care provider's formal education, yet even in medical schools scant attention is paid to death education, which would seem a logical area of study. We recognize that sexist stereotypes are a powerful tradition and there is currently resistance to change, even "backlash" as noted by Faludi (1991). We also recognize the lack of incentive and encouragement to change. Nonetheless, for any health care provider to suggest that she or he is utilizing a feminist approach, the environment must be freed of overgeneralizations towards elderly women.

It is just as important that the environment is emotionally supportive. However, terminally ill older women find themselves in a health care system wherein "the specialization and fragmentation of the health care system does not well-equip or reward professionals for effectively managing older patients, whose health problems are complex, chronic, and tightly interwoven with psychosocial problems and needs" (Sharpe, 1995, p. 12).

Hospitals are organized for managing patients and for curing illnesses, not for palliative care. Physicians, nurses, and hospital staff in general are not trained or inclined to offer the resources needed for emotional support, which is in and of itself, not a problem. What medical personnel often do, however, is make it difficult for others to offer such support. Listening to the terminally ill woman, helping her express her feelings, taking notice of her pain, and acknowledging her grief are all imperative. Even if a terminally ill older woman can choose to die, the more important question for her may be "Can I be assured that someone will stay with me while I am dying?", or "Will I be comforted?"

INCLUSION AND ACCESS FOR ALL WOMEN

Most recently Anderson (1996, p. 699) explored "the contradictions in the discourse on empowerment . . . and drew attention to those for whom the notion of empowerment should be neutral, yet who are least likely to enter into, and benefit from the current discourse." Anderson explored what empowerment might mean for women who had immigrated to Canada, and focused upon the structural inequalities which prevented many of these women from gaining control over their own illnesses. While Anderson "speaks to the practical and pragmatic issues that are part of these women's everyday reality and that shape their experiences as patients" (1996, p. 700), we too must consider the women in our lives who would be easy to exclude, even from a feminist health care perspective.

For decades women have been subjected to both pay discrimination and job segregation, resulting in fewer dollars and fewer resources, such as long term health care benefits. Elderly women are particularly disadvantaged as a lifetime pattern of lower earnings, career disruptions due to caretaking responsibilities, and fewer investments, result in fewer resources during the later years of life and makes the management of a terminal illness more difficult. Elderly black women are among the most severely disadvantaged as the interaction of sex, age, and race further limit earnings and occupational pursuits. In light of the feminization of poverty in this country, it is not surprising to find that far too many elderly women do not have the financial resources to pay for medical services. Medicare's exclusion of chronic care services is another reason medical needs of many elderly women are not met.

Women have also been subjected to educational discrimination. Many older women today, noted as women of the Depression era, were maturing during a time when economic and political events required them to care for family and country. Even for women who obtained formal education, the prevailing philosophy was not far removed from the belief that education was most appropriately a male pursuit.

We also have an ever expanding diversity in our aging population which brings to light issues of cultural differences and language barriers. There are considerable cultural differences in what symptoms are defined as deserving of treatment, whether or not one should seek help outside of the family, and how illness and death is experienced (Johnson, 1995). Yet, "service delivery systems, particularly ones targeted for the elderly, are often not culturally informed or sensitive" (Johnson, 1995, p. 177) nor "accessible in the patient's language" (Anderson, 1996, p. 701).

We must also recognize that service providers for the aged in organizations such as nursing home, hospitals, and senior citizen centers make the assumption that their clients are heterosexual and may be blind to the significant relationships that form the families of lesbians and gay men (Fullmer,1995, p. 103-104). By making such an assumption lesbian women are immediately disadvantaged. When one operates from a heterosexist position, one cannot be sensitive to the life circumstances of lesbian women or the content of their relationships.

Each of these issues impact a woman's experience in the health care setting and, if not taken into consideration, will limit her choices and prevent her from controlling her terminal illness. For poor women, women who have not acquired higher levels of education, ethnic women, and lesbian women, a feminist approach to health care will be meaningless if their life circumstances are not understood.

Nonetheless, introducing feminist principles into the health care of terminally ill older women is not without its problems. A perspective which challenges long held beliefs and well-established patterns of tradition requires investments of time and effort. Advocating for change in the ways we respond to terminally ill older women, and planning and implementing new strategies will not materialize without resistance and antagonism from some. Even for those who embrace such an approach there are economic concerns. Once women of all social classes become the focus of care, and the quality of care takes precedence over the quantity, revenue of health care providers can be threatened.

Indeed, a feminist approach to working with terminally ill older women presents challenges, and at present lies outside of the majority interest. But feminists are committed "to develop the conditions that will enable us to control our own political, social, economic, and personal identities" (Ruth, 1998, p. 6). This commitment, we argue, must continue until the moment of death. "For the terminally ill, who may have only a few years, months, or days to live, living fully until death is important, whatever the time span" (Barrow, 1992, p. 306).

REFERENCES

Anderson, J. (1996). Empowering patients: issues and strategies. *Social Science Medicine, 43,* 697-705.

Barrow, G. (1992). *Aging, the individual, and society.* MN: West Publishing.

Basow, S. (1992). *Gender: Stereotypes and Roles.* CA: Brooks/Cole.

Bata, E. and Power, P. (1995) Facilitating health care decisions within aging families. Pgs. 143-157, in G. Smith, S. Tobin, E. Robertson-Tchabo, and P. Power (Eds.) *Strengthening Aging Families.* CA: Sage.

Baylis, F. and Nelson, H. (1997). Access to Health Care for Women. *The New England Journal of Medicine, 336,* 1841.

Belgrave, L. (1993). Discrimination Against Older Women in Health Care. *Journal of Women & Aging, 5,* 181-99.

Berney, B. (1990). In Research, Women Don't Matter." *Progressive, 54,* 24-27.

Boston Women's Health Book Collective. (1984). *The New Our Bodies, Ourselves.* NY: Simon & Schuster.

Faludi, S. (1991). *Backlash: the undeclared war against american women.* NY: Doubleday.

Foster, P. 1989. Improving the doctor/patient relationship: a feminist perspective. *Journal of Social Policy, 18,* 337-361.

Fullmer, E. (1995). Challenging biases against families of older gays and lesbians. Pgs. 99-119, in G. Smith, S. Tobin, E. Robertson-Tchabo, and P. Power (Eds.) *Strengthening Aging Families.* CA: Sage.

Glaser, B and Strauss, A. (1965). *Awareness of Dying.* IL: Aldine.

Hansen, M. (1998). Fen-phenomenal tort battle brewing. *ABA Journal, 84,* 24.

Johnson, T. (1995). Utilizing culture in work with aging families. Pgs. 175-201, in G. Smith, S. Tobin, E. Robertson-Tchabo, and P. Power (Eds.) *Strengthening Aging Families.* CA: Sage.

Kearl, M. (1989). *Endings: A Sociology of Death and Dying.* NY: Oxford.

Levitt, J. (1997). Men and women as providers of health care. *Social Science and Medicine, 11,* 395-398.

Lips, H. (1993). *Sex and Gender: An Introduction.* CA: Mayfield.

Logue, B. (1991). Taking charge: death control as an emergent women's issue. *Women and Health, 17,* 97-121.

Miles, S. and August, A. (1990) Courts, gender and "the right to die." *Law, Medicine, and Health, 18,* 85-95.

Renzetti, C. and Curran, D. (1995). *Women, Men, and Society.* MA: Allyn and Bacon.

Ruth, S. (1998). *Issues in Feminism.* CA: Mayfield.

Sapiro, V. (1994). *Women in American Society.* CA: Mayfield.

Schneidman, E. (1973). *The Deaths of Man.* NY: Quadrangle.

Schumacher, D. (1990). Hidden death: the sexual effects of hysterectomy. Pgs. 49-67, in E. Rosenthal (Ed.) *Women, Aging, and Ageism.* NY: Harrington Park Press.

Sharpe, P. (1995). Older women and health services: moving from ageism toward empowerment. *Women and Health, 22,* 9-23.

Ward-Griffin, C. and Ploeg, J. (1997). A feminist approach to health promotion for older women. *Canadian Journal on Aging, 16,* 279-296.

Wass, H., Berardo, F. and Neimeyer, R. (1988). Dying: integrating the facts. Pgs. 395-405, in H. Wass, F. Berardo, and R. Neimeyer (Eds.) *Dying: Facing the Facts.* WA: Hemisphere.

Older Women of Color:
A Feminist Exploration of the Intersections
of Personal, Familial and Community Life

Kate Conway-Turner, PhD

SUMMARY. This paper examines the lives of older U.S. women of color who represent racial and ethnic heritages that have a history of unequal access to sources of economic and political power in this country. These women exemplify women with vastly different cultural traditions, but are similar in that they face discrimination as women of color. The combined impact of age, gender, and racial and ethnic background is neglected within our discussions of older women. This paper contributes to our understanding of older women of color by examining the personal, familial, and community aspects of the lives of older women of color. This exploration challenges feminist gerontologists to bring the discussion of this intersection to the center as we explore and seek to comprehend the reality of older women's lives. This scrutiny creates a space for the discussion of both the threats faced by women of color in their unique juncture as old, female, and of color as well as an illumination of the strengths manifested by these women. Further the need to embrace a feminist gerontological framework when practitioners work with these populations is addressed. *[Article copies available for a fee from The Haworth Document Delivery Service: 1-800-342-9678. E-mail address: getinfo@haworthpressinc.com]*

KEYWORDS. Older women of color, feminist gerontology, health concerns, mental health, marital ties, family ties, care giving, community, diversity, culture, adaptive behavior

[Haworth co-indexing entry note]: "Older Women of Color: A Feminist Exploration of the Intersections of Personal, Familial and Community Life." Conway-Turner, Kate. Co-published simultaneously in *Journal of Women & Aging* (The Haworth Press, Inc.) Vol. 11, No. 2/3, 1999, pp. 115-130; and: *Fundamentals of Feminist Gerontology* (ed: J. Dianne Garner) The Haworth Press, Inc., 1999, pp. 115-130. Single or multiple copies of this article are available for a fee from The Haworth Document Delivery Service [1-800-342-9678, 9:00 a.m. - 5:00 p.m. (EST). E-mail address: getinfo@haworthpressinc.com].

What is sometimes considered obvious to some is never entertained as a possibility to others. The relationship of race, gender, and aging on the lives of women is such an issue. For some it goes without question that the critical exploration of the intersection of these constructs is crucial in understanding the lives of women as they move through the lifespan. For others, people of color, women, and the aged are neglected in discussions that paint reality's picture. This historical and continued neglect fosters misconceptions about older women. Stereotypic notions around this juncture are reinforced and supported by long standing biases and discrimination toward people of color (Taylor, 1998), women (Coyle, 1997), and the elderly (Binstock and George, 1990; Conway-Turner, 1995; Padgett, 1995; Padmore, 1997). MacDonald (1989) argues that even women studies scholars neglect older women and particularly older women of color. The investigation of older women of color should be central to a feminist gerontology. The feminist movement and the millions of worldwide voices that have and continue to fight for the analysis and examination of the impact of race, class and gender must be challenged to include issues of old age within this inquiry. Although issues of age and gender (Troll, 1995) and race, class, and gender (Anderson, 1997) are not uncommon, a full discussion of older women within their racial, ethnic, and economic context is rare.

In this discussion older women of color are the focus of a feminist gerontological discussion of the reality of women in this juncture. In this article, women of color is used not solely as a racial descriptor, but as a designation of women who represent racial and ethnic heritages that are generally non-European and who have had a history of unequal access to sources of economic and political power in this country. Many women of color represent the crossing of traditions and heritages, but nevertheless they self designate themselves as belonging to a group typically described as a minority or ethnic group within the United States. These diverse women have received far less systematic study than white males and females and they are subject to even more sweeping generalizations. The cruel manifestations of racism have a long documented history; however, sexism and ageism have more recently come under scrutiny. As longevity has increased and women continue to live longer than men (creating greater numbers of elderly women) and the wisdom that elders possess based on years of experience has been either underestimated or become outdated in fast moving technological fields, sexism and ageism have further sharpened. Thus the combination of "isms" has created a critical intersection that can not be ignored by a feminist gerontology. Here old women of color find themselves in sometimes fulfilling and other times precarious, life threatening or challenging situations.

This paper will explore the ways that the personal, familial, and community aspects of older women of color's lives impact their perceived experience. Specifically I will address both the strength and vulnerability of the location of being old, female and of color within the United States and the importance of this in a feminist understanding of older women. Further I will discuss the importance of this information for practitioners working with older women of color. This paper can not fully explore all experiences of older women of color, but will highlight some of the experiences of African American, Hispanic origin, Asian American and Native American older women.

Let's begin by discussing some general characteristics that shape the reality of women's lives. Similar to white older women, the number of women of color has continued to grow. According to the U.S. Census (Hobbs, 1996) older women are the majority of the aged, and women continue to disproportionately out-live men such that 4/5 of all centenarians are women. The oldest old are a small but rapidly growing segment of the populations of older women of color. The rates of young old (those 65 to 74 years) and those within the old-old (85 and older) have more than doubled. In 1990 African American elders make up 8.0% of the aged and Hispanic origin elders make up 3.7% of those over 65 years of age. However, population projections indicate that both groups will increase with African Americans reaching 8.6% and Hispanic origins elders 7.3% of all aged by the year 2010. The obvious greater projected growth of Hispanic populations are apparent in this figure. It is further projected that in 2030, Hispanic elders will be the largest group of elders of color representing 10.3% of all elders, with African American representing 9.7%. Women will continue to represent the majority of this growth in numbers and will represent a growing need to address the needs of these elder women of color. To understand the reality of the lives of the growing number of older women of color and to provide a understanding within a feminist gerontological framework, let's examine the personal, familial, and community aspects of their lives.

PERSONAL CONSIDERATIONS

Self perceptions of women of color are influenced by many factors and situations that construct the lives of these women. Women find themselves located within the reality of their personality characteristics, their cultural background, and their place within families and society. Marital status is a factor that is often related to a number of situations. Frequently marital status structures much of the experience within older years. Along with a marital tie comes the potential for interpersonal closeness, emotional gratification, an additional source of support during times of stress and upset, increased financial security, and socially sanctioned sexual fulfillment (Chappell and Badger, 1989; Coombs, 1991; Conway-Turner, 1992).

The incidence of divorce, marital disruptions, and longer life expectancy makes marriage, although seen as optimal for many women, unlikely for most. According to the U.S. Census (1993) only 26.4% of African American women over 65 are presently married and 37.1% of Hispanic older women are married. A significant number of older African American women and Hispanic origin women are widowed. Fifty-five percent for African American women and 44.1% Hispanic origin women are widowed. In comparison to older men of color, older women of color are only half as likely to be presently married. The personal lives of these women are shaped by a perspective of widowhood that ties them within a network of both a marital and a birth family.

In the same way that marriage remains an important institution in the lives of women of color (Engram and Lockery, 1993), widowhood creates a personal loss from the role of a marriage partner with the accompanied psycho-social and physical realities of this loss. Even in marriages that are recognized as less than ideal, this loss has major consequences in the remaining partner. The shift from a central role as wife to that of a widow requires, for many, a reordering of priorities, a change in how to utilize the time within a day (many widows have spend years constructing their days around the needs of an ailing husband), decreased financial resources and the acquisition of a new widowed role within the family. Each is influenced by the cultural expectations and background of the older woman. Some widowed women find new adventures to augment their personal lives as widowed women, while other move to participate within family networks or friend community networks more fully.

Personal health is often a central issue of discussion among elders. The self perception of health at times differs from what can be documented by health professions. Edmonds (1990) suggests that it is extremely important to recognize that difference between actual and perceived health. The health of Asian older women varies by cultural group, however, many women across cultures report levels of illness that do not map onto what can be diagnosed. There are consequences to both underestimating the level of illness, as well as inflating disease symptoms. An underestimation can delay needed medical intervention and exacerbate disease, while those who inflate may be met with skepticism when a real medical emergency arises.

In many cases women of color are faced with high levels of malady. High levels of diabetes are seen within Chinese, Filipino, Japanese and Korean older women living within the U.S. (Yee, 1997) as well as among older African American women (Ralston, 1997). Increasing rates of hypertension are noted within many Asian older women and African Africans (Coyle, 1997). The leading causes of death in women from 44 to 85 years of age are similar, however the rates increase dramatically as women age during this period, and women of color are disproportionally affected by many diseases. Heart disease and cancer represent the two greatest contributors to mortality in women of these ages, and in both cases Black women are disproportionally affected (Wykle and Kaskel, 1991; Anderson, 1988). Black women have a higher mortality rate from breast, cervical, and uterine cancer and many women of color face greater difficulty in accessing adequate diagnostic or interventive care. The rate of cervical cancer screening is particularly low among Mexican American older women (Suarez, 1994). In fact, Spanish speaking older women often report not recognizing the meaning of a Pap smear. Mammogram screening is also extremely low among Mexican American elderly (Markides and Black, 1996). Issues of higher levels of morbidity create stresses on individual women both physically as they manage these illnesses, as well as a social impact on daily living.

Presenting at times as physical health concerns, older women sometimes face mental health problems. The most common mental health concern of elders is depression (Turnbull and Mui, 1995). Elders at times mask their depressive symptoms with somatic complaints (Hall 1985; Turnbull and Mui, 1995). This tendency to mask depression can complicate the diagnostic process and lengthen the time required to make diagnostic decisions. Further complicating the mental health status of women of color is the tendency to not report important symptoms. In many cases women see symptoms that could indicate depression as "just" signs of aging. In this manner, sleeping difficulties, fatigue, being unsteady on their feet or even feeling nervous is dismissed as "just" getting old (Brody and Kleban, 1981). Even in situations when women do not dismiss symptoms physicians may. Low socio-economic status is a risk factor for depression and women of color are disproportionately poor. In all of these ways, mental health in general and depression in particular is often complicated to recognize by both individual women and the physicians they utilize. When a mental health problem is perceived, people of color are less likely to seek or utilize mental health services (Kuo, 1984; Steffens, 1997). The legacy of racial discrimination within formal services, language and cultural barriers, and the stigma associated with mental illness contribute to underutilization.

Feminist gerontologists acknowledge that personal considerations have broad impact on the lives of women of color. These considerations affect not only the individual lives of women and the adjustments they make, but also the families they are a part of and the communities where they reside and contribute.

FAMILIAL CONSIDERATIONS

Although most older women of color are not presently married, the majority do not live alone. Among the non-institutionalized population, 37% of African American older women, 35% of Native American older women, 16% of Asian American older women and 27% of Hispanic origin older women report living alone (U.S. Census, 1994). The majority of women of color find themselves living with spouses, children, other relatives, and friends as they move throughout the older years. This is centered on a number of cultural traditions that place family as a significant organizing structure within the lives of many women of color.

The role of the family in the lives of African Americans is well documented (Billingsley, 1968; Stack, 1974; McAdoo, 1997; Taylor, 1988, 1998). The older African American woman finds herself with a broad kin network; when optimally functioning, this network meets the needs of its members across the life course. Exchanges between the generations are quite common such that older women not only receive from younger generations, but participate in providing needed support, services and information to younger generations (Billingsley, 1968; Taylor, 1988; Dilworth-Anderson, 1992). The strong ties between grandmothers and grandchildren are well documented and illustrate how older women can provide enormously to the development of youth (Kivett, 1993: Dilworth-Anderson, 1992).

Native American women are an extremely diverse group; however, John, Blanchard and Hennessy (1997) argue that five central roles exist for older Native women within the family. These roles represent a connection between the elder Native American woman and her family. As a grandmother, elder women hold a central role within the family. Here they provide tangible support to the younger generations and seek to foster the well-being of the youth. Children are significantly connected to their grandmother and often live with them. The educator and wisdom keeper grandmother is closely related to the general grandmother role. In this role, as observed within many racial and ethnic groups, grandmothers pass on central traditions and information to youth. The older woman as leader is yet another central role. In this situation the older woman leads both within and outside the family in ways that acknowledge her importance to both the family and the broader community. Many authors have noted the role of the older woman as artist (Trimble, 1993; Woodhead, 1994). The medium differs for these women, but through an expressive materials these women bring honor to themselves, their families and their communities. Finally the role of dependent elder is seen for woman who are frail and functionally are dependent upon the family to provide for their needs. These five potential roles are at times overlapping, but indicate the centrality of the older Native women in the lives of her family.

Older women of Hispanic origin have also been documented as embracing the family as a central focus (Sanchez-Ayendez, 1986; Facio, 1996). Familism is often discussed as an undergirding philosophy within Chicana families. Facio (1997) argues that although older Chicana women are a strong force within the family and provide both a central role as grandmother and cultural teacher, that they continue to be influenced by the strong patriarchy within the family. Regardless of the strength of the male hierarchy within the family, Chicana older women continue to be a real focus for the extended family, maintain significant care giving roles for the youth, and participate in a shared system of support networks that cross generations. Hispanic elders are more likely to live within multi-generational family systems than all other groups of older women (Cubillos and Prieto, 1987).

The experience of many women of color centers them within a network of children and adults who, by blood line, marriage, or mutual consent, convey a clear and consistent sense of family. However, such reciprocal and desired family ties do not come without a price. Many older women find themselves caring for both the old-old and the young. These multiple levels of care giving responsibilities, even within the context of deep family ties, can be stressful (Cox and Monk, 1996; Burton, 1996). Increasing demands for women of color to care for grandchildren for short and long periods (Strom et al., 1996) goes beyond the support of a nurturing grandparent. These women and families often find themselves parenting, schooling, disciplining and providing for grandchildren throughout their childhood years. The intense care given to grandchildren, in addition to the role of care giver to older relatives, sick family members and friends, and frail spouses creates a cross generational demand that draws upon the deep connection older women of color have with their families. A feminist perspective recognizes that family dynamics for women of color include both a central location as an older woman and a strong role as contributor and care giver within their family systems.

COMMUNITY CONSIDERATIONS

The contribution within the world of paid employment shapes a significant level of community involvement for older women of color. Although women of color are reflected throughout the earned income categories, they disproportionately find themselves within the lower ranks across the life course.

The income of older women of color is related to the overall social economic history of less resources and lifetime wages compared to older men of color, white women, and white men (Hobbs, 1996). African American women have always participated at greater rates within the labor force when compared to white women, although the margin narrows in the 1990s. This tendency of greater participation in full-time employment is consistent across all ages of mature women (women over fifty years). Women, regardless of race or ethnic origin, have increased their labor force participation since 1950. In 1950 34.9% of African American women between 55 and 59 years were in the labor force and in 1990 56.3% of African American women in the same age group were in the labor force. For women 65-69 years of age, 16.4% of African American women were working in 1950 and 18.2% were in 1990.

The earliest census data available for Hispanic origin older women was 1970, but even comparing those figures, we see the same trend for Hispanic older women. In 1970, among women 55-59 years of age 34.7% were in the labor force and by 1990 48.2% reported working full-time. And for women 65-69, 11.2% were in the labor force in 1950 and 15.1% reported full-time employment in 1990. The differences seen here between these women illustrate the diversity in the lived experience of women of color. For African American women the necessity of working has typically outweighed a broader cultural desire to have women remain at home exclusively, apparently a clearer message within the Hispanic origin family. The unemployment rate and the underemployment of men of color frequently takes the choice to work away and makes work a necessity for many Black women and other women of color (Jones, 1995).

Older women of color, although contributing in significant numbers within the labor force have consistently been disadvantaged in garnering resources across the life span. For families of color combined family household and individual income continue to lag behind white combined household and individual income. In 1992, 66.2% of all married African American households (over 65 years) saw an income of $24,999 or less. In fact, data from the U.S. Census (Hobbs, 1996), notes that greater than a third of this 66.2% had household incomes of under $10,000. Comparing the individual incomes of all persons over 65 years, women of color fair the worst. African American women's median income is $4,860, Native American women's median income is $5,100, Asian and Pacific Islander women's income is $5,000 and women of Hispanic origin garner a median income of $4,632. These median incomes are lower than comparable men of color, white women and far behind the income median of $14,760 for white older men (U.S. Census, 1990). The number of women living in poverty increases with each decade of life. This lack of income is most serious for women who are without a spouse to contribute to the household income and thus must manage with fewer financial resources.

However, the transition from full-time work to a retirement occurs, although necessity postpones this transition for many people of color (Silverman, Skirboll and Payne, 1996). Investigations that focus on the retirement patterns of women of color are rare; however, Richardson and Kilty (1996) studies older professional African Americans. They report similar attitudes concerning work and retirement among both men and women. Research indicates that African Americans report a desire to remain working well within the elder years and after retirement they express a desire to return to work (Silverman, Skirboll and Payne, 1996); this seems regardless of the income level. Work is for many women of color not only a source of income, but also a locus for self worth and production and a significant connection to the broader community. Although women of color find themselves disadvantaged frequently within the socio-economic environment they often assume roles within their work that compensate for these economic limitations (Ralston, 1997). Becoming the informal "organizer" at work, taking on greater responsibilities, and acting as a "trainer" to new employees are all ways to gain a sense of worth and peer acknowledgment used by older women. Unfortunately, these extra duties are generally go without monetary reward, although they are of immense benefit to the employer. So both a financial incentive and a need to participate seems to characterize some continuation within the community of work.

Within the community sphere, religious and spiritual behavior often balances the lives of women of color. Across the country, women of color inhabit the pews of churches, mosques and synagogues as well as participating within spiritual endeavors outside of formalized institutions. Many churches find older women sustain the church as a viable organization within the community. Older African American women are documented to play central roles within their churches tying family and community together in an effort to support spirituality as a foundation for the family (Hine, 1993; Conway, 1980). Chicana women report the importance of the church, particularly the Catholic church, within their lives (Facio, 1997). Religiosity has been found to be protective within older populations and in fact religious orientation and involvement is inversely related to depressive symptoms (Turnbull and Mui, 1995). The community involvement of women of color varies across economic status, geographic location, and ethnic lines, but it remains a source of significance for many women.

CONCLUSIONS

Diversity characterizes these women. Inter-group diversity is a repeated theme within all groups and it is difficult to summarize the experiences that captures the lives of such varied groups of women. Within Asian older women, the census data represents large sweeps of women who have extremely different backgrounds. The U.S. Census combines women who are Chinese, East Indian, Filipino, Indochinese, Japanese, Korean and the many Pacific Islanders into one group. These women represent widely different cultures and traditions that inform their experience as older women of color. Similar diversity exist within all the groups discussed here. This cultural and historical diversity is only exasperated by the geographic, education and social economic differences that are seen within these groupings. While I have attempted to summarize the central features of the lives of these women, it is with a constant acknowledgment of the diversity within each example discussed. A feminist gerontological perspective recognizes the distinct cultural differences among these older women, but clearly see significant similarities in their historical and present position within the United States.

The distinctions between the personal, the familial, and the community realm have been provided to structure an understanding of the many systems that influence and are influenced by these women's encounters. The personal realms includes the issues of self, self definition, and perception. Older women of color self define themselves in ways that acknowledge, in varied degrees, their ethnic and racial heritage, their gender and the implications of gender with their lives, and their age as older women. The intersections of these images varies both within and between groups of women of color. It is impossible to create one map to understand the personal representation for all older women of color. Issues of cultural heritage, educational background, economic status, geographic location, immigration status, physical and mental health are but some of the factors that mix to create a personal definition of women of color. As complex as girls are in their youth, age brings with it the many experiences that further distinguish each person as a unique representation of their intersections.

Within the realm of family considerations, women of color are documented to be both central and significant within the lives of their families. Women's roles as kin-keepers and orchestrators of the lives of family are important. Marital status, number of children, family size, proximity of family, and family expectations are all factors that influence the family life of these women. What is particularly apparent is the role of family as both a sense of strength and the family as a source of stress for these women. This is especially prevalent in the care giver role, a role that is common for older women of color. This balance between these two aspects of family is central in understanding the reality of these women's lives. Women with greater resources (education, financial resources, extended family) are often able to more easily maintain the balance between the responsibilities and rewards of family life. However, stress is associated with the reality of the balance. Achieving culturally appropriate ways to handle this stress is of significant importance.

The realm of community life includes many diverse sectors depending on the lives of the women. For many, the world of work connects them to varied levels of involvement outside the immediate personal and family spheres. A feminist gerontological perspective notes that many women find it not a choice but a necessity to be involved in work outside the home as an older woman, due to high levels of underemployment among men of color, low income standing, and needs to assist family members financially. These issues are not issued related solely to the lives of younger women, but follow the women throughout their lifespan. Regardless of the many ways that women of color give to their community, they are disproportionally poor and are economically more vulnerable within the older years. Along with the job related sector of community lives, these women have other aspects that have been reported to provide fulfillment for older women of color. Two examples are the church as a life force in the lives of many and the informal (non-paid) work that advances the community. In both, albeit differently, women of color are able to find a sense of connection to the community environment that allows for a contribution and a connection that has served to enrich their lives.

For those who work to serve the needs of older women of color, it is essential to be aware of the balance within the lives of these women. Using a feminist lens to recognize both the strengths of the location of being old, female and of color and the vulnerabilities provide a more complete understanding of these women. Although, women of color are faced with serious hardships that can jeopardize their quality of life, they also have sources of strength. It is these sources that allow them to face the threatening aspect of the intersection of race, gender, and age. The personal, family, and community concerns that women of color face are at times both serious and threatening. A recognition of these concerns and the impact of being old, female, and of color as contributors to the reality of this situation is central to a feminist gerontological perspective. Multiple tiers of discrimination can exacerbate existing issues. However, these women hold unique cultural strengths, adaptive behaviors, and ties within their families and communities that can be of assistance in times of stress. The challenge is to acknowledge both the strengths and vulnerabilities of vastly different older women as their needs are being met. Drawing upon cultural strengths, practitioners can tap into the natural systems of women of color and both provide and assist women in ways that feel familiar, that are consistent with the cultures of women of color, and that demonstrate an understanding of the distinct cultural fabric held by each individual woman. It is important for feminist gerontologists to not marginalize older women of color, but to bring them to the center of our discussions of older women. By focusing on the realities of these complex and diverse women we can recognize the similarities between women of color, as well as acknowledging the historical and cultural differences that also shape their lives.

REFERENCES

Andersen, M. (1997). Thinking about Women: Sociological Perspectives on Sex and Gender. Boston: Allyn and Bacon.

Anderson, M. (1988). Aging and Hypertension among Blacks: A Multidimensional Perspective. In: J. Jackson. *The Black American Elderly: Research on Physical and Psychological Health*. New York, NY: Springer Publications.

Billingsley, A. (1968). *Black Families in White America*. Englewood Cliffs, NJ: Prentice Hall.

Brody, E. and Kleban M. (1981). Physical and Mental Symptoms of Older People: Who Do They Tell? *Journal of American Geriatric Society*. 29, pg. 442-49.

Burton, L. (1996). The timing of childbearing, family structure, and the responsibilities of aging Black women. In Hetherington, E. And Blechman, E. *Stress, Coping, and Resiliency in Children and Families*. Mahmah, NJ: Lawrence Erlbaum Associates. pg. 155-172.

Chappell, N. and Badger M. (1989). Social Isolation and Well-Being. *The Journal of Gerontology*, 44(5), pp. S169-S176.

Coombs, R. (1991). Marital Status and Personal Well-Being: A Literature Review. *Family Relations.* 40, pg. 97-102.

Conway, K. (1980). The Position and Role of Black and White Aged in Rural Churches. *The Journal of Minority Aging.* 5 (March), pg. 242-248.

Conway-Turner, K. (1992) Sex, Intimacy and Self Esteem in African American Older Women. *Journal of Women & Aging.* 4(1), pg. 91-104.

Conway-Turner, K. (1995). Inclusion of Black Studies in Gerontology Courses: Uncovering and Transcending Stereotypes. *Journal of Black Studies.* 25(5), pg. 577-588.

Cox, C. and Monk, A. (1996). Strain among Care givers: Comparing the Experiences of African American and Hispanic Care givers of Alzheimer's Relatives. *International Journal of Aging and Human Development.* 43(2), pg. 93-105.

Coyle, J. (1997). *Handbook on Women & Aging.* Westport, CT: Greenwood Press.

Cubillos, H. and Prieto, M. (1987). *The Hispanic Elderly: A Demographic Profile.* La Raza, Washington: National Council of La Raza, Washington.

Dilworth, P. (1992). Extended Kin Networks in Black Families. *Generations*, 16(3), pg. 29-32.

Edmonds, M. (1990). The health of black aged female. In Z. Harel, E. McKinney and M. Williams (Eds). *Black Aged Understanding Diversity and Service Needs.* Newbury Park, CA: Sage.

Engram, E. And Lockery, S. Intimate Partnerships, In J. Jackson, L. Chatters and R. Taylor (EDS). *Aging in Black American.* Newbury Park, CA: Sage.

Facio, E. (1996). *Understanding Older Chicanas: Sociological and Policy Perspectives.* Thousand Oaks, CA: Sage.

Facio, E. (1997). Chicanas and Aging: Toward Definitions of Womanhood. In Jean Coyle's (Ed). *Handbook on Women and Aging.* Westport, Connecticut: Greenwood Press, pg. 335-350.

Hall, W. (1982). Correlates of depression in the elderly: Sex differences and similarities. *Journal of Clinical Psychology.* 38, pg. 253-257.

Hine, D. (1993). *Black Women in America: An Historical encyclopedia.* Brooklyn, NY: Carlson.

Kivett, V. (1993). Racial Comparisons of the Grandmother Role: Implications for strengthening the family support system of older black women. *Family Relations*, 42, pg. 165-172.

John, R., Blanchard, P. and Hennessy, C. (1997). Hidden Lives: Aging and Contemporary American Indian Women. In Jean Coyles (Ed). *Handbook of Women and Aging.* Westport, Connecticut: Greenwood Press. pg. 291-316.

Jones, J. (1995). *Labor of Love, Labor of Sorrow: Black Women, Work, and the Family From Slavery to the Present.* New York: Vintage.

Kuo, W. (1984). The prevalence of depression among Asian Americans. *Journal of Nervous and Mental Disease*, 172, pg. 449-457.

Markides, K. and Black, S. (1996). Aging and Health Behaviors in Mexican Americans. *Family Community Health*, 19(2), pg. 11-18.

McAdoo, H. (1997). *Black Families.* Thousand Oaks, CA: Sage.

MacDonald, B. (1989). Outside the Sisterhood: Ageism in Women's Studies. *Women's Studies Quarterly.* 17(1-2), pg. 6-11.

Padgett, D. (1995). *Handbook on Ethnicity, Aging and Mental Health.* Westport, CT: Greenwood Press.

Padmore, E. (1997). Sexism and Ageism. In Jean Coyles, *Handbook on Women and Aging.* Westport, CT: Greenwood Press.

Ralston, P. (1997). Midlife and Older Black Women. In Jean Coyles, *Handbook on Women and Aging.* Westport, CT: Greenwood Press.

Richardson, V. and Kilty, K. (1992). Retirement intentions among black professionals: Implications for Practice with Older Black Adults. *The Gerontologist.* 32, pg. 7-16.

Sanchez-Ayendez, M. (1986). Puerto Rican Elderly Women: Shared meanings and informal support networks. In J. Cole (Ed). *All American Women: Lines that Divide, Ties that Bind.* NY: Free Press. pg. 172-186.

Silverman, M., Skirboll, E., Payne. J. (1996). An Examination of Women's Retirement: African American Women. *Journal of Cross Cultural Gerontology.* 11(4), pg. 319-334.

Stack, C. (1974). *All Our Kin: Strategies for Survival in the Black Community.* New York, NY: Harper Row.

Steffens, D. Artigues, D. Ornstein, K., and Rama Krishnan, K. (1997). A Review of Racial Differences in Geriatric Depression: Implications for Care and Clinical Research. *Journal of National Medical Association.* 89(11), pg. 731-736.

Strom, R., Strom, S., Collingsworth, P., and Strom P. (1996). Black Grandparents Curriculum Development. *International Journal of Aging and Human Development.* 43(2), pg. 119-134.

Suarez, L. (1994). Pap Smear and Mammogram Screening in Mexican American Women: The Effects of Acculturation. *American Journal of Public Health.* 84, pg. 742-746.

Taylor, R. (1988). Aging and supportive relationships among black Americans. In J. Jackson (Ed). *The Black American Elderly: Research on Physical and psychological Health.* NY: Springer.

Taylor, R. (1998). *Minority Families in the United States: A Multi-cultural Perspective.* Upper Saddle River, NJ: Prentice Hall.

Trimble, S. (1993). *The People: Indians of the American Southwest.* Santa Fe: SAR Press.

Turnbull, J. And Mui, A. (1995). Mental Health Status and Needs of Black and White Elderly: Differences in Depression. In D. Padgett (Ed). *Handbook on Ethnicity, Aging and Mental Health.* Westport, CT: Greenwood Press.

Turner, B. and Troll, L. (1994). *Women Growing Older: Psychological Perspectives.* Thousand Oaks, CA: Sage Publications.

U.S. Bureau of Census (1993). Marital Status and Living Arrangement. March 1993. *Current Populations Reports,* P20-478, Table 1. Washington D.C: US Government Printing Office.

U.S. Bureau of Census (1994). Marital Status and Living Arrangement. *Current Population Reports,* P20-479, Table 7, Washington, D.C.: US Government Printing Office.

Waxman, H. and Carner, E. (1984). Underutilization of Mental Health professionals by community elderly. *Gerontologist.* 24, pg. 24-40.

Woodhead, H. (1994). *The American Indians: Cycle of Life*, Alexandria, VA: Time Life Books.

Yee, D. (1997). Issues and Trends Affecting Asian Americans, Women and Aging. In Jean Coyle's (Ed). *Handbook on Women and Aging.* Westport, CT: Greenwood Press.

Negating Identity:
A Feminist Analysis
of the Social Invisibility
# of Older Lesbians

Elise M. Fullmer, PhD
Dena Shenk, PhD
Lynette J. Eastland, PhD

SUMMARY. Older lesbians are invisible both within and outside of the lesbian community. Using a postmodern and lesbian feminist approach, in this article we identify a paradox in our society which defines lesbians in terms of their sexuality while older women are generally viewed as asexual. We suggest that this paradox contributes to the invisibility of older lesbians. Our focus is on the interactive nature of the relationship between personal and public constructions of lesbianism in the lives of older women. Finally, we discuss the potential impact of invisibility on self-identity, and using a feminist gerontological framework suggest implications for the empowerment of older lesbians. *[Article copies available for a fee from The Haworth Document Delivery Service: 1-800-342-9678. E-mail address: getinfo@haworthpressinc.com]*

KEYWORDS. Lesbian, aging, social construction, feminism

Consider the experience of seeing three old women together at a grocery store. Most people will probably make a number of conscious and unconscious assumptions about these people like, "grandmother," "non-sexual," "widowed," and "heterosexual." What as-

---

[Haworth co-indexing entry note]: "Negating Identity: A Feminist Analysis of the Social Invisibility of Older Lesbians." Fullmer, Elise M., Dena Shenk, and Lynette J. Eastland. Co-published simultaneously in *Journal of Women & Aging* (The Haworth Press, Inc.) Vol. 11, No. 2/3, 1999, pp. 131-148; and: *Fundamentals of Feminist Gerontology* (ed: J. Dianne Garner) The Haworth Press, Inc., 1999, pp. 131-148. Single or multiple copies of this article are available for a fee from The Haworth Document Delivery Service [1-800-342-9678, 9:00 a.m. - 5:00 p.m. (EST). E-mail address: getinfo@haworthpressinc.com].

131

pects of their identity might be negated by these assumptions? Feminist theories are uniquely suited to exploration of this question, because central to current feminist thought is the assertion that by uncovering fallacies in our essentialist understandings of people's lives, we can reclaim marginalized or repressed knowledge particularly as this knowledge relates to the experiences of disenfranchised groups (Van Den Bergh, 1995). Through this process a more holistic and inclusive understanding of people can be developed; we can identify socially constructed meanings that serve to oppress particular peoples; and can encourage dialogue that empowers rather than disenpowers marginalized groups.

This task becomes more speculative, however, when the people in question are beyond public consciousness and the primary avenue for understanding them is a collage of assumptions pieced together indirectly and even, perhaps, unconsciously. As the previous example suggests, older lesbians represent such a group. They are absent from public consciousness, and with few exceptions (Adelman, 1987; Cooper, 1988; Kehoe, 1989; Macdonald, B. & Rich, C., 1983; Martin, D. & Lyon, P., 1970; Poor, 1982), absent from scholarly dialogue as well. Feminist dialogue on older lesbians is even more limited (Cooper, 1988; Macdonald, B & Rich,1983). Within the lesbian community itself, older lesbians, to a large degree, are out of sight and out of mind (Cooper, 1988; Shenk & Fullmer, 1996). As expanded on below, our purpose here is to examine structures in our society that contribute to the invisibility of older lesbians and suggest avenues for social change.

In the last several years it has become common to see articles in the popular media about lesbians and, concurrently, lesbians are increasingly becoming the subject of public dialogue. Openly lesbian figures like Ellen Degeneres, k. d. lang and others have addressed their sexual orientation in ways that have touched public consciousness. Lesbians, at least youthful lesbians, are being acknowledged (albeit, this notice is not necessarily positive) as a class of people in American society. There is an intrinsic assumption, however, among many Americans that sexuality is the dominant and most essential aspect of lesbianism (Wolf, 1980), and like all stereotypes, this formula reduces beliefs about lesbian culture to a simplistic level. As we listen to the public discourse about these celebrities, it is not about who they are as people or their way of life, but with whom they sleep.

An issue important to feminist gerontology is the fact that the media, as a major expression of and stimulus of culture, has typically not focused on women who show signs of aging. Whether heterosexual or homosexual, gray hair and lined faces have been perceived as aesthetically displeasing, particularly for women, and so older women have been of secondary interest and until recently, unworthy of attention at all. Since popular stereotypes suggest that older women are not sexual and women's value is based largely on their sexual appeal, older women have been given little public attention. It is no surprise, therefore, that as the media focuses on lesbianism they also focus on those women who are young and seen as sexual beings. In this article we use postmodern and lesbian feminist perspectives to discuss the relationship between women's sexuality, aging, and lesbians. Our purpose is to discuss the social constructs that contribute to the invisibility of older lesbians. We examine the social understandings available to older lesbians for making sense of and defining themselves within the context of postmodern conceptions of identity. It is our contention that a combination of prevailing social constructs of sexuality, lesbianism, gender and age serve to make older lesbians invisible both within and outside of the lesbian community. We further contend that the lives of lesbians in general, and younger lesbians in particular, are considered salient only in so far as they reflect male interests and concerns. Sexuality, including women's sexuality, is perceived as a masculine domain and is a place where older women presumably play little or no role. To address these issues, we begin with a discussion of the construction of identity and a consideration of public media portrayals of lesbians. This will be followed by a discussion of the social construction of the invisibility of older lesbians through public and private consciousness of lesbian identity. We discuss the invisibility of older lesbians even within the lesbian community. Finally, we discuss the implications of invisibility to older lesbians and consider the need for a (re)consideration of the definitions and meanings of sexuality for older lesbians.

POSTMODERN CONSTRUCTIONS
OF IDENTITY AND NEGATING THE OLDER LESBIAN

An assumption of this paper is that who we are and how we construct ourselves takes place within a cultural/historical context.

Identities, social constructionists claim, are formed through social processes and "maintained, modified, or even reshaped by social relations" (Berger and Luckman, 1967, p. 173). Gergen (1991) talks about identity *production*. He claims we are entering a new era of self-conception: "We bid adieu to the modernist concept of the concrete self and move into the postmodern reconstruction of self as relationship" (p. 145). As a relational concept, self is embedded in relations of power and our conceptions of self are to some degree determined by the choices, both our own and others, and by the array of potential selves that populate our social world.

Closely related to this idea is the assumption that the primary medium within which identities are created and have their currency is textual. In other words, "persons are largely ascribed their identities according to the manner of their embedding within a discourse–in their own or in the discourse of others" (Shotter & Gergen, 1989, p. ix). Cultural texts, then, furnish the resources for the formation of selves. They "lay out an array of enabling potentials, while simultaneously establishing a set of constraining boundaries beyond which selves cannot be easily made" (Shotter & Gergen, 1989, p. ix).

The issue of lesbian identity has been the subject of an ongoing discussion since the 1970s. Radical lesbian feminist, Jill Johnston, a central figure in the early women's movement observed, "Identity is what you can say you are according to what they say you can be" (Johnston, 1973). Identities are not "the freely created products of introspection, or the unproblematic reflections of the private sanctum of the inner self, but are conceived within certain ideological frameworks" (Kitzinger, 1989, p. 82). We "make" ourselves according to the scripts provided us by society. Identities, as such, are inherently cultural and political.

In fact, issues of identity are at the core of the current cultural war involving the rights of homosexual persons. Eastland (1996a) discusses the Oregon Citizen's Alliance campaign as an effort to "redefine" and ultimately "conceptually liquidate" homosexuals in terms of discourse around their identity. A major contention of the campaign is that homosexuality is a behavior as opposed to an identity. Visibility is also a vital aspect of the issues involved in this cultural debate.

Within the discourse of North American culture, one of the most important aspects of lesbian identity is the sexual behavior of such women, which is regarded as abnormal or, within the context of the male gaze, regarded as titillating. That lesbianism (as well as homo-sexuality) is a *behavior* as opposed to an *identity* is clearly a primary argument of the numerous conservative anti-homosexual political campaigns currently raging in this culture (Eastland, 1996b). On the other hand, lesbian identity involves more than a sexual behavior and an argument can be made that there is something uniquely different in the worldview of women whose primary sexual and/or affectional relations are with other women (Kitzinger, 1989; Shenk & Fullmer, 1996; Wolf, 1980).

THE CREATION OF PUBLIC
AND PRIVATE CONSCIOUSNESS OF OLDER LESBIANS

Factors that influence public perceptions and internal self-construc-tions of aging and lesbianism are elemental to understanding the issues involved in the social construction of identity for older lesbians. De-fining oneself as a lesbian is a complex process shaped by a combina-tion of factors which include related personal, cultural and historical factors. Central to this process is the eventual conscious acceptance of a lesbian identity as a part of one's self-definition. To say precisely what it means to incorporate lesbianism into one's self-definition or to live as a lesbian, however, is elusive because the term lesbian may have different meanings for different people based on their personal and culturally-based understanding of the concept.

Most studies of older lesbians discuss lesbian identity in terms of the accommodations and adaptations these women make in their day-to-day lives; that is, on social constructions and their impact on the *behavior* of individuals. Few have dealt with the relationship between public definitions and personal constructions of identity, or on the ways in which individuals seek to create understandings of who they are in the world (Shenk and Fullmer 1996). Eastland's (1996a) study is an exception. She discusses personal identity and public constructions within the context of the current cultural war against homosexuals and the impact of aspects of the campaign on the lives of members of the gay community. The framework used considers these public defini-tions in terms of *disempowerment*, and response on the part of individ-uals in terms of *empowerment*. Empowerment as used here involves the ability of an individual (or group) to exercise free will. This ability evolves from the belief and hope that a person has control over the direction of her/his life. As pointed out by Germain and Gitterman (1995), empowerment occurs through "the creation of maximal opportunities for choice, decision making, and action consonant with age, physical and emotional states, capacities, and cultural patterns" (p. 496). Conversely a person or group is disempowered when a combination of internal and external factors serves to limit opportunities for choice, thus limiting their ability to exercise free will.

We believe that there is a strong relationship between the *absence* of public definitions, and personal constructions of identity by many older lesbians. Our contention is that lesbian elders are hindered in relating their life experience to the contemporary definitions of self available in either the broader culture or in the lesbian community and, therefore, sometimes fail to work out a definition of the relational aspect of self. The cultural construction of the concept of lesbianism refers to the development of a definition of lesbianism within the public societal domain, while the personal construction of the concept refers to the development of a definition of lesbianism within the private domain. These constructions are, of course, closely interrelated. At its foundation, cultural constructions of older lesbians cannot be meaningfully separated from issues of gender. The root, after all, of beliefs and misconceptions about homosexuality is in sexism. In an interesting discussion on "tomboys" and "sissies" Russo (1985) points out:

> Weakness in men rather than strength in women has consistently been seen as the connection between sex role behavior and deviant sexuality. And while sissy men have always signaled a rank betrayal of the myth of male superiority, tomboy women have seemed to reinforce that myth and have been indulged in acting it out. In celebrating maleness, the rendering invisible of all else has caused lesbianism to disappear behind a male vision of sex in general. The stigma of tomboy has been less than that of sissy because lesbianism is never allowed to become a threatening reality any more then female sexuality of other kinds.

MULTIPLE HIERARCHICAL IDENTITIES: AGING WOMEN, SEXUALITY AND LESBIANS

Women in this male-dominated society are often defined in terms of their relationships with men, first as daughter, and later as girl-friend or spouse. Heterosexual women have an investment in maintaining relationships with men, because they partially define their own self-identity and are known to others, in terms of these primary relationships with men. Women who do not have primary relationships with men as adults, may have more flexibility in creating their identities, because they cannot use the approach of formulating their self-identity based on men. Older women, on the other hand, are perceived as both asexual and sexually unattractive. This is due to the fact that it is difficult for many younger people to imagine that anyone who is old is still sexually attractive or active. The older woman that most of us know best is our mother who we could never imagine as a sexual being in any case. Although literature has suggested that older women continue to be sexual and have sexual interests, the public perception persists.

The sexuality and multiple identities of older lesbians is basically misunderstood, for a number of reasons. First, older women are perceived as asexual while older lesbians are defined in terms of their "unusual" sexuality. This is a major paradox which is central to our discussion. Women are defined in our society, at least in part, through their sexuality. Older women as a group are viewed as asexual. Since lesbians are defined primarily in terms of their sexuality, older lesbians are primarily defined through their "unusual" (read unacceptable) sexuality. The paradox then, is that older women as a group are viewed as asexual, while older lesbians are defined, when they are at all, in terms of their sexuality. Why is their sexuality so important if they are perceived to be asexual as older women?

Another reason is that many older lesbians have never "come out" publicly, or as we will discuss below, developed a personal sense of their identity as a lesbian. In fact, a secondary definition of lesbian in Webster's dictionary is "secret or hidden." Older lesbians may have come out in late life and they may have children, ex-husbands, and for all intents and purposes be thought of as heterosexual.

Another popular stereotype about lesbians that contributes to their invisibility is that they do not have children and they have never had sexual experiences with men. If we see women only in relational terms, particularly relational terms with men, their involvement with men may be the primary premise upon which we base our assumptions. Many lesbians do have children either from previous marriages or heterosexual relationships, artificial insemination or adoption (Laird,

1995). In one of the first major studies on homosexuality, conducted over two decades ago, (Bell & Weinberg, 1978) about a third of the white lesbians (n = 229) and one-half of the black lesbians (n = 64) had been heterosexually married at least once. When an old women has children or has been heterosexually married does it blur all subsequent developments in her life, and how does it affect her development of a lesbian identity?

LESBIANS IN FILM AND BOOKS

Until quite recently, novels and films that included lesbians existed to satisfy the sexual fantasies of heterosexual men and most often portrayed young lesbians. It was not uncommon to find pulp novels as well as movies that had a lesbian as the main character. While the primary marketing target for these books and film was heterosexual men, lesbians were attracted to these media too. With few publicly open lesbian role models, many lesbians had to rely, at least in part, on the popular media to fill the gap. The themes of books and movies during the time when today's older lesbians were young were fairly standard: lonely young girl meets "young dyke," lonely young girl has sordid relationship with "young dyke," young girl leaves "young dyke" for a man and finds true love.[1]

A particularly popular series of books written by Ann Bannon featured a character named Beebo Brinker. Beebo was described as masculine and attracted to more "feminine" women. The primary focus of these books was her love affairs and sexual relationships with other women. Beebo and her partners were chronologically young and developmentally in the process of exploring their identities as lesbians. As lesbian pulp novels go, the Beebo books were more sensitive to the issues of lesbian women, probably because their author is a lesbian (Russo, 1985). This sensitivity likely accounts for their popularity among lesbian women. At the same time, these novels as a whole are very youth-oriented. That is, older women play little part in the sultry underground world of lesbians. They are non-existent and invisible. When older women do fleetingly appear, it is in terms of the hopelessness of their fate, and additionally, it is usually heterosexual women who are the focus. In one of the few films that does feature a mid-life lesbian, *The Killing of Sister George*, an aging soap opera star (who plays the character in the soap opera "Sister George") is a lesbian. In this movie the main character, who is an alcoholic, is in a relationship with a younger women. When her character, Sister George, is killed in the soap opera (presumably because Sister George is becoming old and useless) the main character in the movie commits suicide. Several conjectures are worthy of note in regard to this movie. First, there is the notion that as women become older they become useless. Second, that lesbians (like aging men) will be in relationships with younger women rather than women of their own age. This is a particularly interesting assumption because the underlying premise is based on commonality between the relationships of men and lesbians. Third, that as one ages, particularly if she is a lesbian, she will ultimately become lonely and desperate. This seems to relate to the assumption that older women are unattractive and asexual and remember that sexuality is seen by the public as core to the definition of a lesbian identity. In many ways this particular film is a metaphor for older lesbian existence in our culture.

DISTINCTIONS BETWEEN THE GAY AND LESBIAN COMMUNITIES AND THE SOCIAL MEANING OF "GAY"

While lesbians are gaining public attention, the distinctions between gay men and lesbians remain unclear. In a male dominated society, women and even lesbians, are always seen as extensions of male interests and male concerns. As a result, there is little overt public recognition of the fact that lesbians and gay men represent two distinct communities. As a society there is more seriousness placed on the sexual deviance of men, specifically the perceived betrayal of masculinity by gay men, than on the "deviance" of gay women. It is intriguing to wonder if a situation comedy exclusively about gay men could gain acceptance on prime time television. Would a situation comedy featuring older gay men be more acceptable because the elderly are viewed as asexual?

For the most part, however, there is little recognition that lesbians exist apart from gay males. Most often when the issue of sexual orientation is publicly addressed it is done so using as a model the stereotypes about gay men. The assumption seems to be that the lesbian and gay communities are essentially the same, and one group's issues are synonymous with the others. Or, as is often the case with women in general, the issues of women are only important so far as they mirror, or compare with, the issues of men.

INVISIBILITY OF OLDER LESBIANS IN LESBIAN CULTURE

Older lesbians who were young adults prior to the women's movement of the 1970s sometimes are unable to relate to current lesbian culture. Even lesbians raised in the 1980s, who now find themselves aging, feel alienated from the youth-oriented lesbian culture. Lesbians are clearly not immune to the influences of a sexist, ageist culture. Cooper (1988, 1997) describes getting older *within* the lesbian community:

> Our community is so ill-prepared for this that old lesbians find themselves disappearing right off the edge of reality. The ageism we encounter teaches us that we are obsolete; that we should not be able to imagine ourselves powerful, either physically or socially. It is a standard default assumption of the lesbian political community that old lesbians are conservative (or at least politically incorrect) and inflexible. Above all else we are expected to be submissive to women younger than ourselves who are the "right" age to exert power within the lesbian world. We are asked to be walking contradictions to the cliches of lesbian identity which all of us are in the process of inventing. Unless old lesbians are remembered as sexual, attractive, useful, integral parts of the woman-loving world, current lesbian identity is a temporary mirage, not a new social statement of female empowerment. (p. 123)

Cooper sees this ageism as destructive to the lesbian community: "I believe that there is an important reservoir of lesbian energy denied by this false consciousness, this 'othering' of the older lesbian" (p. 122). She sees lesbians, like everyone else, as getting older and the ways in which the lesbian community copes, mirror the destructive ways in which the rest of our culture deals with aging. "Our community," she says, "is so ill-prepared for this that old lesbians find themselves disappearing right off the edge of reality (p. 123).

CULTURAL CONSTRUCTION OF LESBIANISM

The cultural construction of lesbianism involves the historical and environmental context within which the meaning of lesbianism is framed in society. For older women in this culture this requires consideration of the understandings of homosexuality prevalent earlier in this century. What it means to be a lesbian has varied over time and across cultures. Faderman (1981) for example, points out that in sixteenth century England, women were not thought to be sexual beings and so were able to express sensuality toward one another without suspicion. In more recent times women have used the term "lesbian" to refer to political solidarity with other women. In the 1970s some feminists declared themselves "political lesbians" in their stance against patriarchy but were not necessarily involved with other women sexually (Adam, 1987). More recently, the cultural war against gay men and lesbians seeks to define homosexuality as exclusively a "behavioral choice" (Eastland, 1996b). This perspective suggests that a woman chooses to "be" a lesbian and could choose not to be one.

Other women, particularly older women who have had to endure prejudice and discrimination against homosexuals in much more hostile times, may have abandoned terms such as lesbian or homosexual altogether in an attempt to dissociate themselves from negative stereotypes and social stigma or because they did not want to be so narrowly defined. Many of these older women carefully hid their relationships with other women and limited their contact with lesbian and gay people (Adelman, 1987; Clunis & Green, 1988). This is not particularly surprising given the cultural context within which they lived. Wolf (1980) remarks about the reality of life for the generations of homosexual women in America who are now older: Most of them experienced oppression, potential arrest and exposure, and an internalized view of lesbianism as a social stain. The only public place to socialize with other lesbians, if one dared risk periodic arrests, was the gay bar, even though bar life was not comfortable for many women (p. 26).

Before the 1970s only larger cities had organizations catering to lesbians and for this reason rural women and women in smaller towns had to develop alternate ways of being in the world that did not necessarily follow patterns of women in larger urban areas. Friendship networks and social ties in rural areas were often made up of close-knit support networks and women may have had to depend on hetero-sexual neighbors for friendship and support. Furthermore, for most women prior to the 1970s there were also few, if any role models available aside from the heterosexual relationships that surrounded them. In rural communities, there is often a strong sense of personal independence within the context of the interdependence between friends and neighbors. There are also guidelines and expectations of close social ties and how they are to be maintained within an environment where everybody knows everyone else. These cultural values and expectations clearly affected the lives of lesbians living within that context.

The following case for example, is taken from a research report on homeless elders. One woman who is now in her seventies spent the majority of her life living with a female partner in a rural area of Utah and explained the circumstances of their life as a couple:

> We met at age 16 in school. Our parents were farmers and we hadn't been exposed to much beyond our hometown. We were instantly attracted to each other and I don't think we spent more than a few days alone from the time we met. When my father died he left me the farm and Mary moved in a few months later. No one ever questioned us about our relationship. I don't think anyone particularly cared as long as we didn't talk about it openly. We didn't even talk about it much to each other. . . . it just was. I had heard some about other women in Los Angeles but I couldn't relate. It was only after Mary died that I got lonely enough to sell the farm and move to Salt Lake. (Fullmer, 1987)

This case illustrates the fact that a personal definition of oneself as a lesbian is based on negotiation of personal feelings and experiences as they developed within the cultural context. Here, the *absence* of cultural understandings of the specifics of their experience has led to the absence of personal and interpersonal constructions.

PERSONAL CONSTRUCTION OF LESBIANISM

While the social definition of lesbianism focuses on sexuality, personal definition as a lesbian is much more broadly structured with the primary emphasis on the relationship, such as family and community, aside from the sexual aspects. There is, of course, great diversity among the lifestyles and experiences of older lesbians.

Family

Kimmel (1992) suggests that there are three most typical family types within which gay men and lesbians grow older. These include (1) long-term committed relationships or "companionships"; (2) social networks of friends, significant others and selected biological family members who provide mutual support of various kinds; and (3) special roles in their family of origin that reflect their unique social position. Patterns in forming intimate relationships also vary, but typically a preference for a long term committed relation with one other person is expressed (see, for example, Bell & Weinberg, 1978; Kehoe, 1989) and long term committed relationships seem to be more common than is typically assumed (Kimmel, 1992). This is not surprising, given that a committed relationship with one other person is the accepted norm in the dominant culture (Fullmer, 1995 p. 101).

Older lesbians who are involved in a long-term committed relationship generally provide each other with a comprehensive, mutual support system and the economic advantages of sharing home and resources (Fullmer, 1995 p. 102). In spite of the broad nature of their interaction and mutual commitment, they may never openly acknowledge the nature of their relationship, or use the word lesbian, gay or homosexual. The cultural construction of lesbianism and the political reality of the world within which they live has constrained their personal construction of the concept of lesbianism.

For older women, adjustments to the transitions and losses that often accompany aging are different within a lesbian relationship, because of the lack of acknowledgment of the existence or the nature of the relationship between the women. If the relationship has never been clearly defined by the participants or by others significant to either partner, others may fail to acknowledge the severity and nature of the loss. The loss of a partner in this instance may also mean the loss of material possessions or financial supports that have previously been considered joint. It might also mean that the partner may seek to hide the grieving process from others to hide the unusual character of the relationship (Fullmer, 1995; Shenk 1998).

Self-Discovery

How people discover themselves as lesbian or bisexual or make the choice to define their same-sex relationships or feelings in other terms must be considered within the context of their environment and the social constructions prevalent in that environment. Literature on the "coming out" or self discovery and disclosure process is quite prevalent (see for example, Bell & Weinberg, 1978; Cass, 1984; Coleman, 1981-1982) but this literature largely aims to develop theories of self-disclosure and self-identification as a developmental and psychological process where the experience of women, men, ethnic minorities, young people and old people are assumed to be similar. The unique concerns of older lesbians are blurred in this literature. A number of questions are particularly relevant to the nature of this process of self-discovery and self definition by older women and they have not been asked in any substantive way. At what point in a person's life course does she begin to explore her sexual orientation? It makes sense that a person who defines herself as lesbian at age 12 will have different experiences than a person who grapples with these issues at age 65. How do cultural differences influence the self defining process? In addition to gender socialization, it is likely that issues such as class, race and even geographic location will be influences in this process. What was/is the social/political climate in which the self-defining process evolves? Again, women living during or self-defining during the first half of this century had a qualitatively different experience than women going through this process in the 1970s or 1990s. What was it like for women coming out in the 1950s during, for example, the McCarthy Era, and for a woman coming out in the 1970s when the women's movement was a central theme in society?

FEMINIST GERONTOLOGICAL APPROACHES TO WORKING WITH OLDER FEMINISTS

Last year the first author came in contact with a seventy year-old woman (for the purposes of this article we will call her Pat) who, as a mutual friend put it, was "re-discovering herself." Pat had opted to spend several days in a car to drive across country because after reading an article written by the first author she wanted to discuss her sexual orientation "face to face." Pat explained that for the ten years before her retirement she had lived with a "roommate" and they had become very close. Eventually, however, her roommate started to identify as "gay" and wanted "more" from the relationship than Pat was prepared to give. For this reason they "separated." According to Pat she had been "very lonely for [her roommate]" ever since. Pat explained that although she had several male friends she had never been "particularly fond of dating men." All of her life, her closest relationships had been with women. Pat asked numerous questions about everything from defining what it means to be a lesbian to strategies for connecting with older lesbians, dating and sexuality. During this period of questioning she made a statement that seemed to sum up many of her concerns about her awakening discovery of herself as an older lesbian: "Now that I am old and dried up what am I to do with all of this? If I just could have figured this out earlier on." Pat seemed to be struggling with understanding her past life in a new context and expressed concern that she was too old to actually "be a lesbian" now.

The central question raised in this paper is the extent to which the identity and well-being of older lesbians may be influenced by competing social constructions of lesbians and elder women. Pat provides one example of how these social constructions might manifest themselves as she begins to explore her identity. To our knowledge this question has not been explicitly addressed in research, and yet it is critical to our understanding of the lives of older lesbians, including older lesbians who discover their sexual orientation later in life. Given the many social stigmas associated with homosexuality, for many women later life identification of a same sex sexual orientation is probably not uncommon (Fullmer, 1998; Fullmer, 1995; Shenk and Fullmer, 1996). As suggested, older lesbians are faced with competing stereotypes encompassing lesbianism, gender, aging and sexuality. A paradox exists in that social constructs of lesbians emphasize sexuality while social constructs of aging women emphasize passivity and loss of sexuality. We suspect that this paradox serves to contribute to the invisibility of older lesbians in both heterosexual and lesbian communities.

The potential negative consequence of invisibility for older lesbians at the macro level is obvious because to be invisible is to be ignored in both policy and practice. Aging service providers often make assumptions about older women that are rooted in heterosexuality. For example, in one senior citizens center where the first author volunteered time, older women had a choice of two primary activities: constructing arts and crafts projects to serve as gifts to children and grandchildren and participating in organized dances for older women and men. Clearly additional avenues need to be available to meet the needs of older lesbians. An equally important issue is the extent to which older women are constrained in their development of their personal identities by these social constructions of lesbianism.

The issues and concerns of feminist gerontology are exacerbated for older lesbians who are both older women and members of the disenfranchised group of lesbians. As we seek social change and enhanced opportunities for older lesbians, the lessons from and approaches of feminist gerontology serve us well. Three key foci are education, empowerment and advocacy.

First, there is an obvious need for education of practitioners about the special issues, needs and life situations of older lesbians. We would suggest, for example, the development of a manual that lays out the current knowledge and includes case studies to sensitive practitioners to their special needs and recommends a range of approaches to reaching out to older lesbians within their service delivery area. Workshops and training modules would also be effective avenues to increased knowledge about the unique situations and needs of older lesbians.

A second emphasis should be on empowerment of older lesbians themselves, as a subgroup of older women with both similar and different concerns. Empowerment of older lesbians should begin with education and the use of groups to provide a venue for exploring shared experiences and concerns, and sharing effective strategies for personal "success." The sharing of life stories among both separate "lesbian-only" and "mixed" groups would be an important part of this process.

Finally, both education and empowerment can be used to prepare for the final goal of advocating for the rights of older lesbians. Through both of these avenues, practitioners and older lesbians themselves, with the support of other older women and younger lesbians, can ready themselves to undertake advocacy efforts on behalf of older lesbians. It is hoped that this article will serve as a starting point for exploring these issues and preparing practitioners to work more effectively with older lesbians.

NOTE

1. For examples of this see *The Fox and Personal Best*, movies produced in the 1970's and 1980's respectively. *The Well of Loneliness* by Radclyffe Hall (written in 1929) is a classic example.

REFERENCES

Adam, B. D. (1987). *The rise of a gay and lesbian movement*. Boston: Twayne.

Adelman, M. (1987). *Long time passing: Lives of older lesbians*. Boston: Alyson.

Bell, A. & Weinberg, M. S. (1978). *Homosexuality*. New York: Simon & Schuster.

Berger, P., & Luckman, T. (1967). *The social construction of reality*. New York: Anchor Press.

Cass, V. (1984). Homosexual identity formation: A theoretical model. *Journal of Homosexuality*, 4, 219-236.

Clunis, D. M. & Green, G. D. (1988), *Lesbian couples*. Seattle: Seal Press.

Coleman, E. (1981-1982). Developmental stages of the coming out process. *Journal of Homosexuality*, 7 (2/3), 31-43.

Cooper, B. (1998). *Over the hill: Reflections on ageism between women*. New York: the Crossing Press.

Cooper, B. (1997). The view from over the hill. In M. Pearsall, *The Other Within Us*. (pp. 121-134). Boulder, CO: Westview Press.

Eastland, L. (1996a). Defending Identity in radical right contexts. In E.B. Ray, *Case Studies in Communication and Disenfranchisement*. (pp. 1-20). Mahwah, New Jersey: Lawrence Erlbaum Associates.

Eastland, L. (1996b). The reconstruction of identity: Strategies of the Oregon Citizen's Alliance. In E.B. Ray, *Communication and Disenfranchisement: Social Health Issues and Implications*. (pp. 59-78). Mahwah, New Jersey: Lawrence Erlbaum Associates.

Faderman, L. (1981). *Surpassing the love of men*. New York: Marrow.

Fullmer, E. M. (1998). Working an extra step: Recovery and aging of an ethnic minority lesbian. In L. J. Eastland, S. Herndon, and J. Barr. *Communication and Recovery: Studies of Twelve-Step Programs*. New Jersey: Hampton Press.

Fullmer, E. M. (1995). Challenging biases against families of older gays and lesbians. In G. C. Smith, S. S. Tobin, E. A. Robertson-Tchabo, & P. W. Power, *Strengthening Aging Families: Diversity in Practice and Policy*. (pp. 99-119). Thousand Oaks, CA: Sage.

Fullmer, E. M. (1987). *Homeless elders: A group in need of services*. Salt Lake City, Utah: Report to Utah Department of Social Services.

Gergen, K. (1991). *The Saturated Self: Dilemmas of Identity in Contemporary Life*. New York: Basic Books.

Germain, C. B. & Gitterman, A. (1995). Ecological perpsective. *Encyclopedia of Social Work*, 19th edition. (pp. 816-824). Washington, D.C.: National Association of Social Workers Press.

Johnston, J. (1973). *Lesbian Nation: The Feminist Solution*. New York: Simon and Schuster.

Kehoe, M. (1989). *Lesbians over sixty speak for themselves*. New York: The Haworth Press, Inc.

Kimmel, D. C. (1992, Summer). The families of older gay men and lesbians. *Generations*, 37-38.

Kitzinger, C. (1989) Liberal humanism as an ideology of social control: The regulation of lesbian identities. In J. Shotter & K. Gergen. *Texts of Identity*. London: Sage Publications.

Laird, J. (1995) Lesbians: Parenting. In R. L Edwards (Ed.), *Encyclopedia of Social Work*. 19th Ed. Vol. 2, Washington, DC: NASW Press.

Macdonald, B & Rich, C. (1983). *Look me in the eye. Old women, aging, and agism*. San Francisco: Spinsters Inc.

Martin, D. & Lyon, P. (1970). The older lesbian. In B. Berzon (Ed.), *Positively gay*. Los Angeles: Media Mix.

Poor, M. (1982). *The older lesbian*. In M. Cruikshank (Ed.), *Lesbian studies*. (pp. 1965-173). Old Westbury, N. Y.: Feminist Press.

Russo, V. (1985). *The celluloid closet: Homosexuality in the movies*. New York: Harper & Row.

Shenk, D. & Fullmer, E. M. (1996). Significant relationships among older women: Cultural and personal constructions of lesbianism. *Journal of Women & Aging*, 8(3/4), 75-89. (Published simultaneously as Significant relationships among older women: Cultural and personal constructions of lesbianism in *Relationships Between Women in Later Life*, (Ed. Karen Roberto), (pp. 75-89). The Haworth Press, Inc. 1996.)

Shenk, D. (1998). *Someone to Lend a Helping Hand: Women Growing Old in Rural America*. Newark, N.J.: Gordon and Breach.

Shotter, J. & Gergen, K. (Eds.). (1989). *Texts of Identity*. London: Sage.

Van Den Bergh, N. (1995). *Feminist Practice in the 21st Century*. Washington, DC, NASW Press.

Wolf, D. G. (1980). *The lesbian community*. Berkeley: University of California Press.

A Feminist Model of Family Care: Practice and Policy Directions

Nancy R. Hooyman, PhD
Judith G. Gonyea, PhD

SUMMARY. Using a feminist perspective, this article examines women's experiences in caring for older family members with chronic illnesses or disabilities. Central to this analysis are the concepts of the social construction of gender-based inequities in caring, the interconnections between generations of women as givers and receivers of care, and variations in family care by gender, race, ethnicity, social class and sexual orientation. The authors critique current practice interventions and policies and purpose models for the elimination of gender-based inequities in caregiving and the provision of caregiver choice and empowerment for women and men, including feminist models of practice with women caregivers and economic and long-term care supports. *[Article copies available for a fee from The Haworth Document Delivery Service: 1-800-342-9678. E-mail address: getinfo@haworthpressinc.com]*

KEYWORDS. Feminism, family caregiving, elder care, community-based care, long-term policy

INTRODUCTION

Concerns about the public costs or burdens of the "graying" U.S. population has heightened attention on the role of families in providing care to dependent older adults. Equally significant is that these

[Haworth co-indexing entry note]: "A Feminist Model of Family Care: Practice and Policy Directions." Hooyman, Nancy R., and Judith G. Gonyea. Co-published simultaneously in *Journal of Women & Aging* (The Haworth Press, Inc.) Vol. 11, No. 2/3, 1999, pp. 149-169; and: *Fundamentals of Feminist Gerontology* (ed: J. Dianne Garner) The Haworth Press, Inc., 1999, pp. 149-169. Single or multiple copies of this article are available for a fee from The Haworth Document Delivery Service [1-800-342-9678, 9:00 a.m. - 5:00 p.m. (EST). E-mail address: getinfo@haworthpressinc.com].

discussions are occurring in a broader social and political climate that emphasizes "personal responsibility" or "self-reliance." During the past decade, we have witnessed the decentralization and devolution of the federal government's role in caring for vulnerable members of society and a shrinking of the public "safety net." Smeeding (1998, p. 24), for example, notes that increasingly the "locus of responsibility for costs, above and beyond those which the federal government decides it can afford, will be shifted to other parties: lower levels of government (states and localities) in the case of AFDC and Medicaid, and thence to individuals and their families (Medicare, AFDC, and Medicaid)." Yet, hidden in most of these discussions by the very use of the word "family" is the fact that women disproportionately bear the negative repercussions of this shift in America's social contract to an ethos of self-reliance since caregiving remains predominantly women's work. Although families provide 70 to 80 percent of the in-home care to older people with chronic illness, it is clearly women–mothers, daughters, daughters-in-laws, wives, and granddaughters–who provide the majority of this support (National Alliance for Caregiving and AARP, 1997).

The care of older adults with chronic illness is a central feminist issue not only because this work remains largely the unpaid and unsupported care of women, but also because the recipients of this care are overwhelmingly female, especially the very-old. In fact, as a woman ages, the likelihood that she will receive assistance from a female relative increases dramatically. Although we typically turn first to our spouse in times of need, many of the women among the ranks of the oldest-old have simply outlived their husbands. Approximately 64 percent of women age 75 and older are widowed, and 52 percent live alone. Accordingly, it is more common to find adult daughters caring for aging mothers than for aging fathers. In fact, the crucial role of gender in the hierarchy of obligation to older family members is reflected in the fact that after spouses and daughters, it is daughters-in-law and not sons, and sisters versus brothers, who are likely to provide the care (Dailey, 1998; Ingersoll-Dayton, Starrels, and Dowler, 1996; Qureshi and Walker, 1989). This pattern reflects the societal expectation and ideology that caring is a natural female characteristic (Dailey, 1998; Hooyman and Gonyea, 1995).

This paper begins by defining a feminist perspective on family care of older adults and then examines how changing demographic, social and economic conditions are impacting women's caregiving experiences. Using a feminist framework, we offer a number of practice and policy change strategies to eliminate gender-based inequities in caregiving and to provide caregiver choice and empowerment for both women and men, thereby moving toward a goal gender justice. Throughout this chapter, caregiving work is defined as custodial or maintenance help or services, rendered for the well being of individuals who cannot perform such activities themselves (Waerness, 1985). Yet caregiving work is more than meeting physical needs; the very use of the word "care" implies intimacy and connection. In examining the caregiving phenomenon, a useful distinction is between *caring for* and *caring about*; caring about implies affection and perhaps a sense of psychological responsibility, whereas caring for encompasses both the performance or supervision of concrete tasks and a sense of psychological responsibility. The integration of caring about with caring for, between love and labor, often intensifies the stress experienced by family caregivers, particularly by women (Hooyman and Gonyea, 1995; Dalley, 1988; Lewis and Meredith, 1988).

WHY A FEMINIST PERSPECTIVE?

A feminist approach to family care recognizes that women have historically been oppressed within the home and the labor market. This devaluation is reflected both in the invisibility and lack of compensation for their work at home and women's low wages in the marketplace (Marshall, 1996; Davis, 1994). Women are expected to be the primary caregivers and relatively little notice has been paid to the psychological and financial effects on women's lives. Typically, social policies and practice interventions have defined the problems faced by women as personal or private concerns. Little attention has been directed toward understanding how existing structural arrangements create women's dependency and limit their choices in old age. In contrast, a feminist analysis challenges the status quo and stresses the absolute necessity of changes in social institutions, attitudes, and values to improve women's lives. Accordingly, feminists do not define demographic and social changes, such as the growth in the percent of the older population or the large-scale entry of women in the paid labor market, as "problems." Instead, a feminist model is oriented toward fundamental systemic changes that accord greater societal recognition to the work of caring and assure flexibility and choice for both those who require care and those who provide it (Calasanti and Hendricks, 1993; Abel, 1991). These changes include a stronger public and governmental presence than currently exists to assure a comprehensive range of social, economic, health care and workplace services and supports for caregivers.

Central to our feminist analysis is the concept of gender and how it creates socially constructed structural, relational, and symbolic differentiation between men and women, including the amount and type of assistance given and the differential consequences of such gender-based responsibilities. Thus, a feminist approach seeks to make visible and validate the importance of women's daily experiences as caregivers. It argues for major changes in the way that society defines, distributes and rewards work. Ultimately, feminism is concerned with changing men and women's roles to ensure that both have choices in how they balance caregiving and employment. Economic and social strategies are needed to integrate women into the public sphere (i.e., to move women into the labor force at wages comparable to their male counterparts) and to extend the imperative of caring to men as well as to women (i.e., to increase the number of men who are primary caregivers).

A feminist perspective also recognizes the connectedness in women's lives as carers across the life course and of the interaction between the needs of care givers and receivers, both of whom are typically women. The roles of caregiver and receiver must be rebalanced in a manner that recognizes the worth of both. These interconnections are especially salient for feminists who are often caught between the desire to challenge the exploitation of women's unpaid labor as carers with the desire to see that frail elders, many of whom are women, are cared for in nonpaternalistic ways (Dalley, 1988). A life span view is also central because issues affecting younger women as mothers, especially their lower economic status, are played out across their lives in caring for older adults. Feminist strategies build on the interconnections between young and old, recognizing that with increased life expectancy there will be no substantial life stages for average adult women that are free of potential caregiving demands (Hooyman and Gonyea, 1995). A feminist analysis makes explicit how caring for family across the life span has severe negative repercussions for women's health and economic status in old age, when many women lack choice in determining the conditions of their own aging. Gender-based inequities in care responsibilities have limited women's economic independence and personal rights, resulting in their higher rates of poverty across the life span, and especially in old age (Arber and Ginn, 1995; Calassanti and Hendricks, 1993).

A feminist analysis takes account of variations in family caregiving not only by gender but also by race, ethnicity, class, and sexual orientation. By recognizing that not all women have the same experiences, feminism acknowledges how inequities created by social policies affect low-income women of color, for example. The incidence of chronic disease and disability is higher among poor and minority women; they form the largest proportion of older people who need care but are the most likely to lack access to formal services. From a feminist perspective, the reasons for these inequities are structural–the ways in which the devaluation of caregiving work in the home and in the marketplace intersects with racism to exploit women's unpaid caring work (Hooyman and Gonyea, 1995).

WOMEN AS PRIMARY CAREGIVERS OF OLDER ADULTS

The prominence of women in the caregiving role should not obscure the efforts of men who are primary caregivers. Husbands, for example, frequently provide care for wives with disabilities (Bengtson Rosenthal and Burton, 1996). Yet, as noted above, female adult children are more likely than men to provide the time consuming and emotionally demanding personal care. Men generally become involved in personal "hands on" care and instrumental tasks of cooking and cleaning only when no female relative is available. Similarly, sons are less likely than daughters to share their households with a dependent parent.

In understanding the stresses that caregivers experience, it is helpful to distinguish between "objective" and "subjective" burdens (Braithwaite, 1992; Bengtson et al., 1996). Objective burden refers to the actual demands that confront caregivers, such as the symptomatic behaviors of the illness, disruptions in family relationships, income and social life, and problems with service systems. Subjective burden refers to feelings aroused in caregivers as they fulfill their functions, such as worry, sadness, resentment, anger or guilt. This distinction recognizes that burden is a subjective phenomenon; what is difficult for one caregiver may not be difficult for another. Rather, the extent to which caregiving is experienced as stressful or burdensome is mediated by the extent of social support, coping strategies, cultural values, and religious beliefs (Lynch, 1998; Connell and Gibson, 1997; Araada and Knight, 1997; Miller, Campbell, Farron, Kaufman and Davis, 1995). In fact, the emotional burdens of feeling alone, isolated, worrying about the care recipient and without time for oneself appear to be greater than the physical or financial demands of care. These feelings are experienced more frequently by women than men (Cohler, 1997; Miller and Cafasso, 1992; Baines, Evans and Neysmith, 1991; Parks and Pilisuk, 1991).

The importance of social supports in helping individuals cope with the caregiving experience cannot be overstated. Lack of support resources can heighten caregivers' feelings of isolation and, in turn, of stress. In fact, feelings of burden have been found to be related primarily to the availability of external helping resources and social support, not to the severity of the illness (Bass, Noelker and Rechlen, 1996). Yet, often as a result of caregiving responsibilities, relationships with other family members and friends are disrupted. Many caregivers report that no one in their network of family or friends regularly assists them with hands on care; even when they help, the timing and frequency of their well-intended actions may fail to be supportive (Lynch, 1998; Pearlin, Aneshensel, Mullon and Whitlatch, 1996). Men who are caregivers are more likely than women to be part of a larger network of services and to utilize more formal supports. Many women, internalizing the societal message that caregiving is a natural female role, are less likely to seek out formal services (Ingersoll-Dayton, Starrels, and Dowler, 1996; Kramer and Kipnis, 1995; Mui, 1995; Twiggs and Atkin, 1994). Given this sense of responsibility, it is not surprising that women report higher levels of burden than men.

THE SOCIAL CONTEXT OF CAREGIVING

The responsibilities facing women as carers are intensifying because of the following trends: the growth of the oldest-old, changes in the family, the increased movement of women into the labor force, and public policies such as the devolution of responsibility from the federal level to local government, privatization of care, and increased emphasis on community-based and family-focused care for older adults.

The oldest-old are the fastest growing segment of the overall U.S. population and the aging population itself. As a result of the dramatically increased life expectancy, middle aged and young-old adults can anticipate thirty or more years shared with their aging parents. In fact, today the average American woman can expect to spend 18 years caring for an older family member compared to 17 years for her children (Pavalko and Artis, 1997). Again, what is significant from a feminist perspective is that the oldest-old, who have the greatest rate of disability, are predominantly female. Not only do women age 75 and over outnumber men two to one, but older women are also more prone to chronic illness and require greater assistance with activities of daily living (Dailey, 1998). For example among community-based persons age 75 and older, 30 percent of women need help with the activities of daily living as compared to only 17 percent of men. By age 85, if those in nursing homes are included, the need for personal assistance with everyday activities climbs to 45 percent (Bould, Longino and Worley, 1997; Camacho et al., 1993).

A number of changes that are occurring in American families, including the increase in single-parent households and the delay of childbearing, may also impact women's ability to care for aging parents. In the 1990s, a single parent maintained almost one-third of all households with children under the age of 18, most likely a mother. In fact, for African-American children, the one-parent household is now the most common family structure. A woman carrying the dual roles of sole breadwinner and sole parent may encounter difficulties also supporting an aging parent. The delay of childbearing has also increased the number of women who are caring for, or "sandwiched" between two generations needing support.

Women caregivers are also increasingly likely to be employed, often out of economic necessity, either because they are single or because the incomes of two workers have become essential for maintaining an adequate family income. Despite the growing numbers of women in the work force, gender-based wage inequity persists. In 1996, women earned on average 74 cents for every dollar men earned. And this wage gap is even greater for women of color. African American women earn only 65 cents, and Hispanic women only 57 cents for every dollar men earned (National Committee on Pay Equity, 1997). This income gap persists across low-wage, professional and managerial jobs, and follows women into retirement.

One factor contributing to this wage gap is that women are more likely than men to move in and out of the workforce across the life span in order to assume care responsibilities. Women caregivers are more likely than their male counterparts to give up employment, modify their work schedules or forgo promotions or career development opportunities to accommodate care responsibilities (Neal, Inger-soll-Dayton, and Starrels, 1997; Pavalko and Artis, 1997). Regardless of their particular configuration of responsibilities, women generally do not reduce the amount of assistance given, but manage their multiple responsibilities by maintaining rigid schedules, negotiating care tasks around their employment or children, or giving up their free time or reducing hours worked. Not surprisingly, work disruptions and economic strains are significant predictors of stress for female caregivers (Orodenker, 1990; Neal et al. 1997). Such movement in and out of the work force has economic costs not only in terms of reduced current income, but also lower Social Security and pension benefits in retirement. Although women now represent almost half the workforce, they have double the rate of poverty in old age as compared to men: 16 percent versus 8 percent (Hobbs and Damon, 1996; National Policy and Resource Center on Women and Aging, 1996).

The increasing devolution of responsibility from the federal to local levels along with cutbacks in federal funding, the privatization of care and the growing emphasis on community-based care have all increased the burdens faced by women as caregivers. Since the 1980s, there has been a decline in the role of public providers and an infusion of for-profit providers into the service delivery system. The trend toward privatization is most pronounced among home health care agencies, nursing homes, board and care homes and hospitals. The growth of home health care, primarily in the proprietary realm, has resulted in services being oriented more often toward high-tech interventions for acute care rather than long-term care for chronic illness. This gap has resulted in the "informalization of care," a phenomenon where care is transferred from the formal delivery system of hospitals and agencies to the informal arenas of home and community (Estes, Swan and Associates, 1993). A consequence of informalization is the transfer of the provision of long-term care services to women, whether as unpaid relatives, neighbors or volunteers (Hooyman and Gonyea, 1995).

A FEMINIST CRITIQUE
OF CURRENT PRACTICE WITH FAMILY CAREGIVERS

Practice interventions with women as caregivers have tended to fall into an individualistic model to reduce caregiver stress, whether through counseling, education, or support groups. Such psychoeducational interventions can be effective in several ways: increasing carers' knowledge of problems faced by their relatives and of available resources, creating feelings of support, and teaching coping strategies, including ways to address secondary strains in the workplace and other areas of their lives. Yet research suggests that many of these practice interventions do not reduce the overall stress of caregiving (Hugen, 1993; Abel, 1991; Smith, Smith and Toseland, 1991; Whitlach, Zarit and von Eye, 1991).

From a feminist perspective, these short-term interventions are limited, primarily because their underlying rationale is to inform caregivers about ways to operate more effectively within the constraints of existing service systems. The primary focus is on "individual solutions" (e.g., if caregivers learn to operate more efficiently and become more skilled at coping, their stress will be reduced) versus systemic change (e.g., the development of more effective delivery models). The cost-effectiveness of such interventions is often measured by whether they prolong the caring relationship rather than by the impact on the caregivers' well being. By focusing on effective ways to live with and manage a relative's illness, education and training may reinforce traditional gender-based inequities in care responsibilities. For example, stress management techniques can reinforce the belief that the priority should be to help caregivers adjust to unavoidable burdens. Similarly, counseling interventions which focus on individual attitudes and behaviors, on cognitive restructuring of the caregiver experience, and on personal change may obscure the underlying gender-based structures that cause caregiver burden and inequities (Jenkins, Hofer and Chebra, 1994).

Educational groups are a relatively inexpensive means to inform caregivers about community resources, but they do not address inadequate policies, program funding, or health or long-term care insurance; in other words, they cannot resolve the structural causes of caregiver stress. Although such interventions may ease stress on a short-term basis, they still assume that caring is primarily the responsi-

bility of individual family members and offer no long-range, collective solutions that address underlying structural factors. Abel (1991)
contends that the critical question for evaluating such psychoeducational interventions is not whether programs make caregivers feel
better about themselves, but whether they improve the quality of the
carers' lives and minimize the sacrifices involved.

Support groups for caregivers may also serve to promote individual
competence, coping, and personal adjustment skills–for example, cognitive restructuring techniques to alter how women think about the
caring experience. However, mixed findings regarding the long-term
effectiveness of support groups suggest that they do not address what
carers perceive to be their problems and needs, such as assistance with
specific tasks, such as arranging community services or home care
(Smith et al., 1991). Given the range, complexity and chronicity of
issues facing family caregivers, it is unrealistic to expect that a limited
number of group sessions will have profoundly affect their lives
(Whitlatch et al., 1991). Similar to educational programs, support
groups can provide an immediate and visible response to families, but
they do not alter structural-based gender inequities in care responsibilities nor necessarily increase the funding and development of appropriate, accessible and affordable services (Hooyman and Gonyea,
1995; Abel and Nelson, 1990).

A FEMINIST MODEL
FOR PRACTICE WITH WOMEN AS CAREGIVERS

The overall goal of a feminist model of practice with women as
caregivers is to assure gender justice in terms of caring responsibilities. Such a model is organized around several key elements: the
opportunity for both men and women to choose roles; information and
advocacy as a basis for caregiver empowerment; and the enhancement
of caregivers' capability to provide quality care, which includes their
rights to a comprehensive range of available, accessible and acceptable services (Hooyman and Gonyea, 1995).

A feminist model of practice with women is founded on the concept
of choice, including the choice *not* to provide care. It is oriented to
enhancing the quality of life for both the caregiver and receiver. This
suggests the importance of care management (not management of a
case), in which the practitioner works with the caregiver to assess

needs and locate appropriate services, including institutional and other residential types of placement when these are the best options for both the caregiver and receiver.

Closely interconnected with the concept of choice is that of empowerment: caregiver control or autonomy over the selection of community supports. As a first step toward empowerment, caregivers need to be educated about their options and to have adequate information by which to identify their preferences about caring. The goal of caregiver education is thus empowerment, not increased efficiency nor cost savings. Because the meaning of caregiving varies among ethnic and racial groups, education needs to occur within the cultural context of the caregiver's beliefs and values and, where possible, to use natural help systems rather than only relying on professionals.

Education about care options needs to be ongoing and available throughout all the stages of caring. Such educational interventions would have a preventive emphasis, and information would be presented early enough in the caring cycle before certain options are closed off. Too often, families have been informed of services too late, after a crisis has occurred or they have reached the breaking point and are seeking institutionalization for their relative. Education may be more effective as an early intervention if it is provided to both current and potential caregivers in natural settings, such as employee assistance programs, family resource centers and parent associations in the schools, adult education in the churches, and neighborhood or community centers. By providing education within such natural contexts, all family members can be included. This more inclusive approach has the potential to promote the development of a larger helping network involving both men and women (Hooyman and Gonyea, 1995; Abramowitz and Cousey, 1989).

The capability to provide quality care necessitates that adequate support services be available in the community. If women choose to provide care and are to be capable providers, they must be supported by a comprehensive range of accessible, integrated and culturally appropriate services that provide a strengthened infrastructure of support (Ansello and Roberto, 1993). In a feminist practice model, families and service providers would be partners or collaborators in tailoring services to the needs and goals of families and care receivers. The care manager would not just be a broker and administrator of services for a "case," but an advocate for mobilizing and changing services to better meet individual client needs and to support caregivers. The practitioner as advocate would seek to influence the quality of care at both the client and the system level (Challis, 1994).

Closely related to the concepts of capacity-building and consumer involvement is the development of support groups as a means to promote social change (Abel and Nelson, 1990). Through open discussion, including consciousness-raising and politicizing techniques, support group members have the opportunity to explore the common systemic roots of their personal problems. Women caregivers can begin to understand the structural factors that underlie the devaluation of their caregiving role. They can be encouraged to seek common solutions to problems previously viewed as private, moving from individual coping and mutual sharing to finding a collective voice, and advocating for increased resources (Hooyman and Gonyea, 1995). Many women's organizations, such as NOW and the Older Women's League, have challenged traditional forms of service delivery. To achieve gender justice, women must be involved at the grass roots level in defining needs and identifying strategies to address caregiving burden.

A FEMINIST MODEL TOWARD ECONOMIC SUPPORTS

Even though flexible and individualized social supports appear to be more important than economic ones for most caregivers' willingness and ability to provide care, there are significant economic costs, especially for women care providers. Because caregiving is both unpaid and underpaid, women who leave paid employment, even temporarily, to assume family care roles, are then often locked into a lower socioeconomic status throughout their lives. In order to address these economic consequences for women, fundamental structural changes are needed in how caring work is valued and rewarded in our society. Modification in the Social Security system to recognize the economic value of years spent out of the labor market to provide care as well as direct economic supports in the form of a caregiver wage or attendant allowance are ways to acknowledge the importance of this work (Hooyman and Gonyea, 1995).

As noted earlier, a long-range goal is not only the integration of women into the public sphere (i.e., to move women into all occupational segments of the labor force) but also to extend the imperative of caring in the private sphere to men. For women to achieve their economic aspirations, a substantial increase in their income-earning capacity is not only required but also societal support for the functions generally performed by women on an unpaid basis. Accordingly, a feminist model assumes that care of dependent relatives is socially important work that must be supported with public resources and shared by both men and women (Sipla and Simon, 1993). All caring work should be adequately compensated, whether by women and men in the home; outside the family in public, voluntary or for-profit organizations; or inside the family through home help or home care nurses (Hooyman and Gonyea, 1995). Adequately reimbursing the caregiver, whether family, neighbor, or public employee, accords societal recognition that caring performed in the home is just as important as the manufacture of automobiles or the generation of electricity. To address the structural inequities of Social Security and private pensions, the provision of benefits to family carers, including health care, retirement and workers' compensation for caregivers, is essential. Payment levels should be indexed relative to inflation in order to insure integrity and incentive value for family members who choose to be paid for their caregiving. While fundamental changes needed in Social Security and pension systems to reduce gender inequities are beyond the scope of this paper, these are long-range issues that must be addressed to reduce the economic costs of care for women.

To attach an economic value to caregiving might also include abandoning the term caregiver itself, which can be disempowering to both the provider and receiver of care: by implying "caring" and "giving" are free, caregiving always leaves the receiver in debt. The concept of attendant for both family and nonfamily providers may be more empowering by "attending" to those aspects of living that cannot be accomplished by the care recipient because of long-term disability. Under the concept of attendant care, one party to the exchange gets a service as well as preserving autonomy in meeting his or her needs, and the other receives an income through an attendant allowance (Hooyman and Gonyea, 1995).

A feminist approach also recognizes that although financial compensation is a necessary first step in legitimizing the important work of caring, it is not sufficient to relieve the burdens experienced by caregivers over time. In a feminist model of care, interconnections must be built with other aspects of the service system. Therefore, an attendant allowance must be one part of a broad-based family approach that includes support services, such as counseling, homemaker, home care, respite, day care, flexible residential care, transportation and assistance with economic expenditures like household alterations, supplies and high-tech equipment. The authors acknowledge that such changes in work, family and public policy will come slowly, if at all, given the larger cultural, historical and political context. However, by raising the possibilities as part of pubic policy discourse, it is hoped that increasing recognition will, over time, be accorded to the economic importance of caregiving work.

A FEMINIST CRITIQUE
OF CURRENT LONG-TERM CARE POLICY

A number of assumptions and values that underlie contemporary long-term care policies have negative consequences for women as caregivers. These include: the older adult with chronic disabilities is the target or unit of care rather than the family system; the emphasis is on community care, which often translates into family care; and the privatization and informalization of care as cost-effective. A primary reason that gender inequities in care responsibilities persist is because promoting the carers' well-being has not been a policy goal, nor have caregivers' rights to public support been legitimized within long-term care policies. Instead, policies have focused on the dependent individual, not on the interconnections between the person with disabilities and those who provide care (Osterbusch, Keigher, Miller and Linsk, 1987). When the individual, not the family system, is viewed as the unit or target of service, the costs of care for caregivers are overlooked.

Government interventions with family caregivers are often construed as a "last resort," after women have exhausted their own resources for care. Accordingly, social and health services have tended to be oriented toward crisis intervention, short-term support and long-term residential care, rather than toward personal care and in-home maintenance for the long haul. When funds are limited, agencies have tended to give priority to providing services to older persons without relatives. For example, under the Medicaid waiver program, personal care services for older adults are reimbursable in some states, but not if a relative provides them. In other states, a child or grandchild may be reimbursed for care, but not an "able and available" spouse (Estes et al., 1993). In sum, the presumption that family members, typically women, are both willing and able to care for relatives with disabilities is, in part, a function of the narrow policy focus on the individual dependent person rather than on the total informal helping system (Abel, 1987).

This focus on the individual has been espoused by policy makers who are concerned with cost containment and who believe that if more services were available, families would overutilize them. Yet most female caregivers do not use services; when they do, they tend to be selective and modest in their requests, asking primarily for a supplement to and respite from what they continually provide. When periodic substitution does occur, as in the case of respite care, the effects may be desirable for both the caregiver and the care receiver by preventing caregiver stress and burnout (Noelker and Bass, 1994). Policy makers' fears about overutilization of formal services overlook the fact that paid services frequently complement and strengthen informal care (Litwak, Jessop and Moulton, 1994; Abel, 1987).

Long-term care in the community by familial providers is assumed to be preferable to institutionalization. Uncompensated care is viewed as more kind, sensitive, attuned to individual needs and compatible with traditional values than that provided by paid care providers (Hooyman and Gonyea, 1995). In reality, care by the community is often perceived by policy makers as less expensive than government involvement. This translates into "care by the community," since a family care network of community services in support of women's caring work in the home does not exist (Gordon and Donald, 1993; Neysmith, 1991). In fact, the growing emphasis on community care has occurred in the context of the overall decline in public funding for such services. From a feminist perspective, community care, as currently constructed, has removed the power of choice from the care receiver and the caregiver, imposing dependency on both of them. In fact, Dalley (1988) contends that the presumed distinction between "care in" and "care by" the community is meaningless when the care–through the provision of public or quasi-public services–is so limited that the physical, emotional or financial costs for family caregivers remain so great.

As noted earlier, privatization is another assumption that underlies current public polices and penalizes women caregivers. Although home care is a rapidly growing industry, there has been a decline in home care provided by public and nonprofit agencies. Privatization has also served to reduce the services available to lower-income individuals traditionally served by public agencies, most of whom are women and minorities. Reductions of public expenditures have meant that gender and racial inequities have been intensified.

Privatization's underlying assumption that caring is a private duty, not a societal responsibility, is also reflected in the emphasis placed on informal care. This shift of labor from persons working within the paid labor force to those working outside it, both in the family and as volunteers, is at the core of our feminist critique. Services of hospitals and community agencies have been transferred out of the formal delivery system into the informal arenas of home and community. Care that was once provided by paid professional providers has shifted to unpaid lay providers, typically women. Government encouragement of the use of volunteers and "natural" helping networks translates into more women providing more care across the life span. The motivations for such a transfer appear to be financial rather than a commitment to building alternative service models (Hooyman and Gonyea, 1995; Neysmith, 1991).

A FEMINIST MODEL FOR LONG-TERM CARE POLICY

A feminist model of long-term care would have family support, empowerment and choice as a centerpiece of the system. Also critical to this model are a partnership between families and formal service providers and universal access to comprehensive community-based care. Central to a feminist approach for long-term care is a broader redefinition of health care that integrates social and health services, physical and mental health care, and addresses prevention as well as treatment. This model would also incorporate a life span approach that builds on the connections across generations. Finally, as noted above, women would be adequately compensated as the primary formal and informal providers of care (Hooyman and Gonyea, 1995; Gill and Ingman, 1994).

Since a feminist approach to long-term care assumes that women's caregiving is integral to the current system, women must have a significant voice in determining how that care is accomplished. A feminist model thus takes account of the additional care burdens that women have disproportionately borne across the life span. It empowers women and men to be able to choose whether to provide care. Supportive nonmedical services would thus be built around both the needs of the care receiver and giver. Services would be psychologically accessible–that is provided in a manner and setting to optimize individual choice about the mix of informal and formal care and to enhance independence, well-being and personal dignity for both the family caregivers and the care recipients.

Choice would also be encouraged through culturally relevant, geographically accessible outreach and education so that people know how to obtain care through local service systems that are perceived as welcoming and appropriate (Gill and Ingman, 1994). Culturally competent care would be accessible in a wide range of community-based settings–hospitals, physicians offices, neighborhood health centers, clinics, long-term care facilities, and hospices. A feminist model would also aim to insure consumer choice regarding the type of providers from among a wide array of nonphysician personnel, including nurse practitioners, clinical nurse specialists, social workers, physical therapists, other allied health practitioners, and non-Western or holistic providers of care. The physician would no longer be the primary gatekeeper to access to services. Care management would link care across time, place and profession in order to ensure access, responsiveness and flexibility (Challis, 1994). In other words, as Callahan (1994) has argued for over a decade, the emphasis should be on care, not on cure. Such a long-term care model would be evaluated in terms of adequacy of results obtained with available resources and what it takes to make possible a decent quality of life, rather than quantitatively equal benefits for all and cost-efficiency as a way to minimize dollar expenditures (Stone and Keigher, 1994).

CONCLUSION

Central to a feminist approach is that long-term care of older adults is defined as a public responsibility to guarantee a minimal level of services to all citizens as a public good in which all citizens should participate without undue burden. Such universal access contrasts markedly with current managed care models (Wiener, Illston and Henley, 1994; Riley and Mollica, 1994). In a feminist model, health is not just an individual personal problem, but also the responsibility of community and government, acting at the local level under national direction, similar to public services of police, fire and public schools (Massachusetts Women's Health Care Coalition, 1994). It presumes that citizens who are structurally disadvantaged by class, race and gender must nonetheless be treated equitably by the health and long-term care systems (Neysmith, 1993). It thus requires a strong public sector presence that takes leadership in defining policy directions to insure entitlement to health care based on rights of citizenship. Such a non-age based approach also recognizes the interdependence of different age groups for care across the life span rather than pitting age groups against one another, as has happened with the current categorical approach to policy (Stone and Keigher, 1993). Caregiving of older adults is thus not a private trouble nor individual stress, but a public or societal responsibility that demands a collective response for enhancing the quality of life of both the caregiver and receiver. As noted throughout, central to achieving this goal is the elimination of gender-based inequities in caregiving and provision of caregiver choice and empowerment for women and men.

REFERENCES

Abel, E. K. (1987). Love is not enough: Family care of the frail elderly. Washington, DC: American Public Health Association.

Abel, E. K. (1990). Informal care for the disabled elderly: A critique of recent literature. *Research on Aging, 12,* 139-157.

Abel, E. K., & Nelson, M. K. (1990). *Circles of care: Work and identity in women's lives.* Albany, NY: State University of New York Press.

Abel, E. K. (1991). *Who cares for the elderly? Public policy and the experiences of adult daughters.* Philadelphia, PA: Temple University Press.

Abramowitz, I. A., & Coursey, R. D. (1989). Impact of an educational support group on family participants who take care of their schizophrenic relatives. *Journal of Consulting and Clinical Psychology, 57,* 232-236.

Ansello, E. F., & Roberto, K. A. (1993). Empowering elderly caregivers: Practice, research and policy directions. In K. A. Roberto (Ed.) *The elderly caregiver: Caring for adults with developmental disabilities* (pp. 173-189). Newbury Park, CA: Sage.

Arber, S. &, Ginn, J., (Eds.). (1995). *Connecting gender and aging: A sociological approach.* Bristol, PA: Open University Press.

Baines, C., Evans, P., & Neysmith, S. (Eds.) (1991). *Women's caring: Feminist perspectives on social welfare.* Toronto, Ontario: McClelland & Stewart, Inc.

Bass, D., Noelker, L. S., & Rechlin, L. (1996). The moderating influence of service use on negative caregiving consequences. *Journal of Gerontology, Social Sciences, 51B,* S121-S131.

Bengston, V. C., Rosenthal, C. J., & Burton, C. (1996). Paradoxes of families and aging. In R. H. Binstock & L. K. George (Eds.), *Handbook of aging and the social sciences*, 4th ed. (pp. 253-282) San Diego, CA: Academic Press.

Bould, S., Longino, Jr., C.F., & Worley, R. (1997). Oldest old women: Endangered by government cutbacks, *International Journal of Sociology and Social Policy, 20*, 142-156.

Braithwaite, V. (1992). Caregiver burden: Making the concept scientifically useful and policy relevant. *Research on Aging, 14*, 3-27.

Braithwaite, V. (1996). Understanding stress in informal caregiving. *Research on Aging, 18*, 139-174.

Callahan, D. (1994). Setting limits: A response. *The Gerontologist, 34*, 393-398.

Calasanti, T. M., & Hendricks, J. (1993). A socialist-feminist approach to aging. *Journal of Aging Studies, 7* (special issue).

Camacho, T. C., Strawbridge, W. J., Cohen, R. D., & Kaplan, G. A. (1993). Functional Ability in the Oldest Old. *Journal of Aging and Health, 5*, 439-454.

Challis, D. (1994). Case Management: A review of UK developments and issues. In M. Titterton (Ed.), *Caring for people in the community: The new welfare* (pp. 91-112). London: Jessica Kingsley

Cohler, B. (1997). Fathers, daughters and caregiving: Perspectives from psychoanalysis and life-course social science. In J. M. Coyle (Ed.), *Handbook on Women and Aging.* (pp. 443-464). Westport, CT: Greenwood Press.

Connell, C. M., & Gibson, G. D. (1997). Racial, ethnic and cultural differences in dementia caregiving: Review and analysis. *The Gerontologist, 37*, 355-364.

Dailey, N. (1998). *When baby boom women retire.* Westport, CT: Praeger.

Dalley, G. (1988). *Ideologies of caring: Rethinking community and collectiveness.* London: Macmillan.

Davis, L. V. (Ed.) (1994). *Building on women's strengths.* New York: The Haworth Press, Inc.

Estes, C., Swan, J., & Associates (1993). *The long-term care crisis.* Newbury Park, CA: Sage Publications.

Gill, D. & Ingman, S. (Eds.) (1994). *Eldercare, distributive justice and the welfare state: Retrenchment or expansion.* Albany, NY: State University of New York.

Ginn, J., & Arber, S. (1995). Only connect: Gender relations and aging. In S. Arber, & J. Ginn (Eds.), *Connecting gender and aging: A sociological approach.* Philadelphia: Open University Press.

Gordon, D., & Donald, J. (1993). *Community social work, older people and informal care.* Aldershot, England: Avebury.

Hobbs, F., & Damon, B. L. (1996). *65+ in the United States.* Washington, D.C.: U.S. Department of Commerce, Bureau of the Census, Current Population Report.

Hooyman, N. R. & Gonyea, J. (1995). *Feminist perspectives on family care: Policies for gender justice.* Thousand Oaks, CA: Sage.

Hugen, B. (1993). The effectiveness of a psycho-educational support service to families of persons with chronic mental illness. *Research on Social Work Practice, 3*, 137-154.

Ingersoll-Dayton, Starrels, M., & Dowler, D. (1996). Caregiving for parents and parents-in-law: Is gender important? *The Gerontologist, 36*, 483-491.

Kramer, B. J., & Kipnis, S. (1995). Eldercare and work-role conflict: Toward an understanding of gender differences in caregiver burden. *The Gerontologist, 35,* 340-347.

Leutz, W. N., Capitman, J. A., MacAdam, M., & Abrahams, R. (1992). *Care for frail elders: Developing community solutions.* Westport, CT: Auburn House.

Lewis, J., & Meredith, B. (1988). *Daughters who care: Daughters caring for mothers at home.* London: Routledge and Kegan Paul.

Litwak, E., Jessop, D., & Moulton, H. (1994). Optional use of formal and informal systems over the life course. In E. Kahana, D. Biegel, & M. Wykle (Eds.), *Family caregiving across the lifespan* (pp. 96-132). Thousand Oaks, CA: Sage.

Lynch, S. (1998). Who supports whom? How age and gender affect the perceived quality of support from family and friends. *The Gerontologist, 38,* 231-239.

Marshall, V. (1996). The state of theory in aging and the social sciences. In R. H. Binstock & L. K. George, (Eds.) *Handbook of aging and the social sciences,* 4th ed. (pp. 12-30) San Diego: Academic Press.

Massachusetts Women's Health Care Coalition. (November 1993). *Statement on Health Care.* Boston, MA: Author.

Meyer, M. H. (1997). Toward a structural, life course agenda for reducing insecurity among women as they age. (book review). *The Gerontologist, 37,* 833-834.

Miller, B., & Cafasso, L. (1992). Gender differences in caregiving: Fact or artifact? *Gerontologist, 32,* 498-507.

Mui, A. C. (1995). Caring for frail elderly parents: A comparison of adult sons and daughters. *The Gerontologist, 35,* 86-93.

National Alliance for Caregiving and American Association of Retired Persons. (1997). *Family caregiving in the U.S.: Findings from a national survey.* Washington, D. C.: Author.

National Committee on Pay Equity. (1997). *The Wage Gap: 1996.* Washington, DC: Author.

National Policy and Resource Center on Women and Aging (1996). *Planning for retirement security* (1, 1-6). Waltham, MA: Brandeis University.

Neal, M. B., Ingersoll-Dayton, B., & Starrels, M.E. (1997). Gender and relationship differences in caregiving patterns and consequences among employed caregivers. *The Gerontologist, 37,* 804-816.

Neysmith, S. (1991). From community care to a social model of care. In C. Barnes, P. Evans & S. Neysmith (Eds.), *Women's caring: Feminist perspectives on social welfare* (pp. 272-299). Toronto, CA: McClelland and Stewart.

Neysmith, S. (1993). Developing a home care system to meet the needs of aging Canadians and their families. In J. Hendricks & C. Rosenthal (Eds.) *The remainder of their days* (pp. 145-168). New York: Garland Publishing.

Noelker, L. S., & Bass, D. (1994). Relationship between the frail elderly informal and formal helpers. In E. Kahana, D. Biegel and M. Wykle (Eds.), *Family caregiving across the lifespan* (pp. 356-385). Thousand Oaks, CA: Sage.

Nolan, M., Grant G., & Keady, J. (1996). *Understanding family care.* Buckingham: Open University Press.

Orodenker, S. (1990). Family caregiving in a changing society: The effects of employment on caregiver stress. *Family and Community Health, 12,* 58-70.

Osterbusch, S., Keigher, S., Miller, B., & Linsk, N. (1987). Community care policies and gender justice. *International Journal of Health Services, 17*, 217-232.

Parks, S. H., & Pilisuk, M. (1991). Caregiver burden: Gender and the psychological costs of caregiving. *American Journal of Orthopsychiatry, 6*, 501-509.

Pavalko, E. K., & Artis, J. E. (1997). Women's caregiving and paid work: Casual relationships in late mid-life. *Journal of Gerontology, 52B*, S 170-S179.

Pearlin, L. I. Aneshensel, C. S., Mullon, J. T., & Whitlatch, C. J. (1996). Caregiving and its social support. In R. H. Binstock & L. K. George (Eds.), *Handbook of Aging and the Social Sciences*, 4th ed. (pp. 283-302). San Diego, CA: Academic Press.

Qureshi, H., & Walker, A. (1989). *The caring relationship: Elderly people and their families*. Philadelphia, PA: University Press.

Riley, T., & Mollica, R. L. (1994). *The impact of health reform on vulnerable adults: Volume II. An Analysis of national health reform proposals*. Waltham, MA: Brandeis University, Center for Vulnerable Populations.

Sipila, J., & Simon, B. (1993). Home care allowances for the frail elderly: For and against. *Journal of Sociology and Social Welfare, 20*, 119-134.

Smeeding, T. M. (1998). Reshuffling responsibility in old age: The United States in comparative perspective. In J. G. Gonyea (Ed.), *Resecuring Social Security and Medicare: Understanding Privatization and Risk* (pp. 24-36). Washington, DC: Gerontological Society of America.

Smith, G. H., Smith, M., & Toseland, R. (1991). Problems identified by family caregivers in counseling. *The Gerontologist, 31*, 15-22.

Twigg, J., & Atkin, K. (1994). *Carers perceived: Policy and practice in informal care*. Buckingham, UK: Open University Press.

Waerness, K. (1985). *Informal and formal care in old age: What is wrong with the new ideology of community care in the Scandinavian welfare state today*. Paper presented at the Conference on Gender Divisions and Policies for Community Care, University of Kent, Canterbury, England.

Researching to Transgress:
The Need for Critical Feminism
in Gerontology

Ruth E. Ray, PhD

SUMMARY. This article defines "empowering research" and argues the need for a critical gerontology informed by feminist and postmodern theories which focus on the connections between language, self, and social action. The author calls for feminist gerontology which evokes critical consciousness on the part of the researcher and participants. Feminist gerontologists are encouraged to engage in self-reflection and self-critique in regards to their own attitudes toward aging and to include personal criticism in their scholarly writings. Examples of feminist research on aging which illustrate these characteristics are provided. *[Article copies available for a fee from The Haworth Document Delivery Service: 1-800-342-9678. E-mail address: getinfo@haworthpressinc.com]*

KEYWORDS. Critical gerontology, women's studies, age studies, feminist research, personal criticism, postmodernism, social constructionism

If there is no other task that feminist activist researchers can accomplish, we must provoke a deep curiosity about, indeed an intolerance for, that which is described as inevitable, immutable, and natural.

–Michele Fine
Disruptive Voices:
The Possibilities of Feminist Research

[Haworth co-indexing entry note]: "Researching to Transgress: The Need for Critical Feminism in Gerontology." Ray, Ruth E. Co-published simultaneously in *Journal of Women & Aging* (The Haworth Press, Inc.) Vol. 11, No. 2/3, 1999, pp. 171-184; and: *Fundamentals of Feminist Gerontology* (ed: J. Dianne Garner) The Haworth Press, Inc., 1999, pp. 171-184. Single or multiple copies of this article are available for a fee from The Haworth Document Delivery Service [1-800-342-9678, 9:00 a.m. - 5:00 p.m. (EST). E-mail address: getinfo@haworthpressinc.com].

A central theme of this collection has been the "empowerment" of older women in different settings and social contexts, as well as the development of empowerment-oriented policies and therapeutic practices among feminists in gerontology. For my own contribution to this discussion, I will consider how the concept of empowerment might also be applied to research and methodology. In this paper, I define "empowering research," arguing for a specific kind of critical gerontology informed by feminism and postmodern theories which direct us to the connections between language, self, and social action. I offer two examples of feminist-inspired research on aging which I consider positively critical–that is, purposely disruptive and transformative. The title of my chapter is inspired by the feminist writings of psychologist Michele Fine and cultural critic bell hooks; by evoking their words, I mean to pay them tribute and call others to action. Ultimately, I'm calling for more personal investment and passionate *activism* in feminist gerontology.

In her collection of essays and conversations entitled *Teaching to Transgress: Education as the Practice of Freedom*, hooks combines personal reflection and theoretical argument to convince us that feminist scholars in all disciplines have the potential, indeed the responsibility, to transgress–to break bonds and overcome restrictive limits and boundaries around what we say and how we speak. I am claiming this same potential and responsibility, as yet largely unclaimed, for feminist gerontology. To begin with, I am suggesting the need for a more critical feminist gerontology, by which I mean a gerontology which questions, challenges, contests, and resists the status quo. Critical feminists not only demand fuller representation of women and women's issues in research, theory, and practice, but also seek methodologies and interpretive strategies that extend current thinking about how knowledge is made and disseminated.

There is little precedent for this kind of gerontology. The contingency of brave scholars doing "critical gerontology"–Thomas R. Cole (1993, 1995), Harry R. Moody (1988, 1992, 1993), and Steven Katz (1996) among the more widely published–have broken fertile ground, but they do not forefront feminism, and they do not critique in the name of *empowerment*. The small group of feminists working in critical gerontology–Meredith Minkler and Carol Estes (1991), Toni Calasanti and Jon Hendricks (1993), to name a few–have taken the approach of political economists, for the most part, and as such have contributed significantly to our knowledge of the economics of aging, particularly caregiving and its long-term effects on older women. We need much more critical work on a wider array of social issues, however, research which is conducted from many theoretical perspectives besides Marxist and post-Marxist. In abbreviated version here, I sketch out the parameters of one kind of critical feminism, informed by postmodern theories. My version of critical feminist gerontology has, at the very least, two characteristics: (1) it challenges the scientific paradigm by being personally "involved" and critical (as opposed to distanced and objective), as well as overtly political (in the sense of advancing an agenda meant to empower both researcher and researched), and (2) it pursues alternative ways to report scholarly findings which are equally "involved" and critical.

EMPOWERMENT
THROUGH CHANGE IN CONSCIOUSNESS

In thinking about how to do critical feminism in gerontology, I have looked to many feminists across the social sciences and humanities. I think it crucial that feminist gerontologists read and draw from the research in many disciplines. We need to be fully interdisciplinary in our orientation. While gerontology as a field is multidisciplinary (researchers from many disciplines working alongside one another but not necessarily influencing each other's thinking or methodology), women's studies has always worked toward interdisciplinarity (researchers from many disciplines working together, borrowing from each other's paradigms and processes, and changing their ways of thinking and knowing through this mutual interaction).[1] Feminist gerontology, still in its formative stages, would do well to follow in the footsteps of women's studies, each of us striving toward interdisciplinarity in every project, article, chapter, and presentation. Feminist gerontologists can take their tutelage from scholarship in philosophy, history, ethics, theology, anthropology, economics, linguistics, education, rhetoric, and literary studies, as well as psychology, sociology, social work, and medicine. We need not recreate the binaries between qualitative and quantitative, "soft" and "hard" science, research and practice, subjective and objective that have so deeply influenced mainstream gerontology. Our "transgressing" can (and should) take the form of disciplinary border crossings, paradigm shifting, and genre-bending, and these crossings can be empowering if we stand on the shoulders of the feminists who came before us.

"Empowerment" in terms of conducting and presenting research, first and foremost entails a change in consciousness. Sondra Farganis explains that empowering feminist research "intends to make people conscious of social arrangements as a prelude to action." At its best, it "is like a transmittal line between self and power. It allows questions to be raised of how a woman comes to think of herself, how she comes to fashion a self, how she comes to know of power and her ability to change or resist it." Such research "helps design an identity by pointing to the social factors that go into the making of an 'I,' a subject, a person with a social map and an historical context" (pp. 10-11). This consciousness-raising must occur for the researcher, as well as the subjects of research. All participants must begin "to discover who they are and to refuse to be what they have been socialized to be" (p. 11) when that culturalization has negated and limited their potential.

Black feminist bell hooks has written and spoken internationally on the subject of empowerment in theory, research, teaching, policy-making, and practice (1984, 1989, 1990, 1994a; 1994b; hooks and West, 1991). She sees a necessary progression in feminist movement from internal empowerment to external empowerment. Informed by anticolonial and feminist theories, the critical pedagogy of Paulo Freire, and the Buddhist teachings of Thich Nhat Hanh, hooks argues that the feminist researcher must become conscious of his/her own oppression and oppressive tendencies first before attempting to "liberate" others. Empowering research, then, is characterized by the researcher's deliberate effort to intervene critically in his/her own life, as well as the lives of others. Personal experience is used as a standpoint on which to base analysis, formulate theory, and motivate action; it is the "spirit that orders the words" of the feminist scholar (hooks, 1994b, p. 91). The empowered researcher is self-reflexive, self-conscious, and self-actualized; from this position of inner knowledge, he/she generates work which is progressive, socially critical, resistant, interventionist, and enabling; and from these beginnings come liberation and transformation.

While Farganis and hooks focus on the material outcomes of critical feminism, Michelle Fine directs her attention to a larger disciplinary critique, challenging the conventional research methods and discourses which have structured the social sciences in general and psychology in particular. These same discourses, associated with the positivist sciences, are the foundations on which gerontology as a research field has been built. Yet Fine argues that feminist inquiry is severely hampered by adherence to the positivist paradigm, namely its "obsessions" with experimental control, separation of researcher and researched, conversion of subjects into objects, search for universal laws, "romance with sterile environments called laboratories," commitment to generalizability to the extent that any consideration of social context is considered "intrusive," and its "fetish with imposed categories, comparisons, hierarchies, and stages" (p. 2). For the purposes of feminist transformation, Fine asserts that a participatory activist inquiry is required–one which is "committed to positioning researchers as self-conscious, critical, and participatory analysts, engaged with but still distinct from [their] informants." Such work changes the way knowledge is created and represented, as well as the material lives of researchers and subjects. It is simultaneously disruptive, transformative, and reflective, because it strives to "resituate our political struggles and our personal passions at the very center of our work, exploring, rather than denying, the nexus of activism and scholarship" (p. x).

If we wish to follow these urgings in building a feminist gerontology, we would do well to align ourselves with both women's studies and what Margaret Gullette (1997) calls "age studies," after current efforts in the humanities toward "cultural studies." In taking the critical turn and assuming an interdisciplinary stance, we must broaden the scope of our publishing beyond the mainstream gerontology journals. Otherwise, we will be forever marginalized in gerontology and constrained by a scientific paradigm that is, by definition, antithetical to the politics of feminism.

THE POWER OF THE PERSONAL

One of the most significant contributions of the feminist movement in and out of academe has been the validation of personal knowledge and experience. Fortunately, in the past 30 years, several intellectual movements in addition to feminism, such as the postmodern challenge to the positivist paradigm and the rise of social constructionism, have converged to make "the personal is political" claim more compelling.[2] Feminism as a political movement has always been grounded in the personal lives of women, as is much feminist theory and criticism. As Camilla Stivers (1993) notes in her "Reflections on the Role of Personal Narrative in Social Science," "feminism demands that those who have been objectified now be able to define themselves, to tell their own stories. This is essentially a claim that each human being occupies a legitimate position from which to experience, interpret and constitute the world" (p. 410).

The need to give voice to personal experience extends beyond the subject of research to include the researcher, as well. Feminist scholars in the humanities, in particular, have begun to articulate their own subjectivity as a research method, constructing what literary scholar Nancy K. Miller calls "personal criticism," defined as an act of cultural or textual analysis which "entails an explicitly autobiographical performance" (p. 1). When writing personal criticism, scholars interweave self-narration into their research accounts by, say, framing an essay with self-revelation, punctuating an argument with a self-portrayal, offering an anecdote to support a claim, or, in a more encompassing way, infusing the text with personal values and political beliefs. Such writing, when done carefully, succeeds in contesting the established systems of power, authority, and knowledge-making in academe. It is meant to reconfigure relationships between the personal (lived experience), the positional (the stances and voices one assumes in research and writing), and the political (the effects of one's scholarship in the world). In short, feminist criticism which "gets personal" recasts the scholar's relationship to self and authority. As Miller observes, "by turning its authorial voice into spectacle, personal writing theorizes the stakes of its own performance," "blows the cover of the impersonal as a masquerade of self-effacement," and "points to the narcissistic fantasy that inheres in the poses of self-sufficiency we identify with theory; notably, those of abstraction" (p. 24). The aim is "believability, not certitude," "enlargement of understanding rather than control" and, ultimately, a change in the way research is conducted and reported (Stivers, p. 424). Personal criticism is both engaged and engaging; it seeks to provoke, incite, excite, and *invite* a passionate, critical response from readers.

So far, feminist gerontology has primarily documented older women's experiences and described the results of interventions created to promote positive interpretations of women's aging. This is necessary work, and we need to do more. But we also need to employ critical theories which lead us to examine older women's personal experiences with an eye toward gaps, inconsistencies, and evasions, and we need to turn this same critical gaze upon ourselves and our interpretations. Without rigorous self-examination, self-articulation, and self-critique, even feminist gerontologists are at risk of becoming "victims of age ideology" and, as such, "perpetrators in our turn" (Gullette, 1997, p. 15). Given the "personal as political" legacy of the feminist movement, feminist gerontologists are perhaps best positioned to conduct this kind of revisionist inquiry.

In the remainder of this paper, I describe two studies of aging that I consider good role models for critical feminism in gerontology. My intention is to motivate both you and me to initiate research projects which involve self-analysis and critique of our own attitudes toward aging; promote a closer, more interactive relationship with our subjects; intervene in established modes of academic discourse in gerontology; and liberate us to build on the knowledge we are creating by generating more critical scholarship. The simple reason we choose to engage in feminist action research, which is admittedly fraught with difficulties and controversy, is, as Shulamit Reinharz (1992) reminds us, to "clarify our vision and improve our decisions" (p. 195) in all aspects of our lives, professional *and* personal.

CRITICAL INTERVENTION
AND THE PERSONAL NARRATIVES OF OLDER WOMEN

One form of research which offers a promising direction for feminist gerontologists is that which is compelled by critical theory to intervene in the ways older women articulate themselves and their lives. I see this kind of work as related to, but distinct from, reminiscence therapy and life review as popularized by gerontological nurses, social workers, clinical psychologists, and educators (Bornat, 1994; Haight and Webster, 1995; Sherman, 1991). As generally practiced in gerontology, life review therapy is motivated by stage theories of adult development and theories of coping. It is therefore concerned with assisting older adults in forming normative, adaptive representations of the life course. The assumption is that the life story is a direct reflection of older adults' mental health and personality adjustment. A critical, postmodern approach to life review, on the other hand, separates the life from the story, focusing on the language and discursive features of self *presentation.* The assumption is not that the text reflects life, but that life *is* a text (Kenyon & Randall, 1997). Thus, one way to improve the quality of people's lives is to change the interpretations and stories they tell about themselves (McNamee & Gergen, 1992; Parry & Doan, 1994; White & Epston, 1990).

The work of Australian educators Barbara Kamler and Susan Felman (1995) provides a unique example of such critical intervention into the life story. Kamler and Feldman developed two six-week writing workshops entitled "Writing Stories of Ageing" for 18 women, ages 58-84. The purpose of these workshops was to "confront the narrow range of negative images of ageing pervasive in our culture, and to provide an opportunity for women to explore how their own autobiographical stories might challenge and disrupt conventional story lines of women and ageing" (p. 3). The researchers created a workshop environment which encouraged participants to engage in self-reflection and to work toward "a collective understanding of the discursive processes that have shaped older women" (p. 4). Kamler and Feldman describe their research as "collective and deconstructive, where the subjects become co-researchers, producing data in the form of stories and subjecting these data to a progressive critical process of reading and theorizing" (p. 4). Among the subjects the women addressed in their life stories were various issues of embodiment, including visibility and invisibility, body image, pain and physical loss, fear of deterioration, power and control over the body, sensuality and sexuality.

I consider Kamler and Feldman's study an important contribution to critical feminist gerontology in at least two ways. First, it is generated by theories which relocate autobiographical writing from an inner personal space to a public cultural space. Most gerontological research in reminiscence and life review focuses on the "inner" self and the levels of "authenticity" approached in narrating the life. In contrast, Kamler and Feldman focus on the effects of social scripting, language, and discourse, asking "what does it mean to voice or come to voice in a culturally critical way?" (Kamler, 1995, p. 7). By moving from the exclusively personal to the socially constructed, Kamler and Feldman open up a space for feminist action and change. Although the older women were initially reluctant to write about their bodies, a disinclination long noted by feminist critics of women's published autobiographies (Smith, 1993), Kamler and Feldman intervened with a series of exercises which oriented the women to their physical selves. One assignment was to complete the phrase, "When I look in the mirror I see . . . " and another encouraged the women to play with the multiple meanings of "She let herself go." Group discussions of the resulting texts provided occasions for the older women to analyze and challenge the social discourses commonly available for describing the female form, most of which are self-judging, ageist, and sexist. The result for many of the participants was a revised body image and an awareness of empowering alternatives to writing the body. Many of the excerpts from the women's writings are remarkable and moving in their growing resistance to normative tellings.

A second way this work is significant is in the authors' willingness to interrogate their own assumptions and personal stances in relation to the women studied. Kamler and Feldman, both in their late 40s, reveal that the workshops had a "profound" effect on them personally and intellectually. They had initially designed the sessions to counter negative images of aging but, through interactions with the older women, discovered that their own views were unconsciously ageist and shaped by the very forces they had intended to overcome. The researchers, for example, became aware of their tendency to group older women as "an undifferentiated mass–as other–as them–not us." They also discovered their unexamined need to overcompensate for negative images by focusing exclusively on the positive, optimistic, and powerful images of aging. The workshop participants refused to let them romanticize late life, however, and insisted on multiple and conflicting representations of old age. "They were adamant in discussions that [the researchers] not glorify ageing or simply reverse the binary and equate old with beautiful" (p. 11). The older women represented *themselves* as constantly changing subjects, not static objects of study. The researchers learned an important lesson: the youth-age binary is vastly simplified and impossible to impose on a real person–an evolving "body in motion" (p. 14).

PERSONAL CRITICISM
AND THE CULTURAL NARRATIVES OF AGING

Another promising direction for critical feminist gerontology is work which combines criticism, self-reflection, and self-critique in regards to the larger cultural narratives of aging. While feminist scholars in the humanities have moved increasingly towards personal criticism, this kind of inquiry is essentially nonexistent in gerontology. Feminist gerontologists wishing to extend the discursive boundaries for writing about age may look to literary critic Margaret Gullette for insight. In her effort to show the social construction of aging and to alter the narrative scripts by which "age identities" are adopted and interpreted, Gullette has written *Declining to Decline: Cultural Combat and the Politics of the Midlife*. The book begins with Gullette's reflection on her own entry into the subject of age identity:

> When I was almost as young as Dante Alighieri at the time he found himself in his dark wood, I realized I was having perplexing inner conversations with myself about aging. A voice would say sharply, "It's too late to even think of starting this new career." Then another voice said, "But you're not even in your prime." Then the first would list all the reasons I should feel belated, and the other would argue back. (p. 1)

Gullette goes on to describe the profound personal conflict, developing in her 30s, between the two poles of decline and progress that ordered her thinking about age. Gullette's ambivalence and anxiety finally led her to embark on a study of how people are "aged by culture in the broadest sense–discourses, feelings, practices, institutions, material conditions," all of which are "saturated with concepts of age and aging" (p. 3). The report of her research is exceptional for its autobiographical revelation as much as its critical content.

Gullette positions herself as a middle-aged writer who uses personal narratives to examine her own "age identity" and by extension that of all other Americans in middle age. From these personal reflections she moves into social and political analysis, instigating change on both individual and collective levels. Gullette argues the need for a specific kind of life story telling she calls "critical age autobiography," which examines and interrogates the negative age ideologies society provides and revises age narratives that no longer seem true. Says Gullette, "I am proposing an active concept of aging as self-narrated experience, the conscious, ongoing story of one's age identity. Once we can firmly distinguish between the culture's aging narrative and our own versions (particularly if we do so within a collective formed for that purpose), we learn that its threats to being and becoming are resistible" (p. 220). In her own personal narratives, Gullette examines the beliefs about age and beauty she held as a child and young adult, her midlife lapses into nostalgia, the ways in which chronic pain has affected her identity (she was diagnosed with osteoarthritis in her forties), differences between the aging experiences of her male and female friends, menopause as cultural "magic marker," and her changing relationships with mother, husband, and son. Gullette's vision is that "once people begin telling stories about their ageist conditioning, we can expect more to gush out in relief, the way the stories of racism and male chauvinism and masculinity training and homophobia gushed out as soon as there was an audience for them. Then there can be truly new accounts of midlife being and becoming" (p. 14). Her writing is passionate and energetic, her intent being to liberate us all from the decline narratives which have circumscribed our understanding of the life course. She urges readers to assume counter positions and go on the offensive.

As a critical theorist, Gullette looks to feminism and social constructionism for empowering ways to re-interpret and re-articulate midlife and beyond. She finds the "feminist midlife," as opposed to the midlife typically represented in the media and the medical professions, to be a period of growth and renewal. Gullette draws on her own experiences, along with feminist discourses, to make this point:

> Like so many women my age, at about forty I started feeling better. It was like convalescence, a slow, midlife cure–as if we were taking tiny homeopathic pills marked Energy, Enlightenment, Self-Delight. . . . Forces inside and outside helped many women age in this unexpected, exhilarating way. . . . The social movements of the Sixties and Seventies have to get a big share of our gratitude: antiwar resistance, black civil rights, women's and gay liberation. For me, it was primarily feminism. Feminism, like a good therapist, envisioned a Next Self. (pp. 60-61)

Gullette sees the feminist midlife as a counternarrative which challenges middle-ageist assumptions that life is all "down hill" after 40. Her assertions resonate for me as a midlife feminist gerontologist. Wouldn't it be wise for me–and others like me who wish to engage in conscious, critical research on older people's lives–to look inward and examine our own aging selves first? Shouldn't we become aware of the decline narratives we have internalized for ourselves before we conduct any kind of research–narrative or otherwise–on the subject of aging?

I read Kamler, Feldman, and Gullette with excitement, and I see a brighter future for feminist gerontology. Their narrative interventions bring about a consciousness-raising that enables and empowers researchers, as well as the older adults they study. These are surely the outcomes we want for a critical feminist gerontology.

CONSIDERATIONS AND CONCLUSIONS

The kind of research I am calling for is not easy. In choosing topics, methodologies, and discursive strategies which challenge the status quo, we risk censure. Established journals in the field–*The Gerontologist, The Journal of Gerontology, Educational Gerontologist*, to name only a few–do not usually publish critical scholarship, much less feminist criticism. And we will find few, if any, compadres in the departments, institutes, and centers in which we work. Many of our colleagues will not even consider critical feminist gerontology to be "scholarly research." They may dismiss it as reactionary and self-obsessed. But these are, and have always been, the challenges of doing feminism in academe. The fact that feminists in gerontology have not fully engaged in the struggles for scholarly respectability suggests at least two things: (1) so far, there haven't been enough feminists doing age research to "matter" (i.e., to make non-feminist researchers stand up and take notice); and (2) the work that feminist gerontologists have done so far has conformed to the standard norms of presentation and thus has not been perceived as a challenge to the status quo. These are not bad things. I am merely saying that, for those of us who are agitating for change in the ways knowledge is made and presented in gerontology, it's time to step out of bounds and do something different.

My call for action, of course, rests on the central premise that generated the women's movement so many years ago–there is great power and potential in working from the margins, including the margins of academe. How to make this position work for feminist gerontologists is an open question. There are many challenges to address as we push for "feminist movement" as a form of action beyond the sedate abstractions of "the feminist movement" (hooks, 1994). To name a few: Who is best situated to write persuasive feminist criticism in gerontology? Only the secure and the tenured? Only those who have "paid their dues" by first writing within the scientific paradigm? Should we encourage our graduate students to develop their disruptive voices, or does this border on negligence and malpractice? Where do we publish and how do we evaluate critical feminism? What characterizes effective personal criticism in age studies? To whom or what are we accountable, if not to the discursive standards of the established journals in gerontology?

I have no responses to these questions. I admit, too, that I have not yet responded to my own call for action. Although I conduct writing workshops with older adults (men and women), I have not intervened critically in their narratives. Nor have I written my own age autobiography, although I have experimented with a little personal criticism in my gerontological writing (Ray, in progress). I'm reaching beyond my grasp here and asking you to do the same. But isn't that what feminists *do?*

NOTES

1. See Klein (1990) on the differences between multidisciplinarity, interdisciplinarity, and transdisciplinarity.

2. See Ray (1996) for a brief review of postmodern approaches across disciplines.

REFERENCES

Bornat, J. (1994). *Reminiscence reviewed: Evaluation, achievements, perspectives.* Buckingham: Open University.

Calasanti, T., & Hendricks, J. (Eds.). (1993). A socialist feminist approach to aging. *Journal of Aging Studies* (Special Issue), 7.

Cole, T. R. (1993). Preface. In T. R. Cole, W. A. Achenbaum, P. L. Jakobi, & R. Kastenbaum (Eds.). *Voices and visions of aging: Toward a critical gerontology* (pp. xii-xi). New York: Springer.

Cole, T. R. (1995). What have we 'made' of aging? *Journal of Gerontology: Social Sciences 50B*, S341-343.

Farganis, S. (1994). *Situating feminism: From thought to action.* Thousand Oaks, CA: Sage.

Fine, M. (1992). *Disruptive voices: The possibilities of feminist research.* Ann Arbor, MI: University of Michigan.

Gullette, M. (1997). *Declining to decline: Cultural combat and the politics of the midlife.* Charlottesville, VA: University of Virginia.

Haight, B. & Webster, J. D. (Eds.). (1995). *The art and science of reminiscing: Theory, research, methods, and applications.* Bristol, PA: Taylor & Francis.

hooks, b. (1984). *Feminist theory from margin to center.* Boston, MA: South End Press.

hooks, b. (1989). *Talking back: Thinking feminist, thinking black.* Boston, MA: South End Press.

hooks, b. (1990). *Yearning: Race, gender, and cultural politics.* Boston, MA: South End Press.

hooks, b. (1994a). *Outlaw culture: Resisting representations.* New York: Routledge.

hooks, b. (1994b). *Teaching to transgress: Education as the practice of freedom.* New York: Routledge.

hooks, b. & West, C. (1991). *Breaking bread: Insurgent black intellectual life.* Boston, MA: South End Press.

Kamler, B. & Feldman, S. (1995). Mirror mirror on the wall: Reflections on ageing. *Australian Cultural History, 14,* 1-22.

Katz, S. (1996). *Disciplining old age.* Charlottesville: University of Virginia.

Kenyon, G. & Randall, W. (1997). *Restorying our lives: Personal growth through autobiographical reflection.* Westport, CN: Praeger.

Klein, J. (1990). *Interdisciplinarity.* Detroit: Wayne State University.

McNamee, S. & Gergen, K. (Eds.) (1992). *Therapy as social construction.* Thousand Oaks, CA: Sage.

Miller, N. K. (1991). *Getting personal: Feminist occasions and other autobiographical acts.* New York: Routledge.

Minkler, M. & Estes, C. (1991). *Critical perspectives on aging.* Amityville, NY: Baywood.

Moody, H. R. (1988). Toward a critical gerontology: The contribution of the humanities to theories of aging. In J. E. Birren & V. L. Bengston (Eds.), *Emergent theories of aging* (pp. 19-40). New York: Springer.

Moody, H. R. (1992). Gerontology and critical theory. *The Gerontologist, 32,* 294-295.

Moody, H. R. (1993). Overview: What is critical gerontology and why is it important? In T. R. Cole, W. A. Achenbaum, P. L. Jakobi, & R. Kastenbaum, (Eds.), *Voices and visions of aging: Toward a critical gerontology* (pp. xv-xli). New York: Springer.

Parry, A. & Doan, R. E. (1994). *Story re-Visions: Narrative therapy in the post-modern world.* New York: Guilford.

Ray, R. (1996). A postmodern perspective on feminist gerontology. *The Gerontologist, 36,* 674-680.

Ray, R. (in process). *Writing a life: Age, gender, and diversity in the life story.*

Reinharz, S. (1992). *Feminist methods in social research.* New York: Oxford University.

Sherman, E. (1991). *Reminiscence and the self in old age.* New York: Springer.

Smith, S. (1993). *Subjectivity, identity, and the body: Women's autobiographical practices in the twentieth century.* Bloomington, IN: Indiana University.

Stivers, C. (1993). Reflections on the role of personal narrative in social science. *Signs, 18,* 408-425.

White, M., & Epston, D. (1990). *Narrative means to therapeutic ends.* New York: Norton.

Conclusions

J. Dianne Garner, DSW

This volume has embarked on a journey exploring the application of principles of feminism to the field of gerontology. It is our hope that reader's have come away with increased awareness and renewed skills in assisting older women realize maximum mastery of their own lives. The areas presented in this work are by no means exclusive. Selection was dictated by both the availability of other literature on particular topics and restrictions on length of the work. For example: the loss of a spouse through death can create financial and psychological burdens for women who are ill-prepared to handle them. These women frequently face poverty, decreased status, and loss of companionship (Conway-Turner and Cherrin, 1998, p. 23). Certainly the application of feminist principles, particularly empowerment, education, inclusion, and egalitarianism, as presented by McCandless and Conner, would be appropriate in working with widowed older women and older women experiencing any emotional disturbance or stressful life event.

We did not specifically delve into therapy, but trusted that our readers can and will apply the skills and theories presented here to their therapeutic intervention whether in a mental health setting, physical health setting, a setting dealing with the abuse or battering of aged women, or in addressing our own systems and organizations that discriminate against or disempower older women. Gaylord's presentation of the "health-giving" benefits of empowerment and the encouragement of self-determination are not limited to any setting or to any particular life stresses. As Richardson points out, "all dimensions are

[Haworth co-indexing entry note]: "Conclusions." Garner, J. Dianne. Co-published simultaneously in *Journal of Women & Aging* (The Haworth Press, Inc.) Vol. 11, No. 2/3, 1999, pp. 185-187; and: *Fundamentals of Feminist Gerontology* (ed: J. Dianne Garner) The Haworth Press, Inc., 1999, pp. 185-187. Single or multiple copies of this article are available for a fee from The Haworth Document Delivery Service [1-800-342-9678, 9:00 a.m. - 5:00 p.m. (EST). E-mail address: getinfo@haworthpressinc.com].

taken into account in empowerment-oriented practice" (p. 61). Whatever the setting and whatever the presenting difficulty, feminist practitioners need to consider the personal, the interpersonal, organizational, and sociopolitical in order to facilitate self-realization by aged women.

In the study conducted by Roberto, Allen, and Bliezner, it is suggested that part of the accomplishment of aging wisely is learning to take on new challenges, guided by a lifetime of considering a sense of self and service to others. They state that through education, consciousness-raising, and other types of empowerment interventions, practitioners can support older women as they continue their lives and encounter new personal, family, and societal situations. Vinton argues for the application of feminist principles consistently employed in working with younger abused women when working with older abused women. McCandless and Conner strongly assert that the commitment to empowerment and to client control of their own political, social, economic, and personal identities must continue until the moment of death.

Conway-Turner tells us that those who work with older women of color must recognize the strengths of being old, female, and of color as well as the vulnerabilities inherent in possessing those characteristics. A recognition of the concerns of old women of color and of the impact of being old, female, and of color, she presents as central to a feminist perspective. She urges us to draw upon cultural strengths to tap into the natural systems of women of color and to bring women of color to the center of our discussions of older women.

Fullmer, Shenk, and Eastland convincingly promote a multi-level focus in working with older lesbians from a feminist perspective. First practitioners must be educated about the special issues, needs, and life situations of older lesbians. Second is an emphasis on empowering older lesbians. And third is the necessity of advocating for the rights of older lesbians within systems and societies that are frequently hostile based solely on the lifestyle of lesbianism.

Hooyman and Gonyea present a feminist model for practice with women as caregivers, including an opportunity to choose roles, information and advocacy as a basis for care giver empowerment, and the enhancement of the caregivers' ability to provide quality care. They critique the current long-term care policy from a feminist perspective and present a feminist model for long-term care policy which includes family support, empowerment, and choice. In addressing the need for public policy which empowers care givers and care receivers, they point out that caregiving of older adults is not a private trouble nor individual stress, but a societal responsibility that necessitates a collective response in order to enhance the quality of life of both care givers and care receivers.

Last, but certainly not least, Ray urges us to step out of bounds and do something different by embracing feminist, empowering research which focuses on the connections between language, self, and social action. She concludes by stating: "I'm reaching beyond my grasp here and asking you to do the same. But isn't that what feminists do?" (p. 185).

In editing this volume, I have had the opportunity to work with a fascinating and diverse group of women and one man, all of whom are committed to the use of feminist theories and methods in working with older women and the systems which devalue them. They are sociologists, psychologists, social workers, gerontologists, and one Professor of English. They have all worked diligently and relentlessly. Some encountered personal tragedies and forged ahead in spite of adversity. At one point, living in the Florida Keys and facing Hurricane Georges, I had to ask authors to be ready to mail new manuscripts to New York just in case my office drowned or was blown away. None were fazed by the possibility of having to duplicate work. Their concern was for my safety and the safety of my family. These are truly empowering people whose first priority is the welfare of others. At the end of this work, I have included a section: *About the Contributors*. Although it does not capture their spirit, it will give you a bit of information about the backgrounds and experiences of our authors.

REFERENCE

Conway-Turner, K. & Cherrin, S. (1998). *Women, families, and feminist politics: A global exploration*. New York: Harrington Park Press.

Overhaul

Ruth Harriet Jacobs, PhD

I have given away
all the clothes that do not fit
or are unfit for the woman I have become.

I have passed on
all the books I will ever read
or reread because my thinking has changed.

I have left at the dump
all the souvenirs of past trips
but not the maps for new journeys to take.

I have gently caught
moths in my house to set them free
when I am old and frail, who will do that for me?

[Haworth co-indexing entry note]: "Overhaul." Jacobs, Ruth Harriet. Co-published simultaneously in *Journal of Women & Aging* (The Haworth Press, Inc.) Vol. 11, No. 2/3, 1999, p. 189; and: *Fundamentals of Feminist Gerontology* (ed: J. Dianne Garner) The Haworth Press, Inc., 1999, p. 189. Single or multiple copies of this article are available for a fee from The Haworth Document Delivery Service [1-800-342-9678, 9:00 a.m. - 5:00 p.m. (EST). E-mail address: getinfo@haworthpressinc.com].

About the Contributors

Katherine R. Allen, PhD, is Professor, Family and Child Development, Virginia Polytechnic Institute and State University. She is a Faculty Affiliate in the Center for Gerontology and a Core Teaching Faculty Member in the Women's Studies Program. Her research and teaching interests include feminism and family studies, qualitative research methods, family pedagogy, and family diversity. She is the author of *Single Women/Family Ties: Life Histories of Older Women*, the co-author of *Women and Families: Feminist Reconstructions*, and co-editor of the *Handbook of Family Diversity*.

Rosemary Blieszner, PhD, is Professor of Gerontology and Family Studies, Department of Family and Child Development, and Associate Director, Center for Gerontology, Virginia Polytechnic Institute and State University. Her research focuses on family and friend relationships, life events, and psychological well being in adulthood and old age. She is co-editor of *Older Adult Friendship: Structure and Process*, and the *Handbook of Aging and the Family*, co-author of *Adult Friendship* and co-author of *Spiritual Resiliency: Listening to Women Who Listen for God*.

Francis (Pick) Conner, ACSW, is Professor of Sociology and Coordinator of the Women's Studies Program, State University of West Georgia where he developed the Master's Degree program in Gerontology. He is widely published in the area of grief. His most recent work *Letting Go: The Grief Experience* continues his focus on grief issues. He is a founding member and former president of the local Hospice and an active participant in community agencies and organizations.

Kate Conway-Turner, PhD, is Professor, Department of Individual and Family Studies and Department of Psychology, University of Delaware. Her research includes international women's health, women's relationships, marital patterns, and the impact of race and culture on women and their families. Dr. Conway-Turner is the past director of the Women's Studies Program, the recipient of the Kellogg's National Leadership Grant and the recipient of an American Council on Education Award. Her most recent book is *Women, Families, and Feminist Politics: A Global Exploration.*

Lynette J. Eastland, PhD, is Associate Professor of Communications at Clemson University in South Carolina. Her primary interest is in issues of identity construction and change. She is editor of *Communication in Recovery: Perspectives on Twelve-Step Groups* (1998) and author of *Communication, Organization, and Change with a Feminist Context* (1991). She has chapters in several books, including *Communication and the Disenfranchised: Social Health Issues and Implications* and articles in several journals including *The Journal of Applied Communication Research and Qualitative Health Research.*

Elise M. Fullmer, PhD, is Associate Professor, Department of Social Work, and a member of the Gerontology Advisory Committee, University of North Carolina at Charlotte. Her primary research emphasis is in gerontology with a focus on gender issues and minority group aging. Recent publications include *The Thirteenth Step: Aging* and *Adaptation by an Ethnic Minority Lesbian, Challenging Biases Against Families of Older Lesbians and Gays,* and *Significant Relationships Among Older Women: Cultural and Personal Constructions of Lesbianism.*

J. Dianne Garner, DSW, is Senior Editor, The Haworth Press, Inc. book program, *Innovations in Feminist Studies* and Editor, *Journal of Women & Aging.* She has written extensively on aging women, including *Women and Healthy Aging: Living Productively in Spite of It All,* with Alice A. Young, and *Women As They Age* with Susan O. Mercer. A second edition of *Women As They Age* is in progress. Dr. Garner is past Professor and Chair, Department of Social Work, past Chair, Center on Aging, Washburn University and past chair of the National Committee on Women's Issues of NASW.

Susan Gaylord, PhD, is Research Assistant Professor, Department of Physical Medicine and Rehabilitation, Adjunct Assistant Professor, Department of Family Medicine, and affiliate, Program on Aging at the University of North Carolina School of Medicine. Dr. Gaylord is also the Director of the Program in Integrative Medicine at the UNC School of Medicine where she teaches principles and practices of alternative and complementary medicine and is establishing an inter-disciplinary program of research, education, and clinical care in alternative and complementary therapies.

Judith G. Gonyea, PhD, is Associate Professor and Chair, Social Welfare Research Department, Boston University School of Social Work. She has written extensively on the stresses American families face and of the health and economic status of older women. In 1995, she co-authored *Feminist Perspectives of Family Care: Policies for Gender Justice* with Nancy R. Hooyman. She was guest editor for a special issue of *Research on Aging* devoted to the topic of work and elder care. Dr. Gonyea currently serves on multiple editorial boards.

Nancy R. Hooyman, PhD, is Professor and Dean, School of Social Work, University of Washington, Seattle. Nationally recognized for her scholarship in aging, family caregiving of older adults, and feminist social work practice, she has co-authored or edited seven books, including *Feminist Perspectives on Family Care: Policies for Gender Justice*. Dean Hooyman has published over 70 articles and chapters related to gerontology and women's issues. Her many activities include past President, National Association of Deans and Directors of Schools of Social Work, and past Chair, CSWE Commission on the Role and Status of Women.

N. Jane McCandless, PhD, is Associate Professor of Sociology, and Director of Graduate Studies, Department of Sociology and Anthropology, State University of West Georgia. She is also the Coordinator of the interdisciplinary Women's Studies Program which she developed. Her research interests are in the area of women's issues, with an emphasis on violence against women. Dr. McCandless plays an active role in the community and works closely with agencies that provide direct services to women.

Ruth E. Ray, PhD, is Associate Professor of English and Faculty Associate in Gerontology at Wayne State University. She was a 1994-97 Brookdale fellow, during which time she conducted participant-observation research with several writing groups in senior centers and nursing homes. Her most recent book is *Writing a Life: Age, Gender, and Diversity in the Life Story*. In addition to her teaching, Dr. Ray is working on integrating age studies into the writing curriculum.

Virginia E. Richardson, PhD, is Professor, College of Social Work and Department of African American and African Studies, The Ohio

State University. She is currently President of the Association of Gerontology Education in Social Work and is on the steering committee for the section on aging of the National Association of Social Workers. Dr. Richardson has published several articles in the area of aging and her book, *Retirement Counseling*, was based on her research on women and retirement. Her new book, *Social Work Practice with Older Persons*, is in progress.

Karen A. Roberto, PhD, is Director of the Center for Gerontology and Professor of Gerontology at Virginia Polytechnic Institute and State University. Her research focuses on older women's adaptation to life with osteoporosis, relationships between family members in later life, and friendships of older men and women. She is the editor/author of four books, including *Relationships Between Women in Later Life* and *Community Resources for Older Adults: Programs and Services in an Era of Change*. Dr. Roberto is widely published in professional journals and other edited works.

Dena Shenk, PhD, is Director, Gerontology Program, Coordinator, Graduate Program, and Professor, Anthropology, University of North Caroline at Charlotte. Her research focuses on diversity within the older population. Recent publications include *Someone to Lend a Helping Hand: Women Growing Old in Rural America* and *Teaching About Aging: Interdisciplinary and Cross-Cultural Perspectives, Third Edition*, co-edited with Jay Sololovsky. Dr. Shenk is a member of the Board of the Association for Gerontology in Higher Education and Chair of the Commission on Age and Aging of the International Union of Anthropological and Ethnological Sciences.

Linda Vinton, PhD, is Associate Professor, Florida State University School of Social Work. Dr. Vinton has published multiple articles in a variety of professional journals, including the *Journal of Women & Aging, The Gerontologist, Journal of Gerontological Social Work, Journal of Family Violence, Journal of Interpersonal Violence*, and *Journal of Violence Against Women*. Her 1991 benchmark article, "Abused Older Women: Battered Women or Abused Elders" in the *Journal of Women & Aging*, spawned a national conference sponsored by AARP which challenged providers to be responsive to the needs of abused and battered older women.

Index

Abuse, of older women, feminist
    perspective of, 85-100
"Abused Elders or Older Battered
    Women," 92
Acupressure, for older women, 40
Acupuncture, for older women, 40
Adorno, T., 53
Age Discrimination Employment Act,
    10
Ageism and Battering for Women of
    Color, 96
Aging
    cultural narratives of, 179-182
    devaluing associated with, 4
    meaning of, 3
    resources and, 4
    women over 65 years, 6-7
Aging women
    Black, incomes of, 24
    education for, 15-18
    egalitarianism in, 18-21
    empowerment of, 21-24
    health care system and, 13-27
    inclusion of, 21-24
    and poverty, 50
    race effects on, 23-24
    sexuality of, 136-138
"Ain't I a Woman," 12
Alexander, F.M., 39
Alexander Technique, for older
    women, 39
Allen, K.R., 11,67
    biographical material on, 191
Alternative therapies, for older
    women, 29-47
    acupressure, 40
    acupuncture, 40
    Alexander Technique, 39
    aromatherapy, 42

biofeedback training, 37-38
bodywork, 39-40
chiropractic adjustment, 38-39
dietary therapies, 41
fasting, 41
Feldenkrais Method, 39
Functional Integration, 39
future of, 45
Ginkgo biloba, 30
herbal medicine, 41-42
homeopathy, 42-43
hypnosis, 38
increase in popularity of, 29-30
juice therapies, 41
laying on of hands, 40
macrobiotics, 41
meditation, 38
mind-body therapies, 37-38
past and present users of, 34-36
principles of, 36-44
process of, 44-45
Reiki, 40
rolfing, 39-40
shamanism, 43-44
St. Johns's Wort, 30
Structural Integration, 39-40
therapeutic massage, 39
therapeutic touch, 40
touch therapies, 40
types of, 36-44
vegetarian diet, 41
Alyn, J., 7
American Association of Retired
    Persons (AARP), 92
American Society of Plastic and
    Reconstructive Surgeons, 16
Anderson, J., 22,108,111
Arber, S., 59
Aromatherapy, for older women, 42

195

TO ORDER: CALL: 1-800-HAWORTH / FAX: 1-800-895-0582 (Outside US/Canada: + 607-771-0012) / **E-MAIL: getinfo@haworthpressinc.com**

Please complete the information below or tape your business card in this area.

☐ **YES, please send me Losses in Later Life**

___ in hard at $39.95 ISBN: 0-7890-0627-8. (Outside US/Canada/Mexico: $48.00)

___ in soft at $19.95 ISBN: 1-56023-0628-6. (Outside US/Canada/Mexico: $24.00)

- Individual orders outside US, Canada, and Mexico must be
  prepaid by check or credit card.
- Discount not applicable on books priced under $15.00.
- Discounts are not available on 5+ text prices and not available in conjunction
  with any other discount.
- 5+ text prices are not available for jobbers and wholesalers.
- Postage & handling: In US: $4.00 for first book; $1.50 for each additional book.
  Outside US: $5.00 for first book; $2.00 for each additional book.
- Canadian residents: please add appropriate sales tax after postage & handling.
  NY, MN, and OH residents: please add 7% GST after postage & handling.
- Payment in UNESCO coupons welcome.
- If paying in Canadian dollars, use current exchange rate to convert to US dollars.
- Please allow 3-4 weeks for delivery after publication.
- Prices and discounts subject to change without notice.

Signature _____

☐ **BILL ME LATER**($5 service charge will be added).

(Not available for individuals outside US/Canada/Mexico. Service charge is
waived for/jobbers/wholesalers/booksellers.)

☐ Check here if billing address is different from shipping address and attach purchase
order and billing address information.

Signature _____

☐ **PAYMENT ENCLOSED $** _____

(Payment must be in US or Canadian dollars by check or money order drawn on a US or Canadian bank.)

☐ **PLEASE BILL MY CREDIT CARD:**

☐ AmExp ☐ Diners Club ☐ Eurocard ☐ Discover ☐ Master Card ☐ Visa

Account Number _____

Expiration Date _____

Signature _____

May we open a confidential credit card account for you for possible future purchases? ( ) Yes ( ) No

THE HAWORTH PRESS, INC., 10 Alice Street, Binghamton, NY 13904-1580 USA

NAME _____

INSTITUTION _____

ADDRESS _____

CITY _____

STATE _____ ZIP _____

COUNTRY _____

COUNTY (NY residents only) _____

E-MAIL _____

May we use your e-mail address for confirmations and other types of information?
( ) Yes ( ) No. We appreciate receiving your e-mail address and fax number. Haworth would like
to e-mail or fax special discount offers to you, as a preferred customer. We will never share, rent, or
exchange your e-mail address or fax number. We regard such actions as an invasion of your privacy.

☐ **YES, please send me Losses in Later Life** (ISBN: 0-7890-0628-6) to consider on a
60-day examination basis. I understand that I will receive an invoice payable within
60 days, or that **if I decide to adopt the book, my invoice will be cancelled. I
understand that I will be billed at the lowest price.** (Offer available only to teaching
faculty in US, Canada, and Mexico.)

Signature _____

Course Title(s) _____

Current Text(s) _____

Enrollment _____

Semester _____ Decision Date _____

Office Tel _____ Hours _____

(06) (15) (14)   07/99   BIC99